PARIS AND ELSEWHERE

L'Armée révolutionnaire parisienne à Lyon et dans la région lyonnaise
(Rachais, Lyon, 1952)

Les Armées révolutionnaires du Midi
(Association Marc Bloch, Toulouse, 1955)

*Les Armées révolutionnaires: instrument de la Terreur dans les
Départements, avril 1793–floréal an II*
(2 vols., Mouton, Paris, 1961 & 1963)
translated by Marianne Elliott as
The People's Armies (Yale University Press, 1987)

Terreur et subsistances 1793–1795 (Librairie Clavreuil, Paris, 1965)

A Second Identity: Essays on France and French history (OUP, 1969)

The Police and the People: French popular protest 1789–1820
(OUP, 1970)

Reactions to the French Revolution (OUP, 1972)

Paris and its Provinces 1792–1802 (OUP, 1975)

A Sense of Place (Duckworth, 1975)

Tour de France (Duckworth, 1976)

Death in Paris 1795–1801 (OUP, 1976)

Promenades: A historian's appreciation of modern French literature
(OUP, 1980)

The Streets of Paris (Duckworth, 1980)

*French and Germans, Germans and French: A personal interpretation of
France under two Occupations 1914–1918/1940–1944*
(University Press of New England, 1983)

Still Life: Sketches from a Tunbridge Wells childhood
(Chatto & Windus, 1983)

A Classical Education (Chatto & Windus, 1985)

People and Places (OUP, 1985)

Something To Hold Onto (John Murray, 1988)

The End of the Line (John Murray, 1997)

The French and Their Revolution
Selected writings edited and introduced by David Gilmour
(John Murray, 1998)

PARIS AND ELSEWHERE

Richard Cobb

*Selected writings edited and
introduced by David Gilmour*

JOHN MURRAY
Albemarle Street, London

© Margaret Cobb 1998

First published in 1998
by John Murray (Publishers) Ltd,
50 Albemarle Street, London W1X 4BD

The moral right of the author has been asserted

A catalogue record for this book is available from the British Library

Cased ISBN 0-7195-5469 1
Paperback ISBN 0-7195-5462 4

Typeset in Sabon by Servis Filmsetting Ltd, Manchester
Printed and bound in Great Britain by The University Press, Cambridge

Contents

Introduction

RICHARD COBB was delighted when Frenchmen mistook his nationality. 'Vous êtes Belge?' they would ask him in a train or a café or a *restaurant d'habitués*. Better still, they might inquire, 'Vous êtes du Nord?' for he loved to be mistaken for a Norman from le Havre or an inhabitant of one of the great textile towns of the north-east. In Paris he sometimes claimed he was *bruxellois*; in Lyon he might pretend to come from Roubaix. But even when his nationality was discovered or admitted (and his gaunt bony features certainly looked very English), he was happy when the stranger beamed and said, 'Monsieur Cobb, vous êtes bilingue' – so long as the compliment was paid by the French, the Belgians or the Vaudois (and not by the Québécois who in his view were not bilingual at all because they managed to massacre both languages).

Cobb was once told that he spoke French with the facility of 'un titi parisien'. Not many people want to be told that they speak a language like an urchin or a teddy-boy – even a French one – but for Cobb, the least pompous and most unpretentious of men, it was the best compliment he ever received. For it demonstrated that he *belonged*, that he had crossed the line and acquired that 'second identity' which enabled him to become such a wonderful writer and historian of France.

As he describes in the opening chapter of this book, Cobb visited Paris for the first time in 1935, at the age of seventeen. During his vacations from Oxford, where he read History at Merton, he regularly returned, and on going down in 1938 he began research on the French Revolution in the Archives Nationales. Had it not been for Hitler, he might have remained permanently in Paris. As it was, he could not resume his research until 1946, although he learnt a good deal about northern France in the months after D-Day, stationed in agreeable and not very dangerous billets in Normandy and the north-east.

After the war he lived in Paris for nine years, working his way through the archives of the capital and the northern *départements*, and publishing his historical articles in French. In 1955 he was enticed home by the offer of a lectureship at Aberystwyth, moving via Manchester and Leeds to Oxford in 1962, where he eventually became Professor of Modern History. But his 'second identity', which he used in the title of his first book in English, remained dominant. He kept his room in the rue de Tournon for long research visits, and his major early works, on *les armées révolutionnaires*, were written in French. Even when he began to publish in English, he went on writing about the social history of the French Revolution: his last work on the subject, *Death in Paris* (1978), won the Wolfson Prize. Only in retirement did he abandon France, preferring to write about his childhood and family background in the south-east of England. He died in Abingdon in January 1996.

Most of Cobb's favourite landscapes were located close to the North Sea or the English Channel. In England they stretched from Tunbridge Wells (where he grew up) through East Anglia and the Fens to Whitby. (But not beyond: he did not like hills and could not see the point of Scotland, which looked on the map as if it had been 'torn out of a piece of paper'; the best thing about my country, he once told me, was that its topography was unsuitable for cricket.) In France he ranged further inland, not just between the bleak sea front of le Havre and the flat country of the Pas de Calais, but to Rouen and Amiens and beyond the Île de France to the wooded valleys of the Yonne and the Upper Seine. He loved Lyon, where he did much of his research, but he seldom went further south, except to Marseille and in later life to Perpignan. Like Maigret he did not care for the heat or the scent of aromatic herbs. You would never find Cobb among the immaculate stone villages of the Dordogne or the Lubéron. He was a winter man with a taste for harsh geography, for the stark angularity of quaysides and canals, the wide horizons of the Beauce, the blackened-brick streets of Roubaix and Lille.

As Raymond Carr once observed, Cobb's history was the work of a poet as well as of an historian. But he was a poet not of the heroic or the romantic or the classically beautiful, but of the opposites of these things – of the banal, the ordinary, the unheroic, of people and their routines, of tramways and railway stations, of townscapes of mills and brick chimneys and back-to-back terraced houses. He himself was very much a creature of routine. Custom and time-tables reassured him: he liked to recognize people in the street, watch them drinking in the *tabac*, overhear them talking on the bus. He was a lonely man, an outsider for whom routine and fixed itineraries were important because they helped him feel that he *belonged* to Paris or Dieppe or wherever he happened to be doing his research. His description of Simenon as a writer of 'loneliness and alienation, of the process of urbanization in individual terms', will do very well for himself.

The pieces collected in this volume are a mixture of autobiography, book reviews and evocations of favourite places. Although he wrote several books on his childhood and upbringing in England, Cobb never, unfortunately, attempted a chronicle of his life in France. Some of it seeped out, of course, in unexpected places over a period of nearly thirty years, in articles and broadcasts and the introductions to his books on the Revolution. But his *experience* of France, his unique encounter with the French, their history and their culture, has been scattered. Its collection here is the justification of the present book.

Cobb would never have aspired to a complete, Braudelian acquaintance with France, geographically, historically or socially. He was not that kind of person. Charlemagne, the aristocracy or the city of Bordeaux were equally alien to him. In spite of his education at Shrewsbury and Oxford, he showed no interest in the French upper classes, in Proust's jaded and dying generation. He moved comfortably between eccentric bourgeois and criminal or anarchic working class; his closest French friend was a deserter and thief. Cheerfully admitting that he himself was not 'officer material', he needed outlets, escapes from authority and 'miserabilism', from Robespierre and Saint-Just, from Enemies of Pleasure and Propagandists of Virtue. He needed feasts and argument and a lot of red wine.

Cobb's France, and especially his Paris, is the landscape of the thirties and forties, of the last moments of the Third Republic and the early years of the Fourth. It is a landscape of what he called 'human proportions', when the markets were still at les Halles, when artisans still lived in the Marais, when even Pompidou himself had not thought of the Pompidou Centre. 'People have not changed much,' he once wrote, 'but places certainly have, and everywhere for the worse.' Like many nostalgic people, he believed that places first seen in his youth were in their prime at that moment, and that all subsequent changes have been bad. This gives his writing an elegiac quality, the historian and the poet combining to record and commemorate a disappearing world. Much of it is necessarily sad, some of it is angry, but as an evocation of place and period, it is both beautiful and unique.

David Gilmour
Edinburgh, January 1998

. . . là où sont les gens, les boutiques, les lumières, la vie,
là se trouve le centre. Il disparaît là où tout s'éteint, où les
façades se ferment ou se spécialisent, là où il n'y a plus
rien à faire et à voir, là où on s'ennuie . . .

Qu'il s'agisse de la Saint-Louis des rois ou du 14 juillet des
Républiques, l'amour est la manière parisienne de se
réjouir collectivement . . .

Louis Chevalier, *Les Parisiens*

PART I

Cobb's Paris

I

Experiences of an Anglo-French Historian*

MANY CASES of specialization are no doubt the result of accident rather than of choice. The late Professor Willie Rose became a specialist in Polish history because, in the late summer of 1914, he was caught, with his wife, in Austrian Galicia, and spent the rest of the war under a liberal system of house arrest with the Polish squirearchical family with whom they had been staying. One of the most distinguished Germanists in Wales went on a return visit to his pen-friend in Kotbus in August 1939; when he reached Dresden, in early September, he discovered that the British Consul-General had already left – a habit of British consuls in times of international crisis that must have caused many similar vocations; in this instance, as he was still under fifteen, he was able to attend the local *Gymnasium*, though he was not allowed to accept invitations from his schoolmates, and to live with the family of his pen-friend for the next six years. He had to report to the police each morning; and when he was eighteen, on completing his exams, he was conscripted to work in a paper-mill. He met with much kindness from the start, and by 1945 even the local police sergeant was reminding him of how well he had been treated by himself and his staff. Later that year, after spending a month in Dresden, in search of a British liaison, hauling corpses by wheelbarrow to mass graves, he made his way to Berlin. By that time, he had forgotten much of his English, thought, dreamt, and counted in German. Of Sir Bernard Pares his son, in a charming essay, writes that, having

---

* First published as the Introduction to *A Second Identity* (1969).

3

gone to Russia by chance, he at once became enamoured of the Russian people, and henceforth spent periods of years in the Empire. 'My father was not an English liberal looking at Russia, but a Russian liberal looking at Russia!' His was perhaps the most successful transference, the most complete acquisition of a second nationality, of a second identity, a crossing of the line that is the most important requisite for the English specialist of the history and culture of a foreign society. Perhaps, in all these cases, the need for *la seconde patrie* was already there; but which country it was to be was largely a matter of accident.

In my own case, I was saved from becoming a 'Namierite' by my headmaster and my housemaster. On receiving my telegram from Oxford, in December 1934, with the news that I had been awarded a Postmastership in History, they both wrote, in almost identical terms, to my mother to emphasize that 'Shrewsbury having done all it could for Richard, it would be better for Shrewsbury if Richard were not to return in January'. It could not have been put more politely, but it was clear that I was no longer wanted. They went on to suggest that a year abroad, before going up, might be the best way of filling this suddenly enforced hiatus in my education.

Neither my parents nor I had ever had any such thing in mind. My knowledge of French was poor; moreover, it was a language I much disliked as being identified with *Hernani* (each country has its *pompier national*, and just as ours is Shakespeare, France's National Bore is Hugo), the *Contes choisis* of the lachrymose, self-righteous François Coppée, and with the works of various nineteenth-century poetical bores. English public schools in the 1930s took every possible precaution to prevent any of their pupils from becoming Francophils. My own interests were with the Shropshire gents, the Duke of Newcastle, and the Member for Bridgnorth; apart from a Greek aunt by marriage, my known world made no allowance for any form of exoticism. My aunt displayed a signed photograph of King George of the Hellenes in a silver frame; I was told that he was more or less an Englishman, near enough at least not to make any difference. And my aunt's nephews had been sent to Eton, apparently at the King's expense. I was quite unenthusiastic at the prospect of being 'sent abroad' for nine or ten months.

4

My parents were equally ill prepared. Germany was ruled out from the start, not because of Hitler, but because some colleague of my father's in Khartoum had told him that German barons were bad and bold and dangerous company for blond young English public school boys. There remained France and Austria, both of which were chosen. My stay in Vienna, however, was brief; after six weeks working for the Quakers, I was arrested, beaten up in a succession of police stations, made to walk very fast through the streets, holding my trousers up, imprisoned for ten days as a Czech student – this went down in the prison register – and, once my identity had been established, accompanied to the Liechtenstein frontier by two men with green velvet tabs on their collars. It appeared that I had been in touch with Otto Bauer and Karl Seitz; my expulsion occurred a little over a year after the assassination of Dollfuss. As a result, I learnt scarcely any German and have retained to this day the strongest dislike for the so-called Austrian *Gemütlichkeit* and for people who dress up in fancy braces and leather shorts and white socks. I was also much flattered by having been taken for a Czech; the Czechoslovak Republic had considerable prestige in my eyes, as a democracy, a friend of the Soviet Union, and an unneighbourly neighbour of Schuschnigg's and Horthy's unpleasant regimes.

This is to anticipate. My Austrian venture was a disaster. My French was not. Yet at first it showed all the signs of becoming one, for in Tunbridge Wells, as in the novels of Anthony Powell, there was a persistent belief, based entirely on myth but widely shared by the English middle classes, that the best French was spoken in Touraine. The effect of this was that several generations of English boys and girls were likely to be packed off to a *colonelle*, or a *commandante*, in Tours, an Army widow who took in *Le Figaro*, *La Croix*, *Ouest-Éclair*, and *Excelsior*, whose other reading was confined to elevating works emanating from Chez Mame,[1] and whose house, shuttered and curtained, draped, pinnacled, *œil-de-bœuf*-ed, *faux Henri III*, the French school primer house for 12-year-olds – see under *maison* in the Dictionnaire Larousse – smelt of the meanness and stuffiness of the right-wing French provincial bourgeoisie of the west. No surer education for life-

---

[1] The name of a celebrated publisher of religious books.

long Francophobia could have been contrived, and I have no doubt that
it may have recruited many to the generation of Appeasement and to
the Germanomania of a section of the English upper middle class
between the wars. For a few days, Tours (a place I had heard about
from a friend at Shrewsbury) hung like a damp cloud over Tunbridge
Wells Common, the Pantiles, Calverley Park, and the Toad Rock. It
was a normal journey from the West Station (the Gateway to the
Continent), via Newhaven, Dieppe, Rouen (a change here), and any
route that would avoid Paris.

Tours was eliminated by further accident. My mother played bridge
several times a week with the widow of a former member of the Indian
Civil Service whose daughter, Philippa, had recently returned from
France. She had spent a year with a family in Paris, had learnt excellent French, and had come back to all intents and appearances much
as she had left. What had been all right for Philippa was all right for
me, so it was decided, over the green tables of the Ladies' Bridge Club
on Mount Ephraim. I owe much to Ely Culbertson, even more to
Philippa.

In January 1935 I was sent to Paris. The family I was to stay with
lived in a large fifth-floor flat facing on to the boulevard Bonne-
Nouvelle, almost opposite the Rex[1] and a little further on from *Le
Matin* and its large blue and red pennant. From the balcony, one could
see the Pâtisseries de la Lune, headed by a grinning moon in neon, a
huge neon Celt smoking Celtique, with real smoke coming out of his
mouth at each puff, the *agent à double barbe*[2] at the porte Saint-Denis,
and the prostitutes in thick clusters at the entries of the hotels in the
rue de la Lune, as it climbed steeply inwards. My bedroom faced
directly on to the Bains Neptuna, with an oblique shot to the Floréal,[3]
on the other side of the boulevard. The flat shook regularly with the
rumble of the *Métro*, the smell of which reached up from the nearby
mouth of the Bonne-Nouvelle station. At night the ceiling flickered
with the neon advertisements, and at weekends one could hear
snatches of *Tout va très bien, Madame la Marquise*, or *Allons les*

---

[1] The Rex is a monster cinema constructed in the 1930s.
[2] The double-bearded policeman was one of the monuments of the Paris scene in the
1920s and 1930s.
[3] The name of a café on the boulevard Bonne-Nouvelle.

pompons, or *Mon frère est poitrinaire*, from the street bands who, with the *baratineurs*,[1] the flame-swallowers, the manacled strong men, then enjoyed *droit de pavé* on the immensely wide pavement just below the flat. One could not have hoped for more Parisian a setting; the press, the theatre, prostitution, particularly in its lower echelons, were within yards, food, pleasure, the *loterie*, the shooting booths within sight, the Halles, the Crédit Lyonnais, the Musée Grévin within ten minutes' walk. This had been the very centre of traditional Paris any time from the eighteenth century to the present day, though since 1914 the centre had tended to move away westwards, towards the Madeleine and the boulevard des Italiens. Below me walked the *badaud*,[2] the *petit bourgeois* from the XIIe, the typists and the shop-girls from the eastern and northern suburbs, and at weekends *les gars de Ménilmontant*, those of Belleville and Aubervilliers. A quarter that seldom slept, that was ceasing to be residential (most of the doors on our staircase bore the plates of *dentistes américains* and of furriers with Polish names). The steppe of the quartier des Invalides and the shuttered silence of the boulevard Malesherbes might have belonged to another continent. I owe to Philippa the fact that, all my life, I have been a *boulevardier*[3] – a term that can only apply to the Right Bank – and that so many of my axes of pleasure and of observation have run from Richelieu-Drouot to Strasbourg-Saint-Denis, the home line, especially above ground.

The family consisted of a widow, Mme Thullier, and her two sons, the elder a law student of twenty-one, the younger, at eighteen, just beginning medicine. The father had been killed at Gallipoli. The maternal grandfather, M. Feuillas, had been a well-to-do stockbroker and private banker who had invested in house property. Boulevard Bonne-Nouvelle had been his city base, but he had also bought a villa in Saint-Mandé – apartment in the Xe, villa in the still fashionable

---

[1] From *baratin*, Parisian slang for talk. A *baratineur* is a street vendor who uses his eloquence to vaunt the merits of a particular product. The nearest equivalent would be the Brooklyn expression, a 'spieler'. Hence the Paris saying: 'Pour avoir la fille, qui est si jolie, c'est à la maman qu'il faut faire du baratin.'

[2] An onlooker, the personification of the Paris spirit of inquisitiveness.

[3] A person who spends his evenings walking along the *grands boulevards*. A member of a declining species.

western fringe of the Bois de Vincennes: this was very much the pattern of Second Empire and early Third Republic middle-class location; there was also a house by the Seine at Samois, and scattered property in the Seine-et-Marne. Mme Thullier owned the whole block at No 26. Her sons, though totally indifferent to her attempts to maintain some sort of order at table or to preserve her Chinese screens from knife-throwing, deferred to her in all financial matters; the elder married, in his early thirties, the daughter of a leading family of the Paris *notariat*, after protracted negotiations between his mother and the girl's grand-mother, and once he was fully established as a *commissaire-priseur*[1] at the Hôtel Drouot. During my stay, there was a succession of mis-tresses: Denise, Micheline, Gaby, Janine – mostly typists or *arpètes*,[2] who were received friendlily by Mme Thullier, in the knowledge that her son would not be likely to marry any of them; *en cas d'accident, on s'arrangerait*. There was also the 122 for special occasions. The medical student took out the prostitutes of the Café Harcourt, near the Faculty.

Three days after my arrival, the boys gave a *surprise-party*. It was a surprise to me, for, having dragged me out of bed, they took me to the bathroom, where a nude girl was being cleaned up. They explained to me that she was an admiral's daughter and that her proper element was thus *la flotte*.[3] The fact that an admiral's daughter could end up naked at a party shocked me beyond words, and for a few days I wanted to return to Tunbridge Wells. The feeling did not last, however. Excellent food (eating has, ever since, been one of the greatest joys of my exist-ence, especially when combined with conversation, with reading *Le Monde*, or with eavesdropping) and plentiful wine helped a great deal. For the first time in my life, I found myself listening to French with pleasure, especially during meals, at which there were generally guests, including an amazingly fat barrister, Mme Thullier's brother-in-law. These people enjoyed talking.

The two boys had taken part with gusto in the *6 février* of the pre-vious year, and claimed to have burnt a bus, which seemed in charac-

---

[1] Auctioneer.
[2] *Arpète*: Parisian slang for a shop-girl.
[3] The Fleet; also a slang word for water.

ter. But they were not committed politically; what they liked most was a chance to get at the police or the *gardes mobiles*.[1] In 1939, the elder joined the *corps francs*[2] and won the Croix de Guerre in the Forêt de Warndt. In 1940, the younger remained with his hospital to look after the wounded; he was the only doctor to do so. After the war, with the formation of the RPF,[*] the auctioneer became a *conseiller municipal* for an elegant western suburb. The doctor, after years in Indo-China and a succession of mistresses that included an Annamite, was eventually induced to settle down; his mother bought him a flat and a practice in the boulevard Malesherbes, and also provided him with a wife, a vague cousin from the Périgord, the nineteen-year-old daughter of an Inspector of Forests. Mme Thullier explained to me on this occasion that she was *sans le sou et un peu conne, mais elle lui fera des enfants*. She had been worried about the current mistress, an actress, who had been in occupation for several years.

Both sons spent part of the weekend playing football with the Stade Français (they had previously been educated at the École des Roches, the nearest French equivalent to an English public school). Sport would be followed by horseplay of various kinds: knives on to silk screens, electric light bulbs down the well of the staircase at 3 a.m., attempting to race the Blue Train on the stretch through Villeneuve-Saint-Georges in their mother's enormous black Panhard-Levassor, throwing fish and salver over the balcony on Fridays to express their anti-clericalism, driving straight at traffic policemen, and fighting with working-class youths from the northern suburbs. They were good-humoured, anarchical, wild, joyful, and resourceful. They enjoyed dressing up and creating a public scandal. They got on very well indeed with girls, especially shop-girls, and they did not boast of their exploits in their mother's presence, nor, indeed, out of it. They had some very nice friends, most of them rich, and as wild as themselves.

My life in France might be divided up into a series of street itineraries, whether in Paris, in Lyon, or in Marseille. My first year in Paris was:

---

[1] The riot police of the 1930s.
[2] French commando units.
[*] Rassemblement du Peuple Français.

boulevard Bonne-Nouvelle, cross, rue d'Aboukir, rue Réaumur, cross, rue du Louvre, place Saint-Germain-l'Auxerrois, quai du Louvre, cross, pont des Arts, quai Conti, Bibliothèque Mazarine (destination), and back, four times a day. My route and my hours were so regular that, for eight months, twice a day always at the same spot, three-quarters of the way down the rue d'Aboukir, I met a sad-faced man coming the other way; we never spoke, but we always nodded. I felt that I fitted into a routine and, by doing so, belonged to a community. From 1936 to 1939, the itinerary was quite different: rue Saint-André-des-Arts, rue Dauphine, Pont-Neuf, the *quais* place de l'Hôtel-de-Ville, under the nose of Étienne Marcel; rue Lobau, rue des Archives (right side), rue des Francs-Bourgeois, Archives Nationales (destination), returning via the pont au Change, the quai aux Fleurs, boulevard du Palais, pont Saint-Michel, place Saint-André-des-Arts. This itinerary is marked with the experience of the Front Populaire, of Weidmann, of *l'Expo*, of the Spanish Civil War, and Munich. After the war, the itinerary went: rue de Tournon, rue de Seine, place Jacques-Callot, rue Guénégaud, with a grateful glance each morning at the charming stone nymph, a smiling fifteen-year-old, eighteenth-century country girl, over the side entrance of the Monnaie, Pont-Neuf, and as before, or with an alternative route quai de l'Horloge, to look at the china. There were, of course, variations to allow for the BN* (via the Palais-Royal), the APP,[1] quai des Orfèvres, the AD Seine,[2] via the rue Saint-Louis-en-Île, Vincennes (by *métro*), and the Bibliothèque Victor-Cousin, over the Sorbonne Library. For several years I took the *métro* at Mabillon at 7.50 a.m. every morning, getting into the middle carriage next to the *Ières*, recognizing the same people – at this hour of the morning, readers of *Le Parisien Libéré*, *L'Aurore*, and *L'Humanité* – and getting out at Duroc, leaving by the exit on the far side of the boulevard des Invalides, near the Enfants-Trouvés, for the avenue de Breteuil and the Centre des Télécommunications. For a brief and unpleasant period I had to take the 7.55 a.m. from the Gare du Nord for Enghien-les-Bains, to teach at the Pensionnat Bigot. In

*Bibliothèque Nationale.

[1] Archives de la Préfecture de Police, in the building of the Police Judiciaire, 36 quai des Orfèvres.

[2] Archives Départementales de la Seine, quai Henri IV.

Lyon, place de la Croix-Rousse, a detour by the Gros Caillou (that I had succeeded in climbing, a test that admitted me as a *croix-roussien d'honneur*, after a dozen *pots* of beaujolais), a striding descent down the montée de la Grande Côte, the *mairie du Ier arrondissement* (with steps between two bored black lions looking *louis-philippard*), rue Bouteille, quai Saint-Vincent, passerelle Saint-Vincent, place Saint-Paul, and up and up montée des Carmes Déchaussés, chemin de Montauban, Archives du Rhône (destination). In Marseille: start at the rue des Couteliers, then quai des Belges, the lower end of the Canebière, cross opposite the sentry outside the Marine Nationale, place de la Bourse, rue Saint-Ferréol, place de la Préfecture (monument to Alexander and Barthou), rue Saint-Sébastien, Archives des Bouches-du-Rhône (destination), an itinerary that could be varied by taking the ferry across the Vieux-Port to Endoum.

The rigid adherence to a daily itinerary gave me a sense of purpose, a feeling of security (there could be no great catastrophe, no war, as long as I stuck on course), and, above all, the sensation that I was an element in the hourly heartbeat of a great city, a unit in the flux and reflux so admirably described in *Le 6 octobre* and in Louis Chevalier's brilliantly imaginative *Les Parisiens*. I was quick to establish similar itineraries in Rouen, le Havre, Dieppe, Lille, Amiens, or, for that matter, anywhere I spent a few days on local research. It is by following fixed routes, like a bus, that one acquires the feeling of a town, perceives the passage of the hours and of the seasons, the shifting of the light, and the regular movement of the crowds. As long as the *lycées* disgorge their noisy hordes, *à heure fixe*, as long as the *cheminots*[1] or the *employés de la Préfecture* pour out at midday, there can be no disaster, no cataclysm, no dreaded lapse back into violence and killing, no corpses left lying in the street. In Lyon, in summer, I swam, from 12.10 p.m. to 1 p.m., at the Club des Nageurs Lyonnais (CNL), below the pont de la Feuillée. Three girls – always the same – were there each day, getting brown on the rafts in the Saône. They smiled at me, but we never spoke.

The work itinerary could be further improved upon by a leisure one, varying day by day, but following a weekly schedule: lunch in the same

---

[1] Railway workers, employees of the SNCF.

restaurant with its regular, and therefore reassuring, clientele of paint-ers and stonemasons in their white hats and white smocks, minor civil servants, *employés de la mairie*, the *parfumeuse* from across the road. For dinner, a greater variety, and with more time to listen and to watch, while reading the *chronique judiciaire* of *Le Monde* or *Le Progrès*. At weekends a sense of involvement could be further enhanced by a trip up the Saône, by the Blue Train to l'Île-Barbe, or by the *ficelle*[1] to Saint-Just, thence to Vaugneray, in the Monts du Lyonnais, in a Wild West sort of train: both places to which the Lyonnais would flock in great numbers, *en famille*, in couples, or as solitary fishermen. It was Simenon country, like the riverside *guinguettes* of the Marne; at least, it was frequented by Simenon-type people, and regularly, for Maigret never seems to have come here. The same people came each weekend, and in this way relations were established.

With two hills – the red and the black – the long peninsula *entre Rhône et Saône*, two rivers, twenty bridges, a wonderland of passage-ways, three *ficelles*, a multitude of tiny squares, perched perilously on some diminutive pocket handkerchief of level ground, Lyon is an endless, inexhaustible invitation to exploration, discovery, and wonderment. In the Croix-Rousse, the long blind windows in peeling ochre façades are those of the *canuts*[2] and of the old prints, *images d'Épinal*, of the 1830s, with the cotton-wool puffs of the cannons of repression. A sense of joy at just being there, in the amazing up-and-down, stepped city, climbing up and up between high, blank, black walls, huge, dark, closed green doorways, yellowing walls surmounted by Greek pots and greenery. As Henri Béraud looks down on the Terreaux from the top of the montée de la Grande Côte, down on the pont de la Boucle, on a dull November day, with the gulls swirling, he exclaims: 'La ville bleue! Ma ville!' Mine too, a beloved place, with friendliness and fraternity *Au Pot des Gônes*,[3] near the Caillou, or *Au Club des Grognards de la Boucle*, where they played bowls.

One could also stay put in Paris; rather than spend a few days in Joinville-le-Pont, it was more adventurous to cross the river and spend

---

[1] Funicular.
[2] Silk-workers of the Croix-Rousse.
[3] *Gône*, Lyon slang for child.

a fortnight in an hotel on the canal Saint-Martin, or in the Batignolles, or off the Ternes, to create a new routine and to observe unfamiliar groups of *habitués*. The *Métro*, curving towards Bolivar and the Buttes-Chaumont, the *ligne 96*, clambering laboriously up the rue de Ménilmontant and the rue du Télégraphe, the *ligne 75*, heading through the button wholesale depots of the Marais, are the most worthwhile *invitations au voyage*; there is no better observation post of the changing world unrolling backwards, than that of the relaxed, leaning comfort of the *plateforme d'autobus*, squeezed between an *agent* and a large man with a drooping cigarette. It is a good platform too for the sharp, North-Parisian wit of the *receveur*, a calling that produces some of the best conversation to be heard in the XXe. There will be little to be heard, nothing to be observed, once the old buses are gone, to be replaced by the closed coffin-like vehicle with automatic doors, with a seated *receveur*, behind glass, like a bureaucrat. If, to emulate Jean Galtier-Boissière, one were to write the recollections of a *vieux Parisien*, or to follow in the steps of Aragon, through the Louis-Philippe arcades of the VIIIe and the IXe, one would be tempted to entitle the book: *Vu d'une plateforme d'autobus*.

In February 1935, sitting at the edge of a concrete-lined lake in the Bois de Vincennes, with *Boule de Suif*, I suddenly realized that for the previous two hours I had been enjoying reading French. It was no longer a burden and had become a pleasure, which, from then onwards, grew and grew, to include *L'Œuvre* and *Le Canard*, and an increasing range of novels. After about a month in Paris, wandering on the boulevard Montmartre, I met my first French friend, Maurice, at the time an unemployed cinema hairdresser from the Épinay studios. We had both been enjoying an argument that had arisen from an accident, in which the car of Mlle Malvy, the Minister's daughter, had been damaged by an ancient Renault driven by a drunken *marchand de bestiaux*, who had both the crowd and numbers on his side; there were four red-faced colleagues with him in the *gambarde*.[1] After the free entertainment, we went to a café. Maurice was a lead-in to the dreaded horrors of military service; he had succeeded in getting himself discharged from the

[1] An old car.

artillery on medical grounds, by distending his stomach on seven litres
of lemonade a day – worth it at the price. He lived in a horrible little
room behind the Gare de l'Est, possibly the most melancholy quarter
of Paris; the floor was covered with back numbers of *Paris-Turf*. He
was a change from the Thullier brothers and we found that we had a
lot to say to each other. I never ceased to marvel at his total rejection
of all authority. After that, we used to meet once or twice a week and
I would offer him a meal in a Greek restaurant in the rue de la Harpe.

About the same time – it was the anniversary of the *12 février*[1] – I
was sitting in the park of Saint-Cloud when a man in a cap came up to
me. 'Lis ça, camarade,' he said, and left me with *L'Humanité*. In April
I went for a holiday in Rouen by myself. One day on the quai Victor, a
small group of dockers, carrying red flags, came past, heading for the
Bourse du Travail; I followed them and attended their meeting in the
courtyard. 'Le patron ne veut rien faire pour nous,' said their leader. A
red-faced docker, who had drunk a lot of calvados, held me by the lapel
and told me how it was to live, in Sotteville or le Grand-Quevilly, on
100 francs a week with a wife and three children. I returned to the rue
Beauvoisine, after having had a row with a taxi-driver; I shouted at
him, called him names. I was over the barrier, could think in French.

My first view of the Latin Quarter was a January day, with the long,
clipped avenues of the Luxembourg disappearing in a cold fog. Lower
down, opposite the medical school, a group of young men wearing
floppy berets and carrying walking sticks with sharp, pointed metal
ends, were chanting: 'La France aux Français, à bas les métèques.' In
the following March, the Austrian dictator, Kurt Schuschnigg, came on
an official visit to France; it was rumoured that he would arrive at the
Gare de l'Est – his carriage was in fact taken off at Noisy-le-Sec – and
there was an immense demonstration, the red banners only just visible
in the gloom, from the boulevard Magenta to the huge neo-Gothic
church. There was a single whistle blast, then the sound of galloping
horses, as the dark-blue, black-helmeted *gardes mobiles* rode into the
crowd, hitting out with their long batons; the first three waves were fol-

---

[1] 12 February 1934. This was the republican counter-demonstration that followed the
attempted fascist *putsch* of 6 February. Organized by the Radical, Socialist, and
Communist parties, by the trade unions and the Ligue des Droits de l'Homme, it might
be seen as the origin of the Grand Alliance of the Front Populaire of 1936.

lowed by fifty or more *paniers à salade*, long dark charabancs of 1920 vintage, into which bleeding demonstrators of all ages and both sexes were literally hurled. After fifteen minutes, the square was quiet and littered with slogans and banners.

It was not difficult to know which side one was on in the France of 1935; and it was easier still in 1936. But I was, above all, appalled by the readiness with which violence was accepted by the Thullier brothers and by most of their friends. They told me that the *passage à tabac*[1] was an old French institution; they did not like the police, but they thought it quite natural that anyone who fell into their hands should have a preliminary beating-up. The father of one of their friends horrified me, at the time of Munich, by saying to me, in the most cheerful manner, as if it were a matter of going on a cross-country run: 'Eh bien! Monsieur Cobb, vous allez bientôt prendre votre fusil!' There did not seem much point explaining to him that this was the very last thing that I wanted to do. I was – and still am – completely puzzled by the reckless readiness of the French to get themselves killed, and equally shocked by their apparent readiness to kill. Fortunately there was Maurice, who had no intention of doing either, and I used to console myself with the thought that there were probably many more like him. In the summer of 1940, he deserted from his unit with a like-minded Parisian, held up a farm to obtain civilian clothes, hitched a lift from a German civilian driving a Darmstadt furniture van; together, they drove eastwards, avoiding the main roads, stopping in village and *bourg*, loading up the contents of deserted houses: furniture, bedding, books, food, silver, wine, typewriters, tyres, *allez oup! et en route!* parting, near Reims: *Gute Reise! Bon voyage et bon retour!* Maurice headed for Paris, serving for a time as a guide to *Wehrmacht* NCOs: *Viele Schweinerei.*

In the Bibliothèque Mazarine, seated facing outwards, on to the back of Condorcet, I discovered first Mathiez, then Jaurès. What appealed to me most in the former was his utter intransigence, his polemical vigour, his capacity to deride, his insistence on taking sides. Mathiez was exciting, because he was quite unlike any other historian I had

[1] A preliminary beating-up.

previously read, he was always uncovering plots, using the Archives like a detective. Robespierre was pure, uncompromising, he loved the common people. By the summer of 1935, I was a convinced *robespierriste*; I was not, however, a Unitarian, for I took in Saint-Just and Couthon as well. My excuse was that I was not yet eighteen. I shed most of Robespierre on resuming research in the mid-1940s; there is no historical personage I now find more repellent, save possibly Saint-Just.

Jaurès had a different and, I like to think, more lasting appeal. I was fired by his rolling eloquence, moved by his immense compassion and generosity. Jaurès was a popular historian, with a wide range of forgiveness; he did not condemn the counter-revolutionary out of hand, but tried to understand him, he did not mock the priesthood, nor denounce deluded women for their 'superstition', he did not think that any of the revolutionary leaders held a monopoly of virtue. He was a warm man with a good heart; he understood poverty.

In 1937, I visited Georges Lefebvre, at his home in Boulogne (avenue Jean-Jaurès) and attended his lectures on the Revolutionary Government in an overcrowded and wildly enthusiastic Sorbonne. There was a total sense of identity between the stiff, red-faced Northerner, extraordinarily effective in his rendering of Marat or of Saint-Just, and an audience that was predominantly Front Populaire. The same year, I was received, Hôtel Saint-James & Albany, by General Herlaut, who had commanded a tank division at Versailles at the time of the 6 *février* and was then in command of the Rouen military division; with his *képi à feuilles de chêne*[1] and a pair of white gloves on a marble table beside him, he called me 'jeune homme', and, after a long tirade against Mussolini and Hitler, ended our interview with the words: 'Vous verrez, jeune homme, tout cela finira dans la boue et dans le sang.' I needed no convincing of that, living as I did with fear, every day, almost every hour.

On going down in June 1938, I returned to Paris and began what is now a thirty years' friendship with the Archives Nationales, one of the most beautiful buildings in Europe and a secure refuge from fear. Violence, one felt, could never lap into that elegant, semi-oblong

[1] A French general's rank is indicated by the oak leaves that fringe his cap.

courtyard. War and revolution must stay outside. The AN remained open from 1939 to 1944; and, after 1940, was regularly attended by a commission of *Wehrmacht* officers classifying the documents concerning the confiscated estates of French Huguenots who, in virtue of the Edict of Potsdam, had entered the Prussian service; nearly all the officers concerned had French names. Theirs must have been the most agreeable war job enjoyed by any Army.

Georges Lefebvre had suggested that I choose as a research subject one of the *hébertiste*[1] leaders, François-Nicolas Vincent, the general secretary of the Ministry of War in the year II. General Herlaut and Georges Javogues gave me invaluable advice as to documentary material. I made one or two interesting discoveries, and espoused, with passion, the strident quarrels of my subject, one of the most violent, most foolish, most sanguinary, and most hysterical of the revolutionary leaders. On returning to England, at the outbreak of war, I wrote up my research. The result was a disaster; I fell into all the usual traps awaiting the biographer, rewriting the whole history of the Revolution around a man who was at best a secondary figure, and bringing down the curtain with his rather well-deserved death. I made claims for his participation in most of the *journées* on the flimsiest of evidence, throwing at my examiners all my material, much of it trifling or irrelevant, subjecting them furthermore to a language barely recognizable as English. When I returned to research in October 1946, I decided to start afresh. Twenty years later, at the end of a lecture that I had been giving at the University of Chicago, I was approached by an elderly lady who handed me a packet containing my abortive excursion into the history of *hébertisme*, which I had sent to Louis Gottschalk in 1940.

When I had finally readjusted to civilian life, I decided to return to research. It was not that I felt any great enthusiasm at the time for academic work (the Army had offered me a varied range of employments, nearly all of which I had enjoyed); but I needed an excuse in my own mind to stay permanently in Paris, and I could not think of a better one. I had seen Georges Lefebvre again in 1944 and 1945, during leaves in Paris, and in 1946 met Pierre Caron. I decided to

---

[1] One of the political groups of the year II.

research on *hébertisme*. In 1947, I was introduced to Albert Soboul, who was then similarly engaged. After a few months working parallel and following each other, not without some mistrust, through the same boxes, we both independently came to the conclusion that *hébertisme* was a non-starter. But, while in its pursuit, we had each stumbled on something else: Soboul, on the Sections[1] and the *sectionnaires*,[2] myself on the Paris Revolutionary Army, and thence to some fifty others, and the *problème des subsistances*.[3] In both instances, our eventual choice of subjects had been largely dictated to us by the nature of our documentary material; Soboul had gone to the *fonds sectionnaires* in search of *hébertisme* as a popular party, and he had discovered an independent popular movement that owed little or nothing to *hébertisme*. I had been after *hébertistes* rather than after *hébertisme* – a line of division that has no doubt always distinguished me from Soboul; I had found few, but I had in the process stumbled on hundreds of *révolutionnaires*,[4] ultras of a less exalted, less self-conscious, more spontaneous kind.

Once he had found his subject, Soboul worked with speed and determination, to a careful plan and with a vigorous refusal to allow himself to be led down any side channels. My own method – this is perhaps not the right word – was very different. I was in no hurry – I was not aiming at any particular career in England; more and more I enjoyed the excitement of research and the acquisition of material, often on quite peripheral subjects, as ends in themselves. I allowed myself to be deflected down unexpected channels, by the chance discovery of a bulky *dossier* – it might be the love letters of a *guillotiné*, or intercepted correspondence from London, or the account-books and samples of a commercial traveller in cotton, or the fate of the English colony in Paris, or eyewitness accounts of the September Massacres or of one of the *journées*. I paused here and there, to write

---

[1] Paris was divided into forty-eight Sections. Originally electoral wards, in 1793 they became the principal unit of popular militancy and remained an effective force until the spring of 1794.

[2] Members of the Sections, hence *sans-culottes*.

[3] This word is difficult to translate; it means mainly the problem of provisioning of the urban markets.

[4] I use this word in the particular sense of 'member of a revolutionary army'.

18

an article, to publish a *glane*, on this or that. And as my research took me to about forty Departments, and especially to Norman ones, the Nord, the Seine-et-Oise, the Oise, the Seine-et-Marne, and the Rhône (there was plenty of material in all these for me, but I also liked being there, so I kept on returning for more) I likewise multiplied excursions into provincial history. It was hard to put down resolutely the register of a municipality at a date in 1794; I wanted to know what followed; inevitably I dribbled over into 1795 – this was first out of curiosity, but later, when I realized what a gold-mine the year III could be on the year II, I did so systematically. Nor was this a stopping point. Much of my material came from individual *dossiers* of officers, in the Archives Administratives de la Guerre; but these did not stop in 1794, some went on to 1820, to 1830, a few to 1840, and with them I went on too. I was interested in individuals rather than groups; and when I could pin down one of them, I naturally wanted to follow him through, to pension and grave, to letters from his widow or children, as the paper, the words on the top, and the handwriting changed, as well as the names and titles of Ministers of War. I was lucky, in this respect, to have had to spend so much time on Army personnel, for soldiers, in France, leave more traces than civilians, and their widows have to be paid. They also tend to live longer; or so it appeared to me.

I researched and wrote for my own enjoyment, taking a particular pleasure in spreading my merchandise over as many provinces as possible. I liked *Annales de Normandie*, *La Revue du Nord*, and *Cahiers d'Histoire* best, because I was happy in Rouen, le Havre and Dieppe, Lille and Lyon; but it gave me particular satisfaction to publish in small reviews like *Présence Ardennaise*; and I preferred *Mémoires: Paris Île-de-France* to a national review, because they represented the history of Paris and the Paris region. And the great strength of French historical research has always been the survival of local reviews. I would have been shocked if anyone had suggested that I should be paid for doing what I enjoyed doing. Nor would I have enjoyed doing it so much, if I had been paid for it. Research was a luxury in which I was able to indulge, by earning money by teaching English to tele-communications engineers, Agro[1] students, and Air France hostesses

[1] Institut National Agronomique.

(this was enjoyable too). I bought my time at the Archives and so valued it more. My brief marriage to a French girl employed by the SNCF facilitated research in local records by the yearly issue of a free ticket, *Ière classe*, usable anywhere on the French internal network. And, if the worst came to the worst, my mother would advance me the odd £50. My approach to historical research was that of a dilettante. I have never understood history other than in terms of human relationships; and I have attempted to judge individuals in their own terms and from what they say about themselves, in their own language.

Most interesting of all, to me, is the individual unrelated to any group, the man, the girl, or the old woman alone in the city, the person who eats alone, though in company, who lives in a furnished room, who receives no mail, who has no visible occupation, and who spends much time wandering the streets. For, apart from the everlasting problem of violence, the principal one that faces a historian like myself is that of loneliness, especially loneliness in the urban context. Hence my inveterate taste for the *chronique judiciaire* of *Le Monde* and, in its day, of *Libération* (the realm of the marvellous, the generous Madeleine Jacob, the warmest of popular historians, the most at home of any in *la correctionelle*). Gaby, from Pézenas, has committed suicide in a *chambre de bonne* in the XVe; the body of Micheline, scantily clad in black underwear, her throat slit, has been discovered in the bedroom of an *hôtel de passe*, rue des Acacias. Madeleine, a Lyonnaise, in Paris only for the previous three months, has been shot dead, coming out of a Cours Pigier. Marcelle has been found stabbed to death, in the Bois de Boulogne; she was from la Ferté-Bernard. And so on. The *concierge*, plied by reporters, can only say: 'Ce fut une jeune fille tranquille, une vraie jeune fille, je ne lui connaissais aucune liaison, elle ne recevait point de visites.' The parents, back home, are bewildered. Sooner or later, the *dossier* is closed. But not for the historian. What road, thus terminating in violence, has been followed by the daughter of a *cheminot* from Saint-Germain-des-Fossés? Into what fearful trap has the lonely provincial girl stumbled? For many years, my favourite historians have been the late Pierre Bénard and Madeleine Jacob.

For myself, history has never been an intellectual debate. This may be due in part to my own insufficiencies, for I am no debater; but also

I have never felt the need of it. For historians should not 'intellectualize' about people often less sophisticated than themselves, and about societies less complicated than those in which we live. In history, intellectual debate can so often be a cover for over-simplification, lack of experience, insufficient culture, lack of involvement and of sympathy, and the impetus to compare and to generalize in cases where comparisons and generalizations are either irrelevant or positively misleading. Why, one wonders, when reading certain sections of *Past and Present*, why do historians spend so much time arguing, imposing definitions, proposing 'models', when they could be getting on with their research?

I have, then, worked on French history because I like being in France and have now reached the second generation of my French friends. To live in France is to live double, every moment counts, the light of the sky of the Île-de-France is unique and a source of joy, there is joy too in a small rectangle of sunshine at the top of a tall, greying, leprous building, the colour of Utrillo, and in the smell of chestnuts that brings the promise of autumn, *la Rentrée*, and the beloved repetition of the Paris year. There is joy in speaking French, and in listening to women, children, Louis Jouvet, and Michel Simon speaking it. Paris is the abode of love, as well as of violence; if, as Louis Chevalier reminds us, the Paris street *sent la poudre*, it is only sometimes, whereas love is there all the time, in a cat arching its back in the sun, and in the eyes of *la belle boulangère* in her white apron. To speak and to write in French is to acquire a second personality and to express oneself not only in another gear, but in a manner other than in one's first. I do not say the same things in French as I do in English, because I am not the same person. For nine years I dispensed with my initial nationality almost entirely, and without any great feeling of deprivation.

My sense of involvement has been further enlarged by the experience of events over a long period, by personal contacts, and by random reading, over the years, of such populist and regionalist novelists as Eugène Dabit (the Paris suburbs), Louis Guilloux (Saint-Brieuc), Maxence van der Meersch (Roubaix), Marc Bernard (Nîmes), Henri Béraud (Lyon), René Fallet (Villeneuve-Saint-Georges), Raymond

Queneau[1] (le Havre, the northern suburbs of Paris, Paris itself), Hervé Bazin (the Craonnais), René Lefèvre (Paris), Julien Blanc (mostly *maisons de redressement* and prisons), Panaït Istrati, and Blaise Cendrars (especially on the subject of Marseille). History is a cultural

[1] THE WRITING GAME

Sir, – Your reviewer (May 25), in his excellent article on Raymond Queneau, has illustrated some of the techniques of an author who is often difficult and has suggested some clues to his mathematical and philosophical riddles. But Queneau is not just a writer, who indulged in intellectual gymnastics, and it would not be quite fair to compare him, even in his most intractable moods, either to Valéry or to Sartre. For he is not deliberately perverse, he is never a fraud, he is more than just clever, and he does not write about sick or try to make his readers it. *Loin de Rueil* is quite the funniest novel in the French language; *Exercices de style* is an encyclopaedia of verbal observation. Queneau is as familiar with the 27 as with the 21, with the 24 as with the 28 – all his lines begin at Saint-Lazare – and the *plateforme d'autobus* – yet another of those amiable, leisurely, lounging institutions now in the process of suppression by the technocrats – is as good a vantage point as *le zinc* – and better than the *Métro*, too crowded for conversation, too noisy for eavesdropping – for the social novelist; and this is what Queneau is, in the happiest populist tradition. For if his extraordinary verbal inventiveness and his joy in rendering speech owe much to a childhood spent in le Havre, during the 1914–18 War, listening – on the tram from school he has certainly made the most of the *transports en commun*! – to English soldiers mauling French, and Havrais girls English, his great qualities as a novelist are his joyful humour, his innocence, his compassion and his enjoyment of unelevated company. Much of his dialogue goes – and has been heard – in the sort of restaurant – *restaurant des chauffeurs*, &c. – in which it was possible, in the 1940s or 1950s, still to get a good *bœuf gros sel* – and which were likely to be found, on small squares, off the rue de Vaugirard, in the XVe. They are too *restaurants d'habitués* – with the painters and builders in their white coats and the horse-slaughterers in their leather jackets. And the conversation is of a kind enjoyed by those who meet daily and who share their allusive jokes. (This is what is so reassuring about such places.) The creator of *Zazie* is very close to his model; and there are sharp, observant and rather naughty children in many of his novels. Like the sturdy characters who eat in the *restaurant des chauffeurs*, and like Zazie, Queneau shakes with fits of uncontrollable laughter.

Finally, unlike so many French novelists, whose approach to Paris has been via the Gare du Lyon or Austerlitz – the first view of the Promised Land of so many *normaliens*, including the creator of Jerphanion – his first contact with the Capital was via the Cour de Rome and the rue du Havre. Sartre found le Havre intolerable – the Havrais, no doubt, were just not clever enough, worse, they may even have seemed happy; Queneau writes of the place with the same warmth as Béraud wrote of a childhood in les Terreaux, between Rhône and Saône, or poor Maxence van der Meersch of Roubaix, its mills, its canal and the long, long rue de Lannoy, during the First World

subject that cannot be disassociated from literature and language. And both resist the attempts of syllabus-merchants to impose upon each the iron frame of periodicity. A great deal of Paris eighteenth-century history, of Lyon nineteenth-century history can be walked, seen, and above all heard, in small restaurants, on the platform at the back of a bus, in cafés, or on the park bench. I have at times been so much aware of this that, in order to improve my chances as an investigator of the past and to cast deeper roots in France, I have been tempted to apply for naturalization. Fortunately, I have been deterred on each occasion by the slowly grinding mills of French bureaucracy, as well as by the thought that I would no more belong in a French institutional frame-work than in an English one. I have tried to have it both ways: to increase my sense of involvement, and to preserve my status of Lone Wolf. It has not always worked very well. But after the *13 mai*, French naturalization lost all its attraction.

Research in revolutionary, or in any other, history, can never be a full-time occupation; nor, indeed, should it be. Even the Archives are not entirely a safe refuge, and the historian, however much he may try, cannot entirely escape from the present. Time and place will affect him, and their influence will inevitably increase with the years, as experience and memory add further layers to the sense of involvement. 1935, however it looks now, was dominated at the time by the constant harping back to the 6 and *12 février*, while the *affaire Stavisky* was given a further lease of death by the endless speculation regarding the disappearance of the *conseiller* Prince, whose body had been found along the railway line near Dijon, at a spot evocatively called la Combe-aux-Fées. 1935 was then as much *l'année Prince*, as it was that of M. Flandin or of *Madame la Marquise*. It was impossible, at the age of nineteen and living alone in a furnished room in the rue Saint-

War or under the Front Populaire. Many of his characters too trail the Seine Maritime behind them, when in Paris or *banlieue Saint-Lazare*. He has come in the best way. Queneau, even in the heart of NRF, is still a provincial, like Louis Guilloux or Hervé Bazin. This too is part of his appeal, especially to the English, for nothing could be more reassuring than le Havre. RICHARD COBB

Balliol College, Oxford

[Published in the *Times Literary Supplement*, 1 June 1967.]

André-des-Arts, not to partake of *la Grande Espérance* of 1936, of the Front Populaire, *les grèves sur le tas*,[1] Léo Lagrange, the first Minister of Sports and Leisure (killed, along with so many other hopes, in 1940), *congés payés* which, for the first time, brought Ménilmontant and Belleville to the Mediterranean and the tandems of athletic campers to the inner recesses of *la Bretagne bretonnante*. In the 14 July procession of that year, one marched hand in hand with Fraternity and Hope. It was impossible too not to feel the utmost revulsion for those Frenchmen – few, but rich, sanguinary, fanatical, and dominated by fear and egoism – who looked on Franco as they had looked on Mussolini, as the potential saviour of *la bourgeoisie française*. Madrid seemed very close to Paris, the Gare d'Austerlitz so often resounded with the incantation: *des avions pour l'Espagne!*

1937 was above all *l'année Expo*. And the *Expo* brought to Paris Weidmann, the young German mass-murderer, who, after killing the American dancer, Joan de Koven, a commercial traveller, a taxi-driver, and various others he had met, generally by chance, stored their effects, including food and clothing, in a villa that he had leased at la Celle-Saint-Cloud (villas were cheap in those days), *banlieue* Saint-Lazare; one can imagine the sort of thing: *faux manoir normand*, with enormous projecting eaves. He was the last man to be guillotined in public, on the place d'Armes in Versailles, an occasion attended by *le Tout-Paris* with champagne suppers, while awaiting the dawn that would see the erection of the death machine. There was something particularly weird about the Weidmann trial, the herald of the violence to come. But something of the spirit of the Front Populaire survived; in 1937 Jean Zay opened the Lycée Claude-Bernard, a monument to the elaborate, copper-covered bad taste of the mid-thirties. It could be classed with *la Normandie* and the current banknotes (with a nude Republic not unlike those on the murals of the Sphinx).[2]

Few can appreciate the deeper, more secret wells of Appeasement if they have not experienced the dreadful, naked panic of the summer of 1938 in Paris: queues outside the banks (and the wealthier the quarter,

---

[1] Strikes accompanied by the occupation of factories.

[2] The Sphinx, the property of the Sarraut brothers, was one of the most celebrated of the *maisons closes* of the inter-war years. Situated behind the Gare du Montparnasse, it was closed in 1945 and has since served as a students' hostel.

the longer the queue; as usual, in times of fear, *la bourgeoisie française* was taking out its gold, prior to running west), the green buses filled to the roof with stretchers, pitiful pails of sand in the wells of stair-cases, fast-moving military ambulances, the semi-civilian, semi-mil-itary, drunken chaos of the Gare de l'Est, choked with *réservistes* in kepis and civilian trousers, large cars loaded with mattresses, the readers of the BN rushing out into the courtyard in the late August 1938, at the sound of a low-flying plane, the evening succession of screamed *Édition Spéciale!* The relief at the news of Munich was phys-ical and visible in the faces of passers-by; no wonder Daladier was wel-comed like a conquering hero. People could sleep undisturbed that night, whatever the future. And, in Paris in 1938, one did not make too big claims on the future, one was grateful for a few more weeks, or a few more months, it was all time gained. I too was physically and morally a *munichois*; even so, if disaster were to come, I preferred that it should come to me in France. I had no inclination to leave Paris in August 1938; the French panic had been mine too. 1939 did not seem quite so bad; it is perhaps difficult to go through the whole process of panic twice, at quite such a short interval; Marcel Déat apparently drew little response, *Match* published impressive photographs of the Polish cavalry, *Paris-Soir*, photographs of WVS organizing canteens and the women of the English upper-middle classes 'going to it' with looks of enormous satisfaction (there was a particular luxury in looking at such pictures and in reading of England's warrior mood from the terrace of a Paris café). But this time, things did not work out as I had hoped. The outbreak of war caught me in England, another accident for which I had not planned. On 9 May 1940 I obtained a visa from the French Consulate in London to return to France. For much of the first year following the Fall of France, I attempted to gain permission to join the FFL[1] (not, I hoped, in any very dangerous capa-city); but I was eventually placed in the British Army, to be trained as a storeman.

A 'lucky' among other 'luckies', most of them lorry-drivers and mechanics from North London, I was placed in a horse-box which I shared with three others, all of whom boasted of their prison

---

[1] Forces Françaises Libres.

experiences. To their *palmarès* of Brixton, Pentonville, the Scrubs, Strangeways, the Mountjoy, Armley, I could only counter with an obscure prison in Vienna and the cells in Tunbridge Wells magistrates' court; it was rather like Sutton Valence or Hurstmonceux competing with Eton and Winchester. They were very decent about it, soon took me in and used their (considerable) influence in the cook-house to get me extra rations and double helpings. After about a fortnight of bantering ('Hoxford, wot wot!'), I was accepted too by the other 'luckies'. My long stay in France had enabled me to acquire a second nationality and to discover fraternity; the Army did me the enormous service of divesting me of class. There was fraternity too in the North, in Scotland, and in South Wales, all places in which I was fortunate enough to be stationed; it was back to the warm kitchen, the tea on the boil. It was quite a new Britain to me. Also, for the first time, I became aware of the infinite guile of the Londoner when it was a matter of avoiding work or of giving the appearance of work to the reality of almost blissful idleness. A long stretch in 'sanitary', emptying latrine buckets spread over an area of many miles, in beautiful rolling countryside, gave me a valuable grounding in the old Army art of making a little go a long way; one could make four or five buckets last out till 4 or 5 p.m., by which time it was possible to return to camp, filthy and suitably stinking, get cleaned up, and go to the pub. I much preferred *les servitudes* to *les grandeurs* of military life; and Jaroslav Hasek and Julian Maclaren-Ross have a much clearer appreciation of the realities of military life, in an unwilling conscript army, than Alfred de Vigny.

The Army, it is well known, 'moves in a mysterious way'. I sought liaison work, still in the hope of gaining access to the FFL. From 'sanitary', I was transferred to the Poles, thence to the Czechoslovak Independent Brigade Group. I did not know either language, but I was not alone in this. At least an extended period with both forces added to my awareness of Europe and of national minorities; some of my closest friends among the Poles were Ukrainians from Wołyn, among the Czechs, Ukrainians from Pod-Karpatska-Rus. At a period when I was making a serious attempt to learn Polish, I was almost persuaded by Professor Willie Rose eventually to invest in Polish history.

In 1943 and 1944, I made a number of broadcasts for Jean Oberlé;

they were sentimental and mushy. I also wrote in French papers published in London. In the spring of 1944, I succeeded in obtaining a transfer to 21st Army Group. This was the first time that things had really come my way, for in April or May, while in a sealed camp somewhere in East Essex, we were all paid 200 francs – the two notes were quite unfamiliar to me, Henri IV and Sully and the bucolic slogan: 'Labourage et pâturage sont les deux mamelles de la France'; if the Maréchal was sinking more and more into dotage, France, it would appear, was going Back to the Land. On receiving the notes, we all concluded that we must be heading for Norway. The notes were a feint. But, of course, they were not. I always wondered where they had been printed, for they were crisp and new.

The Army is the most unpredictable of travel agencies, and has a much wider range to offer than Dean & Dawson, or Swan and the other merchants of sun, sand, and bronzed torsos. It took me first to the Bessin, then to the Nord, then to Ixelles, with several leaves in Paris and Marseille, and fortunately only a few weeks in Germany, at First Corps Headquarters at Iserlöhn (a horrid little town situated in a sinister Grimm-like countryside of thick, pagan pine forests and lakes).

I was in or near Bayeux from July to September 1944 – long enough to make a number of friends in the town, mostly among the *cheminots*, but including a Belgian shoemaker, M. Ploemakers, who had settled there in 1918; long enough too to write regularly for *La Renaissance du Bessin* (the old *Journal de Bayeux* under a new guise, but under much the same management, which was largely royalist); long enough to spend 14 July at a football match and be arrested by the Provost Corps for distributing a news-sheet in French to the Bayeusains; long enough to witness the arrival of groups of black-marketeers from Rouen, Amiens, and Paris, wearing coloured arm-bands and bearing requisition orders in the name of shadowy authorities. Bayeux was experiencing its *heure de gloire*; the Bayeusains were prone to admit that they could well have done without it (and the farmers felt much the same: 'M. le sergent, on fait la guerre en rase campagne, comme l'Argonne ou la Somme, on ne fait pas la guerre dans un pays à herbages, vous savez ce que ça coûte d'abattre 200 poiriers pour faire une piste d'envol?', etc.). The Hôtel du Lion d'Or was crowded in July by an enthusiastic group of young prefects and sub-prefects, even of one or two *commissaires régionaux*,[1] waiting to take up office once their apportioned territories were liberated; the food there was surprisingly good and my civilian friends supplied me with *tickets de pain*. Calvados was easily obtainable in exchange for cigarettes; and I spent much of my time (as I worked at night, I had most of the day free) going from farm to farm – I had my place at the *grande table* in half a dozen; the farms were full of young men who were not from the Bessin. In Barbeville, where I was stationed, I delivered a small cyclostyled news-sheet in French every morning before going to bed to the local *mairie*, which was also the *école communale*. The sheet was thence sent to the neighbouring villages and even as far as Balleroy. Every day, at twelve, a small girl with very fair hair and wearing clogs, came to the *mairie*, from Cothun, seven kilometres away, to pick up a copy. She was sent by the *maire*, an elderly farmer with strong anti-clerical tendencies. To see this small figure as she arrived each day gave me a sense of permanency and the feeling that I had at least one foot in the Bessin. My sheet was widely read, though M. le Curé regarded it with some alarm and the local *châtelain* with distaste.

Most evenings I also had dinner at the *école* with the *institutrice* who was also *secrétaire de la mairie* – this was how I had met her – a girl so blonde that she looked as if she had come down in direct descent from the Vikings. She had taken a liking to me (this was reciprocated) and used to cook me steaks, which we ate out in the vegetable garden, in cream. As I returned to work, in the evening, to the camp, I met long lines of ambulances driving slowly and very gently from the battle area, over the bumpy, unmade, dusty roads. At night one could see the artillery bombardment, but the countryside was dead quiet. I used to think that I was perhaps the luckiest soldier in the British Army. Certainly I must have been one of the happiest. A little before my departure, I heard at dusk the faint rumble of a train – the line between Paris and Cherbourg had been re-established and it was the first to reach Bayeux. The *heure de gloire* was at last over; it was the most

[1] Super-Prefects appointed by the French Provincial Government and entrusted with the task of taking over the administration of liberated territories. Most had very large areas; there was one for Normandy, one for the Nord, one for the Toulouse area, one for the Lyon area, etc. The best known were Yves Farge (Lyon) and Berteaux (Toulouse).

beautiful, reassuring sound I had heard since 1939. The war was receding from the Cotentin, civilian life once more imposed its priorities; and, for me, the sound hinted demobilization, the resumption of freedom as a civilian in France. I was happy for the Bayeusains, who could return to their sleepy existence, made relatively more prosperous by the presence of three large war cemeteries, a greater tourist draw than the *tapisserie* had ever been. The town, which before the Revolution had lived off the Church, could now live off the Allied dead. When my unit left the Bessin for Brussels, there was a girl in white standing outside the *école*, who waved to me as we passed.

There followed a brief, alien interlude in Malines (or, more horribly, Mechelen), an unpleasant Flemish clerical town. We were stationed in the Caserne des Grenadiers, next door to the prison, so that on Thursdays and Sundays, visiting days, we could see the long queues – many fur coats – of the wealthier Malinois, come to visit their sons, *inciviques*[1] who had militated in the VNV[2] or the Flemish SS Legions. We were treated with marked hostility, save by the *cheminots* of the CFB.[3] The Malinois were too, judging from the photographs displayed in windows, mostly *léopoldistes*, which was in character. They showed a marked reluctance to speak French, preferring English. In fact there was not much to be said for them at all; their priests put pressure on the girls to prevent them from attending our dances. At least one could enjoy the sight of Flemish farmers queuing up with suitcases outside the banks, at the time of the Guth Decrees withdrawing the old currency; they must have been hard put to it to explain the sources of their enormous earnings since 1940. The news that we were, in December 1944, to be transferred to Roubaix, was received with general satisfaction and, by me, with joy.

We arrived in Roubaix amidst a snowstorm. In the boulevard de Paris, schoolboys stopped to throw snowballs at our lorries and at the passing trams. It was a guarantee of what was to come, for this was not Malines; here the British Army was treated with enormous friendliness, a friendliness which, in many cases, was based on memory and

---

[1] Belgian for collaborator.
[2] Vlaamsch Nasionaal Verbond.
[3] Chemins de Fer Belges.

experience. In many small houses in the *corons*,[1] there would be photographs, proudly displayed, of British regiments stationed in the city in 1918; on three occasions members of my unit had the surprise of recognizing their fathers, hanging thus, in a spotless, tiled kitchen in the rue de Lannoy or the rue aux Longues Haies. Neither street was, in fact, very far from Bradford, Halifax, Keighley, or Dewsbury. At Christmas 1944 there was not a member of the Army, in the other ranks, who did not have his feet under the table, in some *coron* or other. Many Roubaisiens had to go away unsatisfied, there were not enough British soldiers to go round.

Christmas and New Year, despite so much kindness, were overshadowed by a gnawing fear, felt alike by the inhabitants and by ourselves. The wildest rumours circulated concerning the progress of the Ardennes offensive, German commandos were reported in the suburbs, and we were suddenly reissued with arms – in my case, a sten, which I persisted in leaving in trams, or in civilian houses, to be retrieved the next day ('Monsieur, vous avez laissé chez nous votre parapluie'). The inhabitants were anxious, and became even more so when they witnessed an apparent transformation from a headquarter unit into what was supposed to pass off as a fighting force. Fortunately this was never put to the test. The sense of relief, early in January 1945, was almost as physical as that of September 1938 in Paris.

Roubaix is well off the tourist circuit, though it is well known to Australian wool salesmen and some of its *patrons* and buyers speak English with an Australian accent. Its football team was coached by a Yorkshireman, and in the whole conurbation of LRT (Lille–Roubaix–Tourcoing), the three great textile towns, there were a few score of veterans from the First World War who had married local girls and many of whom, by the late 1940s, had lost their command of English, spoke with the hard *chtimi*[2] accent and had French grandchildren. It was they who had been absorbed by the strong, close-knit family life of the industrial Nord, more akin to Belgium than to France (in both the Nord and the Kingdom, beer and *café à la chicorée* – the

---

[1] *Coron*: a back-to-back in brick, characteristic of the Nord and the Pas-de-Calais industrial belt.
[2] Paris slang for an inhabitant of the Nord.

pot was always to hand and on the boil – predominated; in both, the Saturday night booze-up, on beer or on *genièvre*, gave a noisy, collective, spewy climax to a regular and very laborious week). Indeed, with over thirty frontier posts, and the frontier cutting through a street, sometimes even through a house, so that it was possible to go to an *estaminet* and drink at one bar in the Republic and walk across the room and drink at the other in the Kingdom, it was always rather hard to say where Roubaix ended and Belgium began. The telephone book was full of names under *Van*; many Roubaisiens had brothers or parents over the border, while since 1905 the very pious wool barons had been in the habit of sending their daughters and their sons to schools run by French orders situated often less than a kilometre over the frontier. Some of them had their country houses or their weekend cottages in the Tournésis, and when the *grand patron* thought in terms of pleasure – whether *la table* or *les filles* – it was to Brussels rather than to Paris that he headed. Labour organization, particularly among the SFIO[1] militants, was on the Belgian model; one of the main streets was named after Edgar Anseels, while *Jocisme*[2] had been imported by the Abbé (later Cardinal) Cardijn. There was a constant coming and going of the *gendarmerie nationale* and the *gendarmerie royale*, French *douaniers* operated on the tram routes, the early-morning trams brought in tightly packed *frontaliers*, mostly from the Courtrésis, some of whom had cycled ten or fifteen miles through the dark before taking the tram, and who came to work in France as stonemasons and builders' labourers. Along the canal de Roubaix, in Wasquehal, in Hem, in Watrelos, in Lannoy, the children played *douaniers* and *contrebandiers*; few wanted to be the former, it was a role forced upon tearful little brothers or little sisters by the bigger boys and girls, while at working-class level most families could boast a close relative – often a brother – who gave up most of his time to smuggling in tobacco. Belgian cigarettes were more in evidence than those of the Régie;[3] and while the frontier existed for civilians, it did not for the British Army, a fact which was very rapidly put to lucrative use both by civilians and

[1] Section Française de l'Internationale Ouvrière.
[2] Jeunesses Ouvrières Catholiques.
[3] The French tobacco monopoly.

31

soldiers. There were *estaminets* near the station that specialized in this trade and where Army transporters could be rewarded in cash and in kind – drinks and the *serveuses montantes*. The 21 July was fêted as much as the 14th, and at weekends there were cock-fights in the neutral zone, where it existed between the two countries. Frontiers have their advantages, as well as their romance, and there is much to be said for living on top of one.

A great industrial sprawl, astride two countries, its tramlines disappearing into the misty murk and sticky *pavés* (this is the real grind for the racing cyclist, so many of whom have come to grief on the terrible *Paris–Roubaix*) of January nights, its endless streets and rectangles of *corons* – so like Manchester back-to-backs – offered innumerable opportunities for temporary escape into the many and warm recesses of civilian life, and these did not always mean into the welcoming and well-scrubbed arms of *cardeuses* and *fileuses*, though these too were plentiful. The town was widely acclaimed by the troops as a 'cushy billet', and those who did not have girls (our only casualty, an RSM in the Pay Corps, drove himself and his girl into the canal on VE Day, a watery end to an Anglo-Roubaisien understanding) had their families and a meal waiting for them in well-heated kitchens, at 6 p.m. The Northerner especially felt at once at home. The *estaminets* were cheerful and noisy.

I was particularly fortunate in working at night in the Cercle de l'Industrie, just off the Grand'Place. I even wore civilian clothes that had been given to me by M. Roussel, the director of the establishment, including a jacket, much too big for me, that sported the *ruban rouge*. Most of my days were free, so that I could painlessly move over the gulf – and what a gulf! – that separates the enslaved soldier, the property of a Government, from the free civilian, the envy of every conscript. (I was very careful never to introduce any members of my unit to my French civilian friends.) There was a wide choice of refugees, all of them well out of reach of the Army. At the top were the wool barons, among whom a former acquaintance of undergraduate days, Albert Prouvost, occupied a prominent position. These were the roomy, comfortable, well-heated houses of the boulevard de Paris, the boulevard de Cambrai, and the extravagantly crenellated baronial halls of the parc Barbieux, the pseudo-châteaux of mid-nineteenth-century family prosperity. There was a regular pattern to such establishments: many children, a sister a nun, a brother a priest, or a monk, the others *dans l'Industrie* or married into it, a large modern statue of the Virgin, in cream against a blue background, in a niche in the main room, *Les Grandes Familles de Roubaix-Tourcoing* displayed in evidence on a table. This was a sort of industrial Debrett in which every possible marriage commutation was declined: Prouvost-Prouvost, Prouvost-Wibaux, Prouvost-Glorieux, Wibaux-Florin, Glorieux-Pierrepont, Motte-Masurel, Motte-Motte, Masurel-Toulemonde, Toulemonde-Toulemonde, Toulemonde-Tiberghien, and so on. Every combination had been thought of, and, for younger sons and daughters, there was little chance of escape from a position between the covers of that family litany. Even in death there was a niche for them in monuments the size of mini-Sainte-Chapelles, double-named to eternity. To be introduced to one family was to be introduced to the lot, all doors would open. All were closely related. Few ever looked far beyond *l'Industrie*, though this might take some to Mazamet, to Paris, to Bradford, to Mulhouse, and to Australia. All were deeply attached to the ugly, sprawling, blackened-brick industrial town, and in their intense regionalism, they differed little from the mass of their workers, whom they often knew by their Christian names. They were no doubt relatively good employers, very paternalistic, much concerned with morals and *crèches*, though somewhat suspicious of worker priests and those, like the local novelist, Maxence van der Meersch, whom they described as *Communistes blancs*. But of Maxence they were also proud, like almost everyone else in the town, because he was a regionalist who had written almost exclusively about Roubaix and who had brought honour to the town by winning the Prix Goncourt. He was, in fact, a clumsy stylist, a Christian-Socialist Zola, who wrote off an accumulated stock of *fiches*; but all his characters were identifiable in local terms, and the *patronat* was tickled by this. This is not to give the impression that the *patronat* was absolutely monolithic, even though entirely included between the hard covers of *Les Grandes Familles de Roubaix-Tourcoing*; there were a few rebels. One had written a novel, under a pseudonym, about a family funeral in one of the big houses off the Parc Barbieux, the daughter of another had broken away, taking her *licence* at the Faculté des Lettres in Lille, instead of going to the Institut Catholique there; she eventually went to live in London.

So much for the *patronat*: ecclesiastical gossip, complaints about Paris and its politicians ('Le Nord, c'est la vache à lait de la France entière'), boasts about economic Resistance, plans for slum clearance, a considerable reticence on the subject of the wool industry, a great willingness to demonstrate new techniques to visitors to their mills, lunch quite often with beer (they drank less wine than the Bruxellois, but when they did drink it, it was Burgundy, as in Brussels), bridge in the evening, a manifestation of anglophilia. They read *La Croix du Nord*, and as, in the conditions of 1944–5, the Right had been temporarily driven out of existence, they financed and voted for the MRP.[1] (*Le Sillon* had previously grown deep roots here.)

The *patronat* needed to be savoured in small quantities; it was too invasive, and one had to be too careful, too much on one's best behaviour. I was much more at home in Wasquehal, in Maxence's house by the canal, overlooking the coal barges and the cranes. In the early months of 1945 the barges were frozen hard, and crowds of poor people walked on the ice, pushing prams which they filled up with the captive coal – an episode that would have gone into Maxence's next novel – a study of Roubaix during the Occupation and Liberation periods – but poor Maxence died two years later in 1947.

Maxence, Thérèse, their daughter Sarah, and their little adopted son Valère (the result of a Franco-German liaison), afforded me what is most precious to a soldier: the warmth and security of a family. Maxence took a liking to me, stopped me smoking, made me cut down on drink, even attempted to get me married off to a Lilloise who was worthy, poor, and pious (recommended, *sous tous les rapports*, by the clergy) and insisted that I take my meals at home: home-made bread, potatoes, and everything else boiled. He was tubercular and had fallen under the influence of a medical eccentric who preached under-nourishment as a cure for tuberculosis; his most recent novel was an attack on orthodox medicine. Many of the afternoons were spent upstairs, while Maxence rested and Sarah sang me little songs: *Le Petit Quinquin, Mon mari, qu'il était petit*, and so on. It was not only family life,

[1] Mouvement Républicain Populaire.

but an introduction into the enclosed, secure world of childhood. Maxence's brother-in-law was a *contrebandier*, and when I took Valère out, the men at the lock and the bargees would greet me.

Maxence had a tremendous range of friends quite outside the *patronat*. They included a semi-gangster from Lille, who had done well out of the black market and financed the local Resistance, a sad businessman with wife trouble, a host of people who came to consult the bearded writer about their personal problems (he did have a law degree too), and a large number of men and women who worked in the mills (Thérèse had herself been a *cardeuse*) and who were active *Jocistes* (I never met, through his agency, any socialists or communists). After a month or so, I was so integrated into the spreading van der Meersch network that I found myself regularly attending weddings, baptisms, and, above all, funerals – including one of an infant – in Hem, Lys-lès-Lannoy, and in the *corons*. He also introduced me to some fringe industrialists – *les tapis boulgomme*,[1] and so on – who, not being in wool, nor marriable into the *GFRT*, were more open-minded, more aware of Paris (Maxence too had the deepest distrust of *la Babylone moderne* and its inhabitants: a godless, irreverent, and lazy lot), and, so Maxence assured me, more *social*. Another sector was that of the textile engineers, a few of whom were even anti-clerical and read *La Voix du Nord*. I even knew two doctors and received free medical attention. At the house by the canal, *bonnes à tout faire* came and went with bewildering rapidity. They were all fallen girls, who, after being rehabilitated by *le Bon Pasteur*[2] in Lille, were taken on by Maxence in the belief that the experience of a genuinely Christian household would complete their moral regeneration. In my time, all eight of them went over the wall, on Saturday night, to return, bedraggled, on the Monday morning, after attending the *kermesse* somewhere in northern Roubaix. All were dismissed. One was an enormously fat Pole. Maxence might be kind and generous, but he expected a return on his charity.

The Maxence world, like that of the *patronat*, would have been stifling, had there not been other forms of escape. The way up to

---

[1] Matting in artificial rubber, manufactured by Pennel Flipo et Cie.
[2] A charitable organization run by nuns for the rehabilitation of delinquent girls.

Wasquehal was a very long street, crossed by the line to Paris, lined with *estaminets*, in many of which it was possible to spend the night, for a reasonable fee, with the *serveuse montante*, in the room over the *grande salle* (it was reached by a corkscrew staircase from behind the bar), to wake up to the sound of the early-morning trams or to the crow of cocks or the cooing of pigeons in backyards (the Roubaisiens, even the *cafetiers*, were fanatical *colombophiles*). This was only a Saturday night indulgence, as I worked every other night; but it was a change from a surfeit of virtue and good works, and preserved my sense of freedom.

This, however, I was doing my best to lose. For I asked at least two girls to marry me; one of them was dark, with blue eyes, flower ear-rings and Croix de Lorraine. Her father was *maire* of Lannoy, her cousin a *cardeur*. The father's house was a strange structure, right on the frontier, an admirable setting for a film about smuggling. I think the house, the setting, the cousin, and yet another tiled kitchen with the coffee pot on the stove attracted me as much as the girl. In the next few years, I asked a number of French girls to marry me; they all, fortunately, refused. They were all very nice about it.

Roubaix had sucked me in. I hardly ever thought about Paris, and when I did, it was with some disapproval; and I only rarely took the *Mongy*[1] to Lille. No, my place was with the warm, solid Roubaisiens! I even contemplated settling in Roubaix, or possibly in Lille, after demobilization. Plenty of other Englishmen had done so. I daily exchanged gossip with the *marchand de journaux* of the rue Foch, a political crackpot who was a devotee of Georges Valois. On VE Day I found myself hand in hand with two mill girls, in a huge, whirling circle dancing on the Grand'Place, the apotheosis of our collective joy, just as much as the week of the Ardennes offensive had seen us huddled together in common fear. In the late summer, we were ordered to move to Ixelles. It was just in time. Even so, every time I see the long streets of low brick houses, the advertisements *Bières Motte-Cordonnier*, the sticky *pavé*, and *Les Docks du Nord*, I remember the scrubbed kitchens with large stoves, the blond children neat in their *tabliers*, the noisy es-

---

[1] The high-speed trams from Tourcoing and Roubaix to Lille, named after their inventor.

taminets, the intense, comfortable, protective warmth of regionalism, the frolicking schoolchildren with their burning chestnuts on strings on St Nicholas's Day, and I feel the pull of home. When Maxence died in 1947, I was back in Paris; but I still felt I had lost a close and dear relative.

In Roubaix, my life had been mostly at ground level. In Ixelles, off the Chaussée, the best part of it was at basement level. In Roubaix, Maxence had been the magician who had pulled the front off so many *corons*, to introduce me, *de plein pied*, into the kitchen and the smell of coffee and boiling potatoes. Jean Diederickx, an independent artisan who made toys in his basement flat, which also had a work-shop, rue du Couloir, and who only worked at night – the *café à la chicorée* was again always on the boil – had a more modest, but in human terms, much closer, more integrated range of friends: Marcel Veau, an unemployed tailor, his mistress Reinette, a big, noisy, gusty nurse from Charleroi (plus accent); Charles, a very drunken, savor-ously vulgar Ixellois; Georges, a garage mechanic, who, after serving in the SS, had been condemned to death by a *kriegsauditoriaat*, had been reprieved, was silly, wildly anti-Semitic, terribly mixed-up and ignorant, very generous and completely reliable; a Cossack officer, who stood outside a Russian night-club, porte de Namur, with his rig-out on, and who was waiting for a visa to go to Argentina and join his mistress, a Bruxelloise who had a prosperous *pâtisserie* in Buenos Aires; the *patron*, another White Russian, of the café on the corner of the rue du Couloir and the Chaussée, a place much frequented by the NCOs and soldiers of the nearby Red Army liaison. It was here that I met Jean, on a very cold night, while, with the help of a Red Army sergeant, attempting to revive a corporal from the Argylls, whom we had discovered, dead drunk and his face quite blue, in the snow. The Scot was revived, with slaps and brandy; and Jean took the Soviet soldier and myself back to his basement. And there I remained, for the best part of a year, occasionally sleeping at my billet, avenue de la Cascade (later avenue du Général de Gaulle, the General coming, with the Regent and the *bourgmestre* of Ixelles, to rename it in person). Jean's wife, Émilie, was a big, blonde country girl from Marienbourg, who had come up to Brussels to work at *L'Innovation*. She painted the toys. They had one son called Poum; he rarely went to school, as, like Jean and Émilie, he slept during the day.

Jean was an autodidact, with intellectual pretensions and a dislike of being contradicted, an anarcho-Christian, and a convinced Belgian patriot. Any criticisms of the Kingdom from outside made him very angry, and, like so many Walloons, his attitude to France was strongly conditioned by jealousy. He was a very free man; the family unit only worked seasonally, from October to December, for the St Nicholas and Christmas market, and from January to March, to satisfy Easter demands. They lived mainly off sausage, salami, bread and butter, and coffee; but they had to feed, intermittently, quite a lot of people. They were apolitical, were regularly fined for not voting (in any case, it would have meant getting up in the daytime), and must have been virtually the only Belgians in 1945 not to have any strong views on *la question royale* (on the whole, I think they favoured Prince Charles but only because he was said to have as a mistress a Bruxelloise, the wife of a *garagiste* from the rue Haute). Occasionally, when money was plentiful, in December or in April, they would come above ground and there would follow a round of very heavy drinking, with Charles, Marcel, Georges, and the Cossack, in the neighbouring cafés or in the rue Haute: Export, Stella, and the devastating Gueuse, the most ferocious of all drinks, the most conducive too to the pronouncement of the fatal phrase: *espèce d'architecte*, at once followed by the crash of broken glass and the heavy breathing of a first-class brawl.

As a complete contrast to the basement in the rue du Couloir, and in order to remind myself that *léopoldistes* did exist, that there was another side, and that a few people did read *Septembre*, and did not take their cue from *Le Soir*, there was the Hôtel d'Oursel, a large, eighteenth-century town house, rue aux Herbes, near Saint-Gudule, the Brussels home of the Prince de Croy. Tea and *sablés*, listening to the eldest of the daughters, a loud-voiced girl in the uniform of the Belgian Red Cross, and who had big bones and liked horses. On my rare visits to this archaic world, I always made sure to display *Septembre* well in evidence. After each visit, a rapid plunge, Chez Bastiaan, a very small café almost under the Palais de Justice, as a means of purging myself of the aristos. Jean and Émilie were entertained by my accounts of visits *chez la Princesse*. They were better to talk about than to do.

In later years, when suffering from an overdose of French political intransigence, the rue du Couloir offered me the most effective therapy. There was a serene harmony in the anarchical existence of the underground household, with its own baroque pattern of work and leisure and its odd assortment of knowledge and prejudice. In the 1940s and '50s, the Diederickx family managed to live almost entirely independent of any institution, their contacts were limited to those who were social outlaws like themselves. They were dependent on *L'Innovation* for their orders, but this was their only concession to capitalism. To the State they paid their regular fines as non-voters, from the *commune* they drew relief, during the long months of unemployment. They received occasional help from various ecclesiastical authorities, and were visited every now and then by *une dame patronnesse* from the area of the Bois de la Cambre; they readily accepted her admonitions and her presents of fruit. But they channelled very little back into the Church in return; in general, they were unable to attend Mass as they were asleep at the time. As they were always very short of money, they could very seldom go away. Their year was entirely predictable, the only thing that changed was that Poum got bigger, eventually married, and had twin girls, so that there were three more in the basement. XL remained a harbour of reassurance, to return to, an example too of the Breughelian good humour and joyous vulgarity of the Brussels Saturday night, Chez Jef Denym, the proverbial unwilling soldier, who asked to have inscribed on his grave: *mort contre son gré*.

But Belgium stretched westwards, too, via Hal, to Leuze, Tournai, and the frontier. And there was a stopping-off point at Leuze, at a farm owned by a socialist Senator, a haven of goodwill discovered by a friend of mine who was a dispatch rider. Just outside the small town, on the road to France, there was a small, squat, white café, with a low red roof, Chez Maria, kept by a very dark Flemish woman and her startlingly beautiful daughter, who might have been Spanish. The Leuzois disapproved of the couple, whose clientele consisted of lorry-drivers and commercial travellers. Both the mother and the daughter were said to be *accueillantes*, the café was cool, very dark, and shone with polished brass. It was good Simenon material: the white café on the edge of the small town, another version of the café by the canal lock.

*

Paris 1946, the longed-for return to civilian life, were represented by the rediscovery of Maurice, now visibly prosperous, florid, and even rather fat, a jaunty hat perpetually pushed forward over his eyes, surmounting the perpetual cigarette dangling from his lower lip, all of which with his broad shoulders and his rather washed-out, boiled cod blue eyes, gave him the look of an *inspecteur* from the Mondaine.[1] His appearance was, in fact, so convincing that he was received with a mixture of deference and complicity by the ladies who kept hotels in the quartier des Ternes, when he put his feet on the red staircase carpet, between the potted plants. 'M. Maurice', however uncertain his status, was a well-known figure anywhere from the Étoile to the porte de Champerret. He was one of many, in this area and at that period, who could produce stores of American-printed 100 franc notes – his were printed in Montmartre – US Army red petrol coupons and tyres from Army depots. He was also now well set up in second-hand furniture, and affluent enough to treat me from time to time to an evening out Chez Félix, a black-market restaurant kept by a retired boxer. And he was sufficiently well established to be able to pinch any bottoms to be seen bulging over bar stools from the avenue Wagram to his own base in the rue d'Obligado.

Although I was nominally resident at this time in the boulevard Saint-Michel (the most unpleasant street in Paris), most of it was spent either in the Ternes or waking up in the morning in unknown rooms and trying to guess, from the quality of the light and from the sounds of the street, in which quarter I had landed up on the previous evening. Coming out into the street, in the bustle of 11 a.m. or midday, was always a surprise: it might be the rue de la Boule-Rouge, off the rue du Faubourg-Montmartre, or it might be anywhere in the Ternes network. But the hazards of a night out, with or without Maurice, seldom took me beyond the IXe, the Xe, the XVIe, the VIIIe, or the XVIIe; Pigalle and the place Blanche were never reached. Nor was the Left Bank, so long as the war gratuities lasted.

1947 brought a change of itinerary, as I was now confined to Vanves. I was so reluctant to return there at night that I paused, for hours, in

[1] La Brigade Mondaine: a section of the French Police Judiciaire dealing with prostitution and procuring.

various stopping places on the long, long rue de Vaugirard, to end up, in the early hours of the morning drinking in the various cafés, rue Brancion, opposite the horse slaughter-house, in the company of the slaughterers, big men, clad in long bloody leather aprons, who worked all night. A further itinerary ended in a singularly unattractive street, avenue Verdier, in Montrouge, shadowing the home of a blonde girl called Mauricette, who had gone out with me three successive Sundays, on romantic expeditions to Saint-Nom-la-Bretêche, and who had then suddenly given me the push – '*Pense à moi comme si je n'étais qu'un petit nuage rose*', was her way of putting it. I did not like the bit about the little pink cloud, and spent hours, every evening, in a dreary little café, watching the entrance to her block of flats.

In 1948, the task of supplying me with an evening meal was taken over by the French Communist Party, Albert Soboul having imposed an eating roster on a selected number of *les copains*. So it was the Party almost every night, soup out of plates through which gradually emerged Picasso's dove, entrée plates bearing Picasso's feminine, doe-eyed, moustached, idyllic Stalin – I found it slightly irreverent thus to eat off the coryphaeus of the Arts and the Sciences – cheese plates with another dove. Behind glass-fronted bookcases stood neat ranks of dolls in regional costume: Hungarian girls from the Puszta, Polish mountaineers, Bulgarian peasants, all the *peuples frères* were there, in full folksy-wolksy gear (but, in the same year, the Dalmatian girls, the be-fezzed Bosnians, the Serbs with fierce moustaches, the wide-sleeved Croats, the Slovene milkmaids disappeared from the shelves).

It was not all easy going. I had to talk for my supper, and sign for it too; I had to make the appropriate orthodox noises and to express appropriate indignation at the wicked designs of the US and UK Governments. Round about cheese, the petitions would start to circulate: *libérez Henri Martin, Ridgeway à la porte*, and so on. I signed them all; it was the least I could do. What was much worse was to be subjected to endless discussions, among these revolutionaries, about plans for the summer holidays, or how to fiddle the Assurances Sociales and obtain a *congé de maladie* in la Bourboule, or inside gossip about salary increases for CNRS[1] researchers. I supped with the Party from

[1] Centre National de la Recherche Scientifique.

Monday to Friday; Saturday was my day off, and I much enjoyed the luxury of a non-political meal by myself, in a restaurant, listening to other people's conversation. Sunday too was non-Party. It was often reserved for the meal ticket of families of the French Reformed Church obedience – a different sort of orthodoxy, but also with its own built-in dangers, for the PCF militants did eat and drink quite well, when they had a hand to spare from signing petitions, while with the Huguenots there was always a danger of water, and I knew one HSP[1] family that was so anglophil that they persisted in serving me *la cuisine anglaise*; it did not seem particularly English, but it was very bad.

I was on the Party roster for the next three or four years – an experience that left me with a lasting distaste for the Believer, particularly for the female version: be-plaited or hair in a bun, exuding political *lapalissades*. Party girl guides and Puritans, utterly boring, self-righteous, and totally humourless. The worst thing of all about these people was their inward-looking chumminess; the word *copain* was like a masonic handshake, it was like living among members of a secret society to which one did not belong. I never felt that my efforts to give the impression that I did belong can have sounded very convincing; it was quite apparent that I did not read my daily *L'Huma*, my weekly *Regards*, my monthly *La Pensée*. It says much for the Party discipline of these good people that, Soboul having said they must feed the English historian, the English historian they fed. I never felt in the least bit grateful; the sponger does not manifest *la reconnaissance du ventre*. Reading Mercier, I could later recognize myself in those *abbés* who had their place at table, their napkin and their napkin ring, in the houses of the *dévots*, in the Marais. Like the *abbé*, who knew that the greatest threat to his position would be another *abbé*, I was careful above all to preserve my monopoly as the Only Authorized (and Fed) *camarade anglais*. I viewed with extreme alarm the occasional presence of English militants, over in Paris to look up French brethren. And they eyed me with unconcealed loathing.

If, then, I was hardly a convert and was always relieved to escape, with a full stomach, from these houses of virtue, after 1948 I found much in the Party line to recommend it. In the growing awareness of

---

[1] Haute Société Protestante.

the aggressive intentions of the United States, I became correspondingly sympathetic towards the diplomatic efforts of the Soviet Union,
which I saw primarily as the preservation of peace on the basis of the
Yalta Settlement. At the time of the Rosenberg murders, George Rudé
and I wrote a letter to *Le Monde*, which published it; and in the next
few years, from 1951 to 1955, I wrote regularly in the *Tribune libre* of
that paper, in support of its campaign against German rearmament.
Several of my articles were quoted favourably by *L'Humanité*. When
Stalin died, I attended the commemorative meeting at the Vel d'Hiv,[1]
and, like most people there, I wept. I was deeply shocked when, on
coming out, one of our Japanese friends expressed the intention of
going to look for a prostitute, and disappeared down the *Métro* in the
direction of Montparnasse.

My eating roster was not my only excursion into a community in
which I felt alien and which I did not frequent as a matter of choice. In
1951 I married a colonel's daughter; her uncle was a general. Two of
her brothers were colonels (one of them later made a sort of fame for
himself as one of the leaders of the OAS), another was a naval officer,
one sister had married a *médecin-général* in the medical corps, another
worked for a military laboratory in the Val-de-Grâce. The naval officer
had been on Admiral Estéva's staff during the Occupation, he and his
dog, which he called 'de Gaulle' ('Viens ici, de Gaulle!' 'Ne fais pas caca
là, de Gaulle!', and so on) were well-known figures in the port of Tunis.
Another of the brothers had served on Dentz's staff in Syria. The whole
family – at least among the younger generation – showed an unerring
flair for choosing the wrong side, and then serving it with devotion.
The naval officer was, of course, stripped in 1944, the army officer
was almost shot. (Dentz *was* shot.) They were quite unrepentant,
very brave, very generous, completely un-bourgeois, and, although
Catholics, they had acquired *les mœurs de garnison*, with a succession
of wives and mistresses of various colours. They were very nice indeed
to me. My wife was a kind, gentle person, who believed that the French
Army was the best in the world and who was one of the least ostentatious social workers that I have ever met. On the only occasion that I

---

[1] Vélodrome d'Hiver, Javel. Now destroyed. It was used for political meetings and for
the celebrated six-day cycle race.

stayed with my in-laws, in a broken-down country house situated in a large, weedy park with a lake almost invisible in reeds that contained the remains of a rotting boat, a portrait of Jean Mermoz looked down on me from over the bed, and there were crucifixes in every room. Both were company that made me feel even more uneasy than the Polish dolls. Yet the family had not always been right-wing; in the 1890s, the grandfather had been a Republican Senator for the Sarthe and a great friend of the Caillaux dynasty. While he himself had been an anti-clerical, his son became a *dévot* after going to Saint-Cyr; he was also of the 1914 generation. It was an evolution no doubt typical of many provincial families from the West that gave their sons to the Army and their daughters to Army officers. The break would have come in the 1900s. There was something quite unreal about my presence within such a community; this, too, had been the result of an accident, for Françoise had paid for a meal of mine, at the restaurant at which we both habitually ate, during one of my recurrent periods of *fauche*. Later, she lent me 5,000 francs, later still, had me to supper at her flat. The next day was 1 May and a holiday for employees of the SNCF.

During a very long stay in France, I met with much more kindness than otherwise. In the knowledge that their culture and history are universal, the French are perhaps more sympathetic to foreign scholars than most other peoples, though at times their sympathy might be rather patronizing. At least many of them would be prepared to help materially and with advice.

The only wholly deplorable people that I have met in France are Bordelais, the employees of the Prefecture of Police (especially the sinister-sounding Service de Refoulement), most of them Corsicans, and the females that sit behind the *guichets* in Paris *mairies*, presiding over birth, marriage, and death. France is, after all, the country of *fiches*; and it is impossible even to sleep in an hotel without filling out a condensed autobiography of worthless and uncontrollable information. I was lucky enough not to have been born in France, for I would have given my poor parents endless trouble if I had been. My eldest sons, however, were. I got married in France – a frustrating and formidable process, not unlike a game of Snakes and Ladders. And I hope I do not die in France, for that would be a cruel trick to play on those who had to dispose of my remains. Perhaps the greatest challenge of all is to have someone cremated: *une signature de médecin traitant, une signature de médecin légiste* (a rare bird, not easy to run down at short notice), a document from the deceased, expressing his or her desire to be *incinéré*; I have been through that one too. France is, I imagine, the most difficult country in the world to be born in, to marry in, to die in, to be cremated in. Divorce, too, involves a steeplechase with many runners: *avocats, avoués, huissiers, notaires, juges de première instance, greffiers, employés de la mairie* – many visits to Balzacien *études*, the walls piled high with green boxes: *affaire Bigorneau, affaire Chastellux* – a cascade of paper in various colours and in archaic language (*parlant à sa personne physique* . . .); a journey back into the nineteenth century, confrontation with men wearing celluloid collars, whose *clercs* write at high stools and whose studies have padded doors. I did at least avoid the *contrat de mariage*, as neither party had any possessions to contract about, but I have been interpreter for the reading of one of these monuments to French pessimism: everything was listed, including needles and chamber pots.

The Bibliothèque Nationale is the most difficult place in the world to get a book out of, and its motto has for long been: *dégoûter le lecteur*; much thought, ingenuity, rudeness, and persistence have been employed to reach this end. The catalogues are a cemetery of half-finished schemes and a splendid monument to French perfectionism; they are so complicated that, in the opinion of one of my French friends, one needs at least twenty years' experience to be able to find one's bearings when jumping from one to another. The management even provides a chart, in different colours, rather like the tourist plan of an English cathedral – yellow for Perpendicular, mauve for Decorated – further to confuse the reader.

The *secrétariat* of the Sorbonne adopts similar tactics. The administrative process of presenting a thesis for a *doctorat-ès-lettres* is almost as daunting as that of cremation, and rather more complicated than that of naturalization, at least in the case of a man. (Naturalization for a woman is almost impossible, unless she marries a Frenchman.) After the initial three months of preliminary skirmishing, it so daunted me that I gave up just beyond the stage at which I had unloaded 150 printed copies of my main thesis at the *secrétariat des thèses*. I presume that they are still there, unless they were burnt, in the recent troubles, by the *katangais*.

It is often hard to love a *concierge* – indeed, their function is not to be loved, but to watch, and to report. And just as the main purpose of the Bibliothèque Nationale is not to provide books, the main concern of those who sit in the admission sections of Paris hospitals is to prevent the sick, the dying, and the *accidentés* getting anywhere near the doctors and nurses, and the doctors and nurses anywhere near them. Each patient actually admitted represents a resented and humiliating defeat for these street-level bureaucrats.

France is a very old *pays administré* in which most of the habits of the *ancien régime* and of the First Empire have persisted. The Frenchman, it is true, is nominally a citizen, but his real status is much better described in officialese: he is an *administré*. He must constantly be protected against his own wickedness. It is assumed, for instance, that in the absence of a system by which his true identity can be established, he will assume a false one. Hence a series of paper checks – not just one *carte d'identité*, but a whole pack of them. One can see them bulging in the inside pocket of a jacket, one can catch a sudden flash of transversal colour when an important-looking person flicks his *carte de priorité* as he jumps the queue at a bus-stop. Bigamy, so easy in England, is a very rare crime in France, simply because it is so difficult, save in a period of catastrophe, like 1940, when communications break down. Landru was able to operate only in the favourable circumstances of the First World War. He picked his Departments with great care. Dr Petiot likewise benefited from wartime conditions. There was, it is true, a case a few years ago in Versailles, in which a lady dressed as a man managed to marry her girl-friend; they went through two ceremonies, one at the *mairie* and one at the parish church. The 'husband' had borrowed her brother's identity card, on a visit to her home in Strasbourg. The maid at the honeymoon hotel later admitted, when cross-examined, that, on bringing up the breakfast tray, she had thought that 'Monsieur avait la poitrine un peu forte', but she had given the matter no further thought, and 'Monsieur' had told her, in a gruff voice, to put the tray down on the side table. But, in the home of *fiches*, such fantasies are rare.

The habit of mistrust is so ingrained that it has seeped down from the State to the citizen; I have been denounced on three occasions while in France. In 1945, the Sûreté in Lille was given a tip-off that I was a German deserter masquerading in British uniform. I was arrested by an impressive array of armed men, while having supper with a wool engineer in the rue Sarrail, in Roubaix. The Sûreté men were horrified to discover that the British soldier's brown book contained neither photograph nor fingerprints. How, they asked me, did the Army check on deserters? While staying in a village in the Haute-Saône, I was denounced to the *gendarmerie* as a suspicious character. I had been seen visiting the cottage of a local eccentric, who lived alone in the woods, was known to be a poacher, and was believed to be a magician. And, later, I was denounced by my *concierge* for having spent more than three months in France without a *permis de séjour*. She was unaware that I had spent the previous weekend in Brussels. When the men from the Service de Refoulement walked in on me, very early one morning, I was able to show them the triangular stamp of the Baisieux frontier post. It was so much more simple to take the train to Brussels than to embark on the disagreeable and often dangerous process of obtaining a *permis*.

In *Rue du Havre*, Paul Guimard describes the scene outside Saint-Lazare, between 7.30 and 9.30 a.m., as witnessed by an elderly man, something of a sentimentalist, who lives in a *chambre de bonne* in the XIIe and who, as a war veteran, takes up his daily stand as a lottery ticket salesman, at the street corner. The man, who is utterly lonely, embarks on a series of fantasies in which various regular passers-by in the morning rush are not only identified, but, through the intervention of the stationary witness, introduced to each other, so that their lives are permanently changed. At 7.55 each morning a tall blonde girl – she could be a *bretonne* – her fair hair bobbing in the fast-moving sea of commuters, is carried past the vendor on his raft. At 7.59 there follows a young man, bare-headed, who smokes a pipe. The lottery man becomes attached to the two, looks out for them each day, establishing for them an imaginary itinerary: the girl, he decrees, lives in le Pecq with her widowed mother – or perhaps her grandmother – she takes the train at le Pecq at 7.20, and works for an *agent de change* somewhere near the rue Vivienne. (He has at least been able to ascertain that, on leaving the rue du Havre, she crosses over, left-turns, and disappears behind Le Printemps.) The young man lives in Rueil, taking a direct train from there at 7.30 a.m. He too heads left after Le Printemps; he must be some sort of engineer, working for a big industrial firm. He is unmarried – the old man is sure of this – but does not wish to remain permanently so. The blonde too is thinking eventually in terms of a family, but she has not met the right man. The two can never meet on the same train, and they are never likely to find themselves jostled together in the early-morning crush. Four minutes separate, apparently for ever, the two lives. The witness is powerless, he would like to stop the girl, tell her not to hurry, to wait till she is left in the trough of the wave, to be carried forward in the next swell from the station. He longs for some minor accident: a power failure which would keep her train stuck in le Vésinet or in Chatou for 3½ minutes. There are days when one or other is missing; there is an occasion when the girl is carried along in the 8.12 wave; the old man notices that she is looking pale. And then, after weeks, after months, the miracle happens: both emerge, almost level, at 8.1. The vendor plunges into the crowd, pulls the girl's sleeve, calls to the young man, it is all a matter of seconds, they disappear, talking together, round the left bend. Contact has been established, not only between the girl and the young man, but between what is now the beginnings of a couple and their introducer. All three lives are radically changed, and for a period at least the vendor is pulled out of his loneliness; the young man, who is a *chef de rayon* in Le Printemps – for that is as far as he ever went – secures him a temporary job as Father Christmas in the toy department.

The situation of the old man is similar to that of the historian – or of a certain sort of historian – also a stationary witness, an observer of a swirling collectivity of which he is not a part. He too is lonely, given to fantasy, having to make do with a few scraps of evidence, in an effort to give life to the passing faces. In his passionate desire to know, to establish contacts, there is an element of self-identification; he is both the blonde girl *and* the young man, *and* the red-faced, leather-coated gas man in the peaked cap, *and* the hard-faced woman in her late forties who looks as if she runs her own small business. He too is attempting to break out of loneliness, even if it is a matter of living with the dead. For, to live with the dead, he must live with the living. Loneliness gives him that extra perception, those qualities of curiosity, imagination, and compassion, that are the necessary tools of

48

his trade. I can only speak from experience; and history is experience. One becomes a certain sort of historian because one is a certain sort of person. I have always been a very lonely person, and like others similarly placed, I have sat in restaurants, picking up fragments of conversation, have headed for the café open late at night. In this perpetual attempt to escape from loneliness, the people that one is most likely to meet are themselves lonely. So many of them, after the third or fourth glass of calvados, will push their hats back and begin to give forth, to reminisce and to complain.

The historian then, as I imagine him, is Guimard's hero. He is also the Commissaire Maigret, his old-fashioned Gladstone bag, hastily but neatly packed by Mme Maigret, in his right hand, as he walks through the *salle des pas perdus*[1] of a provincial station, heading for the place de la Gare: a pause to look at the *planisphère* and map out the town, a few indecisive steps to look through the doors of three or four cafés, before deciding on one for breakfast, over the local paper and with ears attuned. An hour or more walking through the town from end to end – the station at one end, the cathedral at the other, the *sous-préfecture* halfway down – for how many French provincial towns resemble thus the simple plan of Fontenay-le-Comte of *Au bout du rouleau*! Having thus completed the exploration of the backbone of the herring, there is time to look at the side-streets, before finally heading, in Maigret's case, for a certain house, for an hotel, in the historian's, for the *mairie*. It is the period at which the Commissaire is content to put his nose to the wind, to establish an ambience and the hour-by-hour clockwork of a small provincial town. Later he will talk to people; but first he must get his bearings, then he can explore assumptions and relationships and find out who is important. It is the most exciting stage of his *enquête*, before anything begins to fall into place, and it is often the most exhilarating stage of research.

There is more too that can be learnt from Maigret, for the Commissaire knows how, with patience, to reconstruct a life, a pattern of work and leisure, even a *vie intime*, from a few scraps of evidence and the inflection of a voice. He is already loaded with a considerable weight of experience, and he is easily at home with small people. He

[1] Entrance hall.

feels uneasy, on the other hand, with the wealthy, the fashionable, the snob; the only foreigners for whom he feels an affinity are the sort of people Simenon's mother used to lodge in Liège: students from Russia and Eastern Europe, Jewish tailors. Though he shouts loud, has a terrible temper, he is not without compassion. For his older customers, *vieux chevaux de retour*, semi-criminals who have made good, set themselves up in the restaurant business, he has a genuine affection, the sort that is derived from shared experiences in the past and from the recollection of old times. He is rather out of sympathy with the young, does not like change, makes no allowance for revolution, believes that things were better when he was a young man in the career; there were fewer clever chaps about then. The Commissaire is an artist in his way who likes seeing things for himself, even if it means staying up most of the night in a café by the canal or opposite the quai des Orfèvres; he does not like paperwork, nor employing assistants. He is an amateur, for he has never been trained in techniques. He does not even use *fiches*. But he knows where to find them, at the top of the PJ.[1]

At 4 o'clock one morning in a *tabac* in the rue du Four, I met a very drunken couple. One was a civilian pilot, who was to fly the next morning, and who had already been threatened with the removal of his licence after a drunken landing. The other was a very well-dressed, rubicund man, with neatly brushed black hair, a hat with a dark band, well-kept hands, and a diamond pin in his tie. He looked professional, and was at first reticent. But by 5 o'clock he was anxious to speak of himself, and gave me a number of hints. 'I am a Belgian; I come to Paris for the summer; I only work here in July, August, and early September; I only work in the XVIe and the XVIIe. My work involves me with Post Offices, female servants, and chauffeurs.' It did not seem very difficult; I told him he was a professional housebreaker. He was delighted, opened a handsome pigskin bag, displaying some hundred instruments on runners. He was a man who enjoyed his work, but he also liked talking about it, and needed an audience.

This is both a personal and an aesthetic view of history. There are, of course, many sorts of history, and the historian makes his choice,

---

[1] The building of the Police Judiciaire.

which will always be dictated to some extent by his own sense of involvement and by a certain feeling of identification with the period and with the country to which he devotes his research. Indeed, I believe that such a sense of involvement is not only inevitable but even necessary, for the historian is not a cold clinician, he is not dealing with steely concepts *à la Saint-Just*, nor with geological 'social structures', he is concerned primarily with human beings. Olwen Hufton can write with such sympathy of Bayeux because she was partly educated there, of women, because she is a woman, of the nuns, because she was taught by them, and she can understand what poverty means to the mother of a large family, because she is aware, from her own experience, of the preponderant place occupied by the Catholic Church in the lives of the female poor. Edward Thompson became the leading historian of a section of the English working class after living for more than fifteen years in Halifax. He also possesses literary gifts which are, unfortunately, rare in an historian.

It is possible to write history that is in no way human. Many economic historians and some diplomatic ones have demonstrated how this can be done. It is no doubt a necessary kind of history, as important as any other. But in the end, history being a cultural subject, one can only judge it by applying to it cultural values. I distrust, when applied to history, such words as 'laboratory', 'workshop', 'group project', just as I distrust those who speak of universities in terms of 'the plant'. Something very alarming occurred in France when, in each university, the old and meaningful title of 'Faculté des Lettres' was given the meaningless and baroque addition of 'et des Sciences Humaines'. For history is not a science, nor should it be written by teams. We can leave that to surgery. The writing of history is one of the fullest and most rewarding expressions of an individual personality.

The historian should, above all, be endlessly inquisitive and prying, constantly attempting to force the privacy of others, and to cross the frontiers of class, nationality, generation, period, and sex. His principal aim is to make the dead live. And, like the American 'mortician', he may allow himself a few artifices of the trade: a touch of rouge here, a pencil-stroke there, a little cotton wool in the cheeks, to make the operation more convincing. Of course, complete understanding is impossible and the historian of the common people, of popular movements, and of individualistic eccentrics can only scratch at the surface of things. He may recapture a mentality; but he cannot probe deeply. He can only make one man witness for many by the selective use of the individual 'case history' as a unit in historical impressionism.

I do not know what history is about, nor what social function it serves. I have never given the matter a thought. There is nothing more boring than books and articles on such themes as 'What is History?', 'The Use of History', 'History and Something Else'. I do, however, find enormous enjoyment in research and in the writing of history. I am happy in it, and that is the main thing. It is always embarrassing and rather impertinent to write at length about oneself. There are the dangers of a jocular whimsicality, or of a studied, pseudo-eighteenth-century reticence, or of false candour, or of endless narration of tri-fling personal experiences. It is not an easy thing to do. And I can hear the objections: 'too much Cobb', 'historical narcissism', 'indecent exposure', 'il s'écoute parler', or, merely, 'what has all this got to do with a book of essays on French history?' My excuse is that I write history subjectively and often, no doubt, with prejudice and that I do not believe it is possible to divorce history from experience. I have not intended to project myself, like a lean shadow, over all that follows, and in what precedes. I have not meant to write about my French friends and acquaintances in terms of their relations with myself; I have tried to keep myself out of it as much as possible and to use individuals: the Thullier brothers, Maurice, Jean, Maxence, and others to illustrate a period, a place, a social climate, the process of change. The people included here have not been selected on account of their personality so much as to illustrate their assumptions and attitudes to a country and to a society in which they were living. The Thullier brothers, for instance, both married late and belonged to a period before the habit of early marriage changed the character of the French *bourgeoisie* and of French society as a whole, by rendering the young couple the hostage to political and social orthodoxy; the change came under Vichy, the Occupation years being the great divide between my genera-tion and those who were born ten years later. In 1944 I returned to a France which, while in rural terms still completely recognizable, had, as far as city life was concerned, undergone changes of appalling dimensions as a result of the strengthening of the family unit, with the advent of the married student, the *jeune ingénieur*, *jeune technocrate* couples – avid, ambitious, and conformist, the unpleasing characters of Christiane Rochefort's *Stances à Sophie* – and the consequent disappearance of the bachelor, the *boulevardier*. After 1944, it would no longer have been possible to enjoy pleasure in the lusty, rumbustious manner of Galtier-Boissière's *La Bonne Vie* – a group of male friends on a night out in Paris: *la table*, *les filles*, the old pleasures. Vichy disappeared, but, unhappily, much of Vichy puritanism has remained, and even Paris is in the process of becoming a dull place. It will be a lifeless one too once les Halles – with the joy, the violence, and the lust that accompany les Halles – have been expelled from the very heart of the city to Ris-Orangis.

In all that I have written I have tried to use individuals in order to illustrate the attitudes and assumptions of a society at a given period. In France in particular, history is perpetual and self-perpetuating; the French Revolution is still going on, there was another one – the fifth or the sixth (if one is prepared to concede the Front Populaire such an illustrious title; Daniel Guérin has called it, perhaps more accurately, the *révolution manquée*) – as recently as May 1968; it still uses the same labels and the same slogans, speaking still in the voice of the year II; the old conflict between 'possibilists' and 'impossibilists', between Jacobin bureaucrats and ultra-revolutionary 'wild men', has been run through once more, like an old film, at breakneck speed, so that what in 1793–4 had been concentrated into weeks and months now became concentrated into hours and days. It is suitable that the French Communist Party should have made a take-over bid on Robespierre; M. Waldeck-Rochet, in the recent crisis, acted as a Jacobin. And, as in 1795, a failed Revolution, or the failure to concretize a revolutionary situation, resulted in Reaction, just as a revolutionary situation was precipitated originally, as in June–July 1789, by the misuse of the repressive powers of Government (too much repression, or too little: my article* on Professor Godechot's book, *The Beginning of the Revolutionary Crisis in Paris*, may have some bearing on the origins of the May Revolution). France is now experiencing yet another of her many Thermidors – the favourite month, just as *homard à la* is the

* See *A Second Identity*, pp. 145–58.

favourite dish, of a selfish and easily frightened French bourgeoisie. Once more, the sheer violence of repression has created an unprecedented and totally unexpected revolutionary opportunity, and yet again, as in the year II and even more in the year III, violence has ultimately proved the most persuasive weapon of a French Government. The police, unfortunately, are always with us, always loathed. It is not only on General de Gaulle that the weight of French history lies heavily. Revolutionary students have looked as much to the *Enragés* as to Che, and much of the discussion *chez Renault* among the young workers echoed the clubs of 1848 and the endless, optimistic *palabres* of the Commune. In 1793–4, the women of the people envisaged equality in a physical and visible form: *à nous maintenant de rouler carrosse*. And in May 1968, the cars of the bourgeois were the principal targets of student violence. How Christiane Rochefort must have applauded such an initiative!

My writing has always been conditioned by my own experience and prejudices, and, above all, by my awareness of the endless variety of French provincialism. Most of my books and articles, like my own life over the last thirty-three years, are so many historical excursions into *le plat pays*, wandering from quarter to quarter. My history is not French history, but French provincial history: Lyonnais history, Norman history, Lille history, Paris history. One French historian, fifteen years ago, said that I wrote, spoke, and thought *comme un titi parisien*. It is the greatest compliment that I have ever received.

So I have been unable to separate my own identity from what I have written. My own identity is something that, despite my *fiche*, I find very difficult to establish as I tend to react to environment rather than to impose my personality upon it or dominate it. The Balliol poem could not apply to me. Balliol did *not* make me. But France did; at least it gave me a new identity, into which I slip almost unconsciously as soon as I cross to the other side. Then I cannot even keep my hands still, and when I lecture over there, I turn down the corners of my mouth. So here too I am *fiché*, pinned down, along with other Parisians, Lyonnais, Roubaisiens, Havrais, Dieppois, Ixellois, all company that I like to keep, all towns that I love.

2

Paris Xe[*]

THERE IS always some danger, I think, both in historical terms and in those of literary localism, of confusing regionalism with provincialism, or even with what I would describe as a pseudo-peasant folklore. Those who react most strongly against the narrowness, the deliberate archaism, and the politically motivated reactionary romanticism of a Charles Péguy or of a Jean Giono – you know the sort of thing: the ancient rural values, a happy and unquestioning paternalism, the idealization of *le labeur* by those who have never put their hands to a plough – will identify such a tradition with appeals both against Paris and against the political system established in Paris.

That sort of regionalism can very often be equated with anti-parliamentarianism, and can best be located in just those areas of France in which an aristocratic nostalgia has, to some extent, survived – for instance, in La Varende's Lower Normandy, in the Bessin, the country round Bayeux; and in Michel de Saint-Pierre's west of France, as illustrated in his *Les Aristocrates*, and so on.

But there is also an abundant literature of Paris that, very far from being in any way national, is as firmly set in a local context as Jean-Louis Bory's celebrated semi-autobiographical book, *Mon Village à l'heure allemande*. To look at what appears to be a conflict between Paris and the rest of France in the perspective, for instance, of a very celebrated polemical piece that came out in the late 1940s – *Paris et le désert français* – is merely to equate Paris with a rather faceless author-

* This chapter was first published in *Promenades* (1980).

ity, with Bureaucracy, and to forget that Paris is itself a whole jumble of quarters and villages, each retaining a very strong sense of identity, even though this is now tending to be lost, each existing in its own right as the framework for childhood, wonder, and exploration.

No literature, in fact, could be more pronouncedly regional than that of Paris and its neighbourhood. And while Léo Larguier's book, *Saint-Germain-des-Prés, mon village*, written in the 1930s, would now appear merely pathetic, as a reminder from a very, very long time back of an innocence and spontaneity long since lost, there is still plenty of life left for the evolution of this or that *arrondissement*, this or that *commune* of the *grande banlieue*. Indeed, Georges Simenon has shown, with great skill, how such a theme as this sudden loss of identity, in personal terms, could still be handled, in his novel *Le Déménagement* – the move from central Paris, from the Marais, to Cachan or Bagneux or Sarcelles or somewhere else farther out, south of Paris on the electric line, *la ligne de Sceaux*: a sociological fact that could be reproduced by thousands and thousands of similar examples.

Even *gauchisme* can readily accommodate the diversity of Parisian geography, and May 1968 was, above all, a phenomenon confined to a couple of *arrondissements* – the Ve and the VIe, on the Left Bank. And it was a phenomenon that brought few enough echoes on the Right Bank, even if many of the most active participants, after revolutionizing all day, were, most nights, in the habit of returning to their homes in the XVIe and XVIIe *arrondissements*, to sleep it off.

Nor could anyone be more provincial and more élitist than *les mandarins*, as described in the memoirs of Simone de Beauvoir: very self-satisfied intellectuals who move in a very narrow physical and social circle. Indeed, they are not all that different from the two *normaliens*, Jallez and Jerphanion, as described in the immense novel *Les Hommes de bonne volonté* of Jules Romains, and from all those who observe the sleeping city from the roof of the rue d'Ulm, which is the street which houses the École Normale Supérieure.

Certainly, *I* have not forgotten Paris, nor its suburbs. I have omitted them so far because I have been speaking* mostly of exiles writing in

---

* In 1978 Cobb gave thirteen talks on Radio 3 on the subject of 'Fiction, Fact and France'.

Paris, and writing with the added nostalgia of absence, lost innocence, and death. How, indeed, could one forget such wealth and diversity as are provided by the tumultuous Paris of childhood? – the sunny, silent, empty Paris of June 1940, the Occupied Paris of the ration cards, of the J3, and of the black market, the Front Populaire of 1936, recalled in the suburbs, Villeneuve-Saint-Georges during the Occupation years, in René Fallet's first novel *Banlieue sud-est*; *Les Enfants d'Aubervilliers*, the title of a very remarkable documentary film of the 1930s about sad, rickety, tubercular children; Charles-Louis Philippe's description of the quartier de la Gaîté, behind the old Montparnasse station, in his novel *Bubu*; the mediocrity and the small-mindedness of the passage des Panoramas, which is where Louis-Ferdinand Céline, Dr Destouches, spent his own rather unhappy childhood and which he exploited both in *Voyage au bout de la nuit* and in *Mort à crédit*.

Paris, on the contrary, must dominate any attempt to explore varieties of regionalism through works of imagination, as indeed it should, for, of all the infinite forms of French and francophone regionalism, that of Paris is the most insistent, imperious, the most cantankerous, the funniest, and, certainly, always the most inventive.

I am very conscious of this and, in my own case, of the strength of my own affiliations, experiences, mishaps, and near disasters, sudden glimpses of absolute happiness, like an April Paris shaft of sunlight all at once lighting up a leprous wall at the top of a house, cut down the side, like a chunk of ice-cream, Utrillo-coloured, and making it appear warm yellow. I remember the surrealist quality of so many Parisian itineraries: Filles-du-Calvaire to Barbès-Rochechouart; Sèvres-Babylone to Marcadet-Poissonniers; Corentin-Cariou to Corentin-Celton; Château-Rouge to Glacière; Strasbourg-Saint-Denis to Richelieu-Drouot; Château-d'Eau to Levallois; Porte-Brancion to Porte des Lilas; Robespierre to Jasmin; La Motte-Picquet-Grenelle to Sully-Morland; De Gaulle to Convention. I remember, too, the *Métro aérien* on green, raised bridges, clanging along at the level of fourth or sixth storey, opening up façades and giving a sort of running view of a bedroom, a kitchen, a dining-room, the figures silhouetted in activity; *Métro à éclipses* suddenly coming out into the light and just as soon disappearing once more into the semi-darkness of tunnel. And I am old enough to have travelled by tram down the boulevard Saint-

Michel in the direction of the Gare de l'Est (and that certainly does date me), and I have, indeed, been so much conditioned by Paris – much more than by any other place, even Ixelles – that I feel it really necessary to place on record my own early subjection to Parisian imperialism.

Whether it is an advantage or a disadvantage I would hesitate to say, but I think there is certainly very much to be said for beginning with the capital of a country, provided one gets round the rest of the country at some later date. In my case, my first exposure to France, its language, its population, its climate, its sudden and terribly alien gusts of violence, and its reassuringly regular movements of work and leisure, of the week and the weekend, the differentiation of class as judged by clothing, came to me in the form of Paris.

My first introduction to Paris was not to the fashionable parts of the city; it was to the Xe *arrondissement*, just where it borders on the IXe, as well as where it borders on the busy quartier du Sentier, the not very reputable rue de la Lune, a steep walk up to vice, almost as steep, but certainly not so long as the climb up to redemption, provided at the top by the hideous Sacré-Cœur, and the ancient theatreland of the boulevard Saint-Martin.

To the north lay a whole maze of *passages*, undetected even by Céline or by Aragon, and so lost to literature. Immediately below the boulevard Bonne-Nouvelle, where I lived, ran a sort of gully that on the day of the execution of Louis XVI, in January 1793, had provided the royalist conspirator, Baron de Batz, with a platform and, as he had hoped, literally a jumping-off ground from which to storm the heavily guarded *berline*, the carriage containing the king and his Irish non-juror confessor, the Abbé Edgeworth.

To the right, a leaden January sky was brightened by the huge black-and-red pennant that flew over the offices of the newspaper *Le Matin*, and by the enormous, apparently fortified Rex, the largest cinema in Paris, a sort of vast, rectangular cube in beige cement that looked like a permanent ice-cream.

Beyond the Rex and beyond *Le Matin* were the salerooms and the offices of auctioneers of the *commissaires-priseurs*, the official valuers, of the Hôtel des Ventes, of the rue Drouot, and their offices in the neighbouring rue Rossini and in the Cité de Trévise, which is partly closed in with glass passages. And there was a female population certainly representative of every province of France and, indeed, pretty well the whole French empire, as well as of francophone Belgium and of Luxembourg, as one approached the Folies-Bergère via the rue du Faubourg-Montmartre.

It was an area of central Paris that had been a *quartier d'agrément* in the time of Baron Haussmann, in the Second Empire, because it was in such convenient proximity to the Bourse, to the Sentier, to the newspaper offices, and to all the theatres of the *grands boulevards*. But, well before 1914, it became an area that was going into a steady social decline. As early as 1900, affluent and middle-class *boursicotiers* and *agents de change*, stockbrokers and so on, and currency speculators had begun moving out from the tall apartment buildings and migrating towards the more fashionable area to the west.

And so at No 26 boulevard Bonne-Nouvelle, where I lived, the impressive double doors to the flats on the first, second, third, and fourth storeys bore the names of Polish furriers and tailors, of private detective agencies, of doctors, though probably not very good doctors – doctors who played safe by specializing in *la sécurité sociale* and *les accidents de travail*.

From my bedroom window I could hear both the dull rumble of the *Métro*, which is very shallow at this point, and the continuous clatter of machinery that sounded as if it might be related to the activities of the Armenian *tapissiers* whom, in a voyage of discovery from fifth to seventh floor, I found to be established towards the top of the house.

The terrible screams and apparent cries for help that had so alarmed me during my first week, inducing me to believe that Paris was undergoing a replay of the September Massacres next door to my bedroom and laid on specially for my benefit, were eventually traced to the presence, on the bottom three floors of the building immediately to the west, of the public baths, the Bains Neptuna.

Immediately below the flat, the pavement widened out so as to include several *kiosques* with elaborate ironwork turrets, selling the newspapers of the world of the 1930s, including *Pravda*, *Izvestia*, and papers from Prague, Warsaw, and so on. At weekends and on public holidays, there were street bands – one or two concertinas, a drum, and a very hoarse singer – selling sheet music of the latest hits.

On Saturdays and Sundays, the very wide *chaussées* were invaded by lugubrious family processions and by noisy, catcalling young men and by girls who had come in from the factory suburbs to the north and the north-east of the city, who were sufficiently ill-informed about the more recent shifts in Parisian fashions to believe that the porte Saint-Denis and the porte Saint-Martin and the *grands boulevards*, from there to Richelieu-Drouot, still constituted the very centre of the capital, the place where all the important things happened and where all the great shops had their frontages.

During the week, the crowds walked fast and humbly, bent down to face the east wind that swept in from the direction of the République. Haussmann, thanks to his east–west grid, succeeded in rendering Paris one of the coldest cities in Western Europe. And when I came to know the Left Bank better, I could appreciate that the area around the *Métro* station Glacière had earned its name doubly.

Crowds poured out of the shallow station Bonne-Nouvelle and headed for the Bourse, the Sentier, the rue Turbigo, the rue Drouot, the newspaper and printing offices of the rue Réaumur, the big shops, the chain restaurants and cafés of the boulevards themselves: *petits employés*, clerks, waiters, shop assistants, tailors, seamstresses, printers, *commissionnaires*, errand boys, armed in the mornings of the 1930s with such papers as *Le Petit Parisien*, *Le Journal*, or *Le Matin*, and armed in the evening with *Paris-Soir* or *L'Intransigeant*. I really never discovered anybody who read *Paris-Midi*, a midday or afternoon paper, apart from those bent either on attending the afternoon races at Vincennes or at Longchamp or on betting on them at the betting-shop, the Pari Mutuel Urbain.

It was an area of what you might call *grand passage*, of work and leisure, a little too far to the east to attract the tourists, whether foreign or provincial, and too far from the Left Bank, from the Palais Bourbon, from the place de la Concorde, the ministries, the embassies, or any of the railway termini, ever to attract a political demonstration or procession. Left-wing processions and demonstrations tended to pack up at the level of the République as their farthest point west. Right-wing demonstrations or processions favoured the boulevard Saint-Michel or the prestigious Champs-Élysées, so that the Xe *arrondissement*, whether by luck or negligence, or as the result of important matters having increasingly tended to pass it by, had consequently fallen into a sort of political apathy.

The family with whom I was staying were survivors from a more prosperous and prestigious period; they had simply not bothered to follow the general current westwards, clinging on to a very commodious flat that had originally been acquired by the maternal grandfather, M. Feuillas, a stockjobber on the Bourse in the lush years of the Third Republic before 1914, and a sufficiently well-known figure in the quartier de la Bourse to have been the subject of several caricatures – bowler hat, spats, long black coat with velvet collar – by famous caricaturists of the turn of the century.

The flat, which was, as I have said, very large, was shaped like an L, with a balconied salon, its two french windows facing on to the boulevard. This room was very seldom used; its furniture, much of the time, was kept under beige covers. There was also a balconied dining-room, round-fronted with a sort of *vue plongeante*, a view from above, right up the boulevard Bonne-Nouvelle past the Bains Neptuna as far as the Théâtre du Gymnase and the Théâtre Sarah Bernhardt. There was a very dark hall which always needed artificial light, and a tiny kitchen facing on to the deep well formed by seven storeys of enclosed *appartements*. Also always lit by electric light was a long, gloomy corridor off which were four bedrooms, themselves equally dark, as only a few feet separated their windows from the tall mass of the building housing the swimming-baths.

The furniture of the salon and of the dining-room, of *faux Louis XVI*, looked as if it had been mostly acquired in one go as a series of sets: *salle à manger, complète*; *entrée, complète*; *chambre à coucher, complète*. And right down to the last detail: *service de table*, several sets of linen, even the bound volumes of the appropriate *grands auteurs*, certainly not designed to be read, but rather to furnish.

Probably, it had all been acquired at the time of Mlle Feuillas' marriage, a suggestion that seemed to be confirmed by the paucity of the kitchen equipment, hinting at a period of purchase many years before the Bazar de l'Hôtel de Ville, the paradise for kitchenware, as far as Paris is concerned, angling for the family unit, began to place the chief emphasis on *la femme au foyer*, and to make its reputation in the furnishing of *les arts ménagers*. When Mlle Feuillas married, the kitchen was still the unvisited prison of the maid, who was exhibited professionally only when she was waiting at table, in her best black silk with white apron.

Later, at Samois-sur-Seine, the village on the Seine where the family had a country house, I discovered something like thirty years of the annual catalogues of the Bon Marché, all of them pre-1914, so my guess would be that the family's furniture, with everything that went with it, had been acquired in a bulk order from that emporium when the young stockjobber and his bride had first set up house.

Certainly, there was little to suggest, in the standard parade of marble-topped tables, wall brackets, and so on, any evidence of personal choice or fantasy. Even the Chinese silk screens looked as though they would have gone with the rest, suggesting a date when Pierre Loti was beginning to seep down to the all-inclusive, regimented tastes of the Bon Marché or of the Grands Magasins du Louvre.

The whole set had seen much better days: the silk screens were torn in innumerable places and, in the salon, most of the arm-rests on the chairs were liable to fall off under the slightest pressure. The bookcases, as I soon discovered, were not designed to be opened. I did manage to prise one of them open, whereupon the whole front came away, revealing, along with the bound Hugos and Balzacs, several bound sets of *Le Petit Journal Illustré*. The chairs themselves were quite safe, but scarcely comfortable.

On the other hand, the silver and table service were both heavy and lavish, and the napkins were the size of the towels in which schoolboys would carry their bathing-trunks to the municipal baths. The glassware was reassuringly abundant, and the dinner-table, when fully laid out, made a very fine late-nineteenth-century showing indeed, under an elaborate cluster of electric lights, which sprouted luxuriantly, like oranges, and were held up by rather dusty, gilt-painted cherubs. There was very little doubt as to what constituted the focal point of an *appartement* that still preserved plenty of mainly unused *signes de grandeur* – fitted corner cupboards, stacked with tureens and flowered plates, much of the ugliest and most massive Sèvres, cut-glass, and fruit-knives.

The maid slept somewhere above the seventh storey, somewhere under the roof, though she seemed to be on call any time from 7.30

a.m. until midnight, save on Saturday afternoons, when she went out with her fiancé, who was a young Alsatian, like herself.

The family had remained in the boulevard Bonne-Nouvelle as a sort of bourgeois enclave in an encroaching sea of *fourreurs, tapissiers, merciers, rubaniers, bimbelotiers, dentistes américains* who, whatever their origin, were certainly not American. Many of the tenants, as far as I could make out, did not live on the premises, but simply used the flats as workshops, returning at night to rooms in the XIe, XIIe or the IVe *arrondissements*. Certainly, at night, the *cage d'escalier* was eerily quiet and one never met anyone coming up or going down after about 8 p.m.

The two sons, however, made up for the surrounding silence and stillness by a maximum amount of noise and bustle, taking the stairs at a furious gallop, and endlessly telephoning their friends, male and female, groping for the Bottin in the pitch-black hall, feebly lit by an anaemic yellowish bulb, to the west and south-west of the city (they had quite a few in the VIIe, some among the parishioners of Sainte-Clothilde, rather more in the VIIIe and the XVIe, or in the far-away Ternes, with cousins, the children of Mme Thullier's artistic sister and a massive barrister, in Saint-Mandé). Édouard was beginning his degree at the Faculty of Medicine; François was preparing to set up in the Hôtel Drouot, as a *commissaire-priseur*, and was thus running through the dreary hoops of a *licence de droit*. Perhaps it was on account of the latter's destined career that they had thus held on to a quarter given over more and more to offices, chain stores, vast cafés, and cinemas, and, in the *passages*, alleyways, *cités*, and small streets to the north of the boulevard, small trades: engravers, printers of visiting cards and *faire-parts*, manufacturers of rubber stamps (by no means a declining industry), sign-painters, stamp-traders, and very small haberdashers.

They were the nearest thing to Parisian one was ever likely to encounter. Both sides of the family had originated from the Seine-et-Marne, first as peasants, then as speculators in national lands; and Mme Thullier still possessed rural properties – a whole street of houses in the Brie, a house in the valley of the Seine, land in that of the Bièvre. But they were rude about most provincials, referred to peasants as *les pecquenots*, employed, often quite unconsciously, a great deal of

Paris slang, particularly when describing women and girls: '*bien fringuée*', '*toute pomponnée*', '*de jolis châssis*', and that sort of thing – some of it acquired, I suppose, in hospital wards, much of it also from the shop-girls whom they ran after at weekends – and possessed an outsize packet of Parisian cheek, particularly well employed by François, once he had become established as an auctioneer, his iron voice brilliantly accompanied by his *aboyeurs*: a veritable orchestra in the long vowels of common Parisian. They were certainly not of a philosophical bent, were not given to pure speculation, were never heard to formulate a general idea or theory, were only peripherally interested in politics, but much engaged in football and in chasing girls, of all conditions, though only French ones: they were quite immune to the exoticism and mystery of *l'âme slave*, preferring a typist from Belleville or Bezons any day, though a Russian accent in French sent them off in peals of laughter. Not for them either the smoky delights of *la peau mate* or *les blondeurs* of the Nordics; in fact, they were remarkably unadventurous in this respect, though, much later in life, when he was a doctor with the French Army in Indochina, Édouard seems to have widened his interests. Although they had been to L'École des Roches as boarders, they did not appear to have even a dis-approving awareness of homosexuality, and the standard French jokes about antique-dealers and dress designers did not figure in their reper-toire. There was then a certain innocence about them even in the totally uninhibited cheek that they displayed in the pursuit of shop-girls or merely female fellow-travellers on *les transports communs*. In this one respect at least I felt myself considerably more worldly-wise than these two hardened and joyful *dragueurs* (there was too a strong element of competitiveness in their sweeping, as in everything else, save, of course, Law and Medicine). They also attached a considerable importance to the joys of eating and drinking; but this certainly did not extend to good behaviour at table; on the contrary, the more important the guests, the worse would be their behaviour. They enjoyed being students, rather than studying, and were complete extroverts. They were sentimental, foolhardy, and potentially very brave. Their courage was not just juvenile *panache*: in 1939, the lawyer volunteered for the Corps Francs, and was probably one of the few sol-diers thoroughly to have enjoyed the period of the phoney war, which, for him, was anything but, consisting of almost daily *coups de main* against German outposts in the Forêt de Warndt; the doctor remained behind, in sole charge of a large military hospital, somewhere in the area of the Maginot Line, in June 1940, and was captured by the Germans. In 1935, my own fear was that they would kill us all there and then: themselves, their mother, the maid, and myself, as a result of the utterly reckless manner in which they drove Mme Thullier's enormous black Panhard-Levassor, on the weekend trips to Samois-sur-Seine.

Although they made rude remarks about peasants, they were also given to boasting about their peasant ancestors – great-grandparents and so on – no doubt as enhancing their own rise to the level of a solid and affluent professional bourgeoisie. They did not often talk about money; but there always seemed to be plenty of it. Clearly, apart from landed and urban property, *le père* Feuillas must have left a substantial fortune in the safer shares. They were certainly not the sort of people who would have fallen in a big way for Russian bonds: *chemins de fer* and *la Rente* were their mother's declared stand-bys.

Both boys much looked forward to the prospect of war, though they did not have any strong ideas as to whom it should be against. As their father had been killed at Gallipoli, they tended on the whole to stick to the Entente system of alliances, mainly out of a sense of family loyalty. But I think that they would have most favoured the Italians as ideal enemies, as they could see themselves giving them a sound trouncing; also *les Ritals* were ridiculous, and their rendering of French represented one of the brothers' favourite party-pieces late on a convivial evening; though I never heard them express any views of Fascism, Ciano was one of their most cherished butts, because he rolled his eyes and brilliantined his hair (they always referred to him as '*le gommeux*'). In fact, *all* Italians were objects of high comedy. Hitler certainly was not that; but he might not have existed, as far as they were concerned, for I cannot recall his name ever having been mentioned in No 26, though they had a number of Austrian friends. But they were apt to make rude remarks about Jews, and were also given to imitations of Jewish furriers, old-clothes merchants, and so on, as they attempted to wrestle with the ambiguities of French. I do not think, however, that they were truly anti-Semitic, it was not so positive as that. Pretty well *anyone* with a foreign accent in French was something of a joke-figure, though none could compete with '*les macaronis*'. There were others within France, too, mostly Marseillais and other southerners, and Bécassine and other female simpletons (*gourdes*) from where she came from in the depths of *la Bretagne bretonnante*.

They also possessed a considerable repertoire of anti-papal and anti-clerical songs and stories. There was one sung saga about the adventures of a Paris prostitute who, repentant, '*est allée voir le Pape à Rome*', finding him, predictably, in a brothel. They regarded priests as poor, hybrid creatures, skirted men who did not serve any useful function in life and were driven to take sex surreptitiously (they claimed to have a detailed knowledge of the specialized clerical brothels in the quartier Saint-Sulpice). I suspect that their most vigorous and scandalous manifestations of anti-clericalism were directed at their mother, whom they greatly loved and indeed, in important matters, respected, but whose totally non-religious attachment to the proprieties of the religious calendar and to very occasional attendance at Mass they easily saw through. In fact, they were no fools, and were quick to detect pretension and hypocrisy, reserving their very worst manners for the occasional visits to dinner of the various literary and artistic luminaries, some of them aspiring *académiciens*, none actually immortalized – not even later on, which was surprising, such was their common mediocrity – most of them of the long-winded and eloquent sort that one would associate with Alliance Française lectures or with fashionable *conférences* in the faubourg Saint-Honoré, who represented Mme Thullier's claim to intellectual status. They were genuinely proud of her artistic achievements and of the official recognition that she had received, as Présidente de la Société des Femmes-Peintres, from la Ville de Paris, the arms of which, *fluctuat nec mergitur*, the *Nef*, and the rest, she wore, on such occasions, as an outsize medal pinned on her dress like a *camée*. They also thought, rightly, that her painting, and her standing with *les femmes-peintres*, kept their mother occupied and reasonably happy. They were good sons. But they had little time for intellectuals, male or female; and I never saw either of them, or Mme Thullier, read a book, whether a novel or the sort of fashionable history dished out by la Maison Hachette.

The brothers were not, however, total philistines, regularly attending each new play at l'Atelier, and having a special admiration for Dullin himself. There was a good deal of theatre – or should it be music-hall? – about their own noisy manner of life, even the simplest gestures being accompanied by the most almighty clatter; and I have never met anyone who derived more genuine pleasure from the sound of breakage, especially that of china or glass, a pleasure which I entirely shared with them, so that I offered a most appreciative audience, and I think the amount of breakage much increased in my time.

I have always believed that François chose the career of *commissaire-priseur* as much for the opportunity it offered him to cut a wonderfully eloquent public figure, from the moment that he made a very rapid and businesslike *entrée* on his rostrum, plunging straight into the sale, with a semi-serious description of some grotesque object held up before him, as if it had been a heraldic symbol, by two of his uniformed acolytes, and acquiring full momentum in the breakneck '*qui dit mieux?*' of the actual bidding, and exercising his machine-gun repartee at the expense of the most faithful attendants, whom he could pick out at a glance, even if they were standing half-hidden right at the back of his *salle*, at that anarchical cult, as to make a lot of money, which he certainly did as well. Each of his appearances at the Hôtel Drouot represented a small masterpiece of Parisian cheek and knockabout humour, with his audience conquered from the start, and the regulars drawn in by name. He also greatly enjoyed the extensive social promiscuity involved in the job, finding himself completely at home with a disparate group ranging from doubtful *brocanteurs*, Greek philatelists, Armenian carpet-dealers, elderly female eccentrics who spent most of their time nosing around the different *salles*, attending every sale of their favourite, Maître Thullier, and never buying anything – their pleasure was purely artistic – of elegant, fastidious, and thin-waisted antique-dealers, and very rough, ill-spoken *ferrailleurs* and *chiffonniers*, in from the flea markets of the porte des Lilas and the porte de Montreuil. He was perhaps the only auctioneer in the place not to have a speciality: carpets, postage stamps, pictures, silver, jewellery, furniture, china, *everything* passed his way, a veritable shower of junk and valuables, the intimacies of past regimes and forbidden, once glorious pleasure-palaces – he put under the hammer a bust of Jean Chiappe, a full-length portrait of Jacques Doriot, standing with his deputy's sash, on a barricade, against a background of red flags, factory chimneys, and clenched fists; at one sale he knocked off, in lots of half a dozen, official photographs of Marshal Pétain, the full uniform of a deceased *immortel* was held up in front of him, commented upon, along with its former wearer, the *bicornes* of *polytechniciens* would be disposed of in company with the shakos of *cyrards*, medals and sashes showered on the table in front of him, immense quantities of female clothing, down to the intimacies of night-wear, knickers, shifts, *soutiens-gorge*, and under-skirts would appear on the anatomical shelves in front of his rostrum, as if this had been an unofficial *morgue*, minus the bodies, with the *clothes* desperately seeking their lost owners, and, in the immediate wake of the *loi Marthe-Richard*, it fell to him to dispose of the entire stock of two of the most celebrated Paris brothels, right down to the erotic lamp-stands and priapic bathroom fittings: a challenge to his descriptive powers which he met with comfortable brilliance, amidst a perfect uproar of hilarity.

His office in the nearby rue Rossini, a sort of antechamber to the real drama, looked as if it had been contrived to the specifications of Salvador Dalí. Like, so it is said, the last Emperor of Germany, he affected to receive customers while seated on a rocking-horse or any other bizarre mount that had come his way, including elaborately decorated commodes or massively Gothic ecclesiastical furniture; and he seemed to expand in the menacing company of springing tigers and panthers, growling leopards, cheetahs with holes in them and the stuffing coming out, bored-looking owls, and a jaded stuffed pike, *aux yeux glauques*, drinker's eyes as boiled as those of one of his *aboyeurs*.[1]

---

[1] In Pagnol's delightful *La Gloire de mon père* (1957) there is the description of the varied contents of the shop of a *bougnat* (*vins charbons*) in Marseille before the First World War: '. . . des remparts d'armoires, des miroirs lépreux, des casques, des pendules, des bêtes empaillées . . . ce robinet col de cygne, *nickelé par galvano-plastic* . . . ce tam-tam de la Côte d'Ivoire . . . un immense drapeau de la Croix-Rouge . . . un billet mauve de cinquante francs . . .', some of the debris, washed up on the Mediterranean shore, and ending up high up in the city, far from the port, indicative of the importance of Marseille as a *dépotoir* of the colonial trade. And a very visual reminder of the changes of period and regime as represented by the altering colours of banknotes, mauve taking one back to the *belle époque*.

Indeed, I suspect that he secretly preferred *le toc* to the real thing, the fancifully hideous extravaganza, of no conceivable use, to the object of rare beauty and great value; and that he liked to live with objects that were bizarre and big, grimacing and in awful colours, as a sort of perpetual student engaged in an everlasting *Bal des Quatz'Arts*, a carnival that for him took place thrice daily, three days a week. He threw himself into his sales, his wild performances on the rostrum, spectacularly aided by his choir of *aboyeurs*, whose muscles were as strong as their stentorian Parisian voices, with a frenetic energy worthy of Pierre Brasseur acting *Kean*. But he was alone on the stage, a one-man act, in which every gesture, every *coup d'œil*, every inflection of the voice was used to maximum effect. No wonder his audience seldom varied; few enough came to buy, a great many came merely to watch, and to be spotted and called out by name.

It was not just the public performance. He enormously enjoyed the haggling, even if it was over some wretched broken telephone, a chair with a leg missing and the seat giving way, or a family photograph album. He spent much of his time chatting with the odd creatures who brought in their daily haul of impossible objects, and was extremely friendly to such a minor operator as my oldest French friend, Maurice Chauvirey. Perhaps, even more, his occasional *voyages à l'intérieur* took him out of the daily round of dust, noise, and flotsam; entry into closed apartments, to make an inventory of furniture, silver, china, linen, the truly astonishing interiors of elderly recluses: bachelor or spinster couples, survivors of noble lineages, shut away in the faubourg Saint-Germain for thirty or forty years, the light penetrating into a fortress closed and shuttered for as long, the ghastly, pathetic, or comical secrets of families gradually unfolding before the washed-out blue, rather globular eyes – his eyes were strikingly like those of the Bourbons – of the auctioneer, the unbelievable smells of old age, avarice, neglect, loneliness, total sloth. Here was a man who had little need to travel, and who could have written, many hundreds of times, *Voyage à travers ma chambre*, save that, better still, each time it would always be someone else's. He liked the *aristos* best – not out of any *bourbonien* affinity or political sympathy, but because their raped interiors were much more unpredictable, always much filthier, often with layers and layers of dirt, and their contents much more bizarre than in the apartment of a banker or an Inspecteur des Finances, where everything would be neat and in place. He had a theory that some elderly *marquises* and *vicomtesses* must have kept themselves in trim well into their eighties by hurling the heads of deer and moose across the room or throwing Sèvres set pieces at one another. He enjoyed the evidence of such posthumous breakage as much as he had enjoyed smashing things, as a young man, when I first met him, No 26, his mother's much-misused flat.

On reflection, I think François was a committed artist, a poet, even a social historian of a kind, endlessly fascinated by breaking into privacy and totting up the balance-sheet of lonely, hidden, and unambitious lives. His favourite customers were those who never bought anything and from whom he never obtained a commission, who came to the Hôtel like gamblers to the green tables, because they had nothing else to do, because they lived in a fantasy world which he helped to create for them. He was not an indifferent man; and his fascination with useless objects came from his own deep humanity, he was not so much interested in the objects as such, but in the people, mostly dead, to whom they had at one time been attached and to whom they had once given pleasure. His curiosity about people was insatiable; and I suppose he will go on in the Hôtel Drouot till he drops, for there is no retiring age in that profession. I have come to understand why he has never felt the urge to read a novel, or even follow the *chronique judiciaire* in a newspaper. It is all there in his *salle* on the second floor: his theatre, his full expression, his realization, to which his chaotic office in the rue Rossini is a *loge*, a place of preparation, meditation, conversation, and, sometimes, rest.

With his brother, a quieter, less flamboyant person, medicine eventually satisfied very different needs. Édouard preferred the quiet parts, away from the limelight, finally setting up as a consultant anaesthetist, on call night and day, as well as in general practice, boulevard Malesherbes, on the fringes of an upper-class and a lower-middle-class quarter, offering then a varied clientele. He was the silent man, the watcher, the giver of sleep. When I first met them, the two boys seemed to have much in common, François being so overpowering that something of him ran off on to his younger brother. But I think Édouard was only making a show of trying to keep up with the spanking pace set by his ebullient elder. Once separated, they developed quite differently, and while François grew in size and in noise and clamour, his brother disappeared to the Far East, only returning at his mother's entreaty. Even so, and though both married, they remained very close. They were in fact very fond of each other and came, in later years, to appreciate one another's differences. Édouard spoke with amused affection of his brother's extraordinary performances on the rostrum. What they did have in common – and retained together – was immense physical courage, a marvellously juvenile irreverence – I had come to the right place early to learn the sense of *épater le bourgeois* – an apparently limitless capacity for enjoyment in such important matters as food, drink, girls, and, as far as François was concerned, in that, related, of war, seen indeed as a sort of prolongation of sport, and a great deal of generosity. Public affairs and politics passed largely beside them, with only muted echoes at No 26.

The Xe *arrondissement*, as far as I know, possesses no literature, and it has been sung about by no poet. Could it be that people simply walk through it in haste to work, in fatigue at the end of the day, along the regular east–west itinerary described in one of Raymond Queneau's novels, *Le Chiendent*, or noisily hitting this outdated *voie triomphale* of music, vice, and pleasure, all three of very low quality, on Saturday nights? As if, indeed, it were but a *lieu de passage*, a sort of surface *Métro*, just like the one following exactly the same route, reflecting the same street intersections, just below the ground. I wonder.

Yet lovers must have met on its broad pavements, domestic dramas dragged along its grim, Sunday expanses, friendships been born between prostitutes and clients on the corner of the rue Faubourg-Montmartre or in the little café opposite the porte Saint-Denis.

It was not murder country. That was farther north: Pigalle, place Blanche, la Chapelle. Or it was farther east: in the old, traditional badlands of the rue de Lappe and 'la Bastoche'. Or it was over on the other side of the river, along the deserted *quai* skirting the Jardin des Plantes. Pigalle and 'la Bastoche', in particular, still attempted to disguise themselves as dangerous territory, certainly convincingly enough to make the tourist on a tour of the *bals musettes* shiver in anticipation of the knives coming out. Nor was it really *faits divers* country, save for the occasional street accident, though I know that suicide often briefly inhabited its loneliness in small hotels situated in side-streets like the rue Mazagran – *voie sans issue*.

For me at least, the Xe *arrondissement* still holds the freshness of relative innocence, of adolescence, and, above all, of discovery and acclimatization, so, perhaps, I am the one who should commemorate it: part of central Paris witnessed both from the fifth floor and at boulevard and *Métro* level. One's home station offers as warmly welcoming a homecoming, as great a sense of belonging, as a return from any familiar itinerary which is regularly followed. For me, the famous *agent à double barbe*, the man who had a huge beard coming down into two points, who was always on traffic duty in the daytime at the porte Saint-Denis, signified the imminence of lunch or dinner. And I could even recognize the man who sold *Paris-Soir* in the long corridor of the *Métro* Bonne-Nouvelle, intoning like a litany, in a voice of monotonous despair, as if the last thing he wanted was ever to sell one of his papers, '*Paris-Soir* . . . *l'Intran* . . . *Sport*,' with a voice falling in a sort of death agony on the last word, as if it signified ultimate doom, rather than Longchamp, Vincennes, Compiègne, and Chantilly, the Vélo d'Hiv and the Palais des Sports, Roland-Garros, and Colombes.

I went to sleep to the tired, dawdling sound of the *métro* heading unhurriedly towards Faubourg-Montmartre and Richelieu-Drouot or the bustling Strasbourg-Saint-Denis. I could distinguish between the wheezing gears of the green bus and the sound of a private car, and I woke to the noise of many heels walking rapidly to work on the wooden boulevard. It was as good an introduction, I think, as one could wish for, offering very few constraints and certainly absolutely no pretensions.

If, indeed, the Xe *arrondissement* has produced any literature, it would not be in French; it would more likely be in Yiddish – a chronicle of lost *Stetl* and of dispersed families from White Russia, Lithuania, Poland, and Romania, populations decimated by the Second World War. I walked up the dark and musty staircase of No 26 sometime late in the 1960s and could find no Polish, Russian, or Romanian names any more, only the names of Armenian carpet-dealers and of dentists.

And yet it was a district of Paris as much deserving of literature as the fashionable literary quarters of Paris or those patronized by populist writers – Ménilmontant, Belleville, or la Goutte-d'Or. The glass *passages* behind the boulevard Bonne-Nouvelle are as bizarre as those enclosed journeys in glass-covered surrealism explored so lovingly by Aragon, in *Le Paysan de Paris*, in the 1920s, farther west in the quartier de la Bourse and the quartier Saint-Lazare. And for sheer ugliness and monumental bad taste, the monster cheap clothing stores that line the street between Bonne-Nouvelle and Richelieu-Drouot must surely be *hors concours*, at least in the highly competitive terms of purely Parisian ugliness.

The quarter, then, would seem to have been crying out for literary commemoration of the same imaginative sympathy and careful observation as two recent works of that great Paris historian, Louis Chevalier, *Les Parisiens* and *L'Assassinat de Paris*, both of them evocations of a Paris which, as he says, is *le paradis perdu* – a Paris already largely lost.

3

Danton 71, 48[*]

'BONJOUR, MONSIEUR Kopp.' 'Bonjour, Monsieur Cobb.' And so it was, the late beginning of a day that offered little promise, as I put my key, *chambre No 25*, right at the top of the steep house, 105 rue Monsieur-le-Prince, on its hook, at the entry to the bar-restaurant on the ground floor. By that time M. Kopp, a totally bald Alsatian with little piggy eyes, would be already standing behind the bar in blue overalls, serving a *vin blanc sec* to one of the regulars, an elderly *appariteur* from the Sorbonne, who in the course of the day would move over *chez Thomas, vins charbons,* on the other side of the street, below the level of the long, hopeless façade of the Lycée Saint-Louis, the grimmest of Paris schools. By then it was generally close to midday, and Mme Kopp would have chalked up the menu for lunch. This had started conventionally with *pot-au-feu* or *biftèque-frites*, but a little before selling up the Kopps made at least a token gesture to the prevailing mode by proposing a *couscous* that was above all peppery and that might ensnare, once only, the occasional passing Swede or Englishman. They would not try again. Christian and I knew better.

'Bonjour, Monsieur Kopp.' 'Bonjour, Monsieur Cobb.' This time, M. Kopp had come up to the fourth floor, to bring me a registered letter: he displayed a natural and quite commendable curiosity about my mail, and the letters bearing the head of the King of Denmark that reached Christian every six weeks or so, for such letters would offer the prospect of the payment of back rent. It was normal for M. Kopp to

[*] This chapter first appeared as the Preamble to *Tour de France* (1976).

be familiar with Copenhagen and its function as a royal capital, but as a result of my mother's much-awaited letters and parcels (containing clothing), his knowledge of English geography extended down to the level of that other royal city, Tunbridge Wells. On the rare and privileged occasion when a letter arrived, he would display an almost deferential affability and a somewhat sickening jollity, even to the extent of offering us a drink at the bar.

But this time the affability, already creased in welcoming wrinkles on his podgy face, was wiped off in a second, as if by the stroke of some invisible towel. The door of my room would only half open against the end of the bed, so that the first and quite unexpected object that caught my landlord's attention was the head, as bald as his own, of a little man, tucked up to the chin, but with his made-up wide bow-tie – the sort of *nœud papillon*, in diagonals, that one would associate with Jules Berry, in one of his more sinister, meaner parts, such as in *Le Jour se lève* – sticking out coyly over the red counterpane. The head was where mine should have been, and it was only by leaning over at a right angle that M. Kopp could take in mine as well, over on the wall side. His piggy eyes starting out of his head, M. Kopp launched into a long, severe tirade about police regulations, introducing unregistered strangers into licensed hotels, one never knew what might happen, there were the other *locataires* to be considered, and so on and so forth. Faced with such unfamiliar vehemence, and believing that he was about to expel me, *je me suis fait tout petit*, explaining that I knew about such regulations but that this had been an exceptional case. But I could see that in fact Kopp, who in many ways was quite an indulgent and even patient landlord, especially on the subject of the alcoholic habits of Christian and myself, did not really have the Prefecture in mind, but that he was deeply disappointed in such a revelation of what he took to be my secret habits. To discover me in bed with a man, at eleven o'clock in the morning, was beyond the limits of his normally blasé Alsatian tolerance. Realizing this, I hastened to pull back the bedclothes, two old blankets reinforced with my overcoat and Army leather jerkin, to reveal my small bow-tied companion fully clothed, even to waistcoat, trousers, suspenders and (holed) socks. He had put his coat and yellow shoes on the end of the bed. Later, when the little man had gone, after thanking me profusely and cadging a *Métro* ticket off me, I went down below and explained to Kopp that I had met him *chez Thomas*, that he was an antique-dealer (though clearly much out of custom, and down in the *Puces* category – for the *Puces* had not yet become fashionable with visiting American academics), that he had been very drunk and had been weeping on my bony and rather unwelcoming shoulder, at a repetitive evocation, shuddering between sobs and hiccoughs, of an empty, uninviting room somewhere in the depths of the wretched XIIe, and that, as the last *métro* had long since departed, I had taken pity on him, deciding that he would never make it back on foot to the horrors of Daumesnil, and had, *en chevalier errant*, offered him half of my bed, an offer accepted with an alacrity that, even in the state I had been in, I had found slightly alarming. But I need not have worried, for *le petit antiquaire* (if that is what he was, which I doubt) had gone right off to sleep, like a child, though during the night he had kept on kicking me convulsively with his hot and sticky socked feet. I think M. Kopp was partially reassured; and I allowed him the luxury of a further homily delivered on the subject of unknown guests: there were a lot of strange people around, antique-dealers with bow-ties were ready suspects, I must moderate my natural hospitality, *les Anglais étaient des naïfs*. Kopp took something of a fatherly interest in his *deux lascars*.

As I climbed up to the fourth floor, after taking the last *métro* from the Ternes, where I had been having my weekly supper with a family, the smell of cheap calvados (*Le Père Magloire*) was wafted down towards me, becoming stronger at each storey. On the landing of the third floor, there was a *signe avant-coureur* of disaster: Christian's rimless spectacles were lying on a stair, one of the glasses broken. At the top, blocking the entrance to his 'room' (it was a sort of cubby-hole with an internal window facing on to the stairs, and a huge bed like a sarcophagus on a red stone pedestal taking up all the space, so that there was not even room for a chair, and when Christian was actually in the room it looked as if he were Lying in State; but this time, and it was not the first, he had not made it), lay his enormous and inert body, as he breathed heavily, emitting sickly waves of calvados at each breath. I went down the street to *chez Thomas*, and got the *bougnat* himself to come up and help me lift the Great Dane on to his tomb-bed. The Copenhagen Mail had clearly come in (he had been meeting

the *Étoile du Nord* each day for the previous week) at last; and with it
cold ham, pickles, cheese, dried fish, in fact enough to keep both of us
going for a week. And, *embarras de richesses*, there had also come a
letter from Christian's uncle in Wisconsin, enclosing a ten-dollar bill,
some of which, as it turned out, had survived the calvados, and was
later to be the means by which I was rescued from a café in les Halles,
where I had been left in pawn, while Christian went off to change five
dollars with my friend Maurice, rue d'Obligado. At least there did not
appear to be any rationing in Denmark.

Those who are condemned to live (or choose to live) in very small,
table-less, and, in the case of my Danish Communist friend (character-
istically he belonged to the *wrong* one of the two rival Danish communist parties), windowless, rooms, are likely to put off returning to
them for as long as possible (this, no doubt, is how I recognized in the
bow-tied antique-dealer a fellow traveller in the night). In our own
case, this generally meant staying in Thomas' tiny, semi-concealed bar
till two or three in the morning. There were three steps down from the
level of the pavement, and, on entry, one was liable to see M. Thomas'
cheery round face and torso emerging from a trap-door in the floor, on
the way up from the cellar. Although behind the bar there was the usual
notice: *La Maison ne fait pas de crédit*, this is just what the Thomas
did, and Christian and I were chalked up *sur l'ardoise*, as well as the
peak-capped *appariteurs* from the Sorbonne, and a female couple in
their fifties, one of whom wore a pair of off-white stockings that were
always falling down round her ankles, revealing the blue geography of
a complicated network of varicose veins; so that there was no danger
of going thirsty, even when the Copenhagen Mail had *not* come in. As
the evening progressed, so would a repertoire, unchangeable and
inexorable in the rigidity of succession: 'Qu'elle est Belle Ma
Normandie' (this, my favourite, would generally come round midnight), 'Les Blés d'Or' (later), 'Le Temps des Cerises' (later still),
something about eating ham with M. le Curé (towards the early
hours), and 'Il ne faut pas rouler par-dessous la table' to cap the
evening before going to bed, often accompanied by a sudden, gentle
slide in that general direction (Christian tended to go down slowly and
majestically, like a huge building, hit slow-motion by dynamite). *Chez
Thomas* supplied all our needs for sociability; it was our family, a fact

emphasized by the presence, often well into the night, of the daughter of the house, a pretty little dark-haired girl of eight, who seemed to find Christian and myself hilariously funny; it was our home, our refuge – and we were allowed into the tiny kitchen at the back, dug apparently into rock and with what appeared to be a medieval vaulted ceiling – and our eating place, for Mme Thomas, a woman of generous girth and disposition, offered a plentiful round of *saucisson d'Auvergne*, brought, like the young red wine, from their own village.

Nor did the function of *chez Thomas* end there. For one of the regular customers was an Italian girl whose marriage had gone on the rocks and who took it out on Thomas' red wine. I can no longer remember her name but she and Christian took an instant fancy to one another, and soon we were a trio, with myself in the role of honorary brother. Anyhow I no longer had to enlist the help of M. Thomas to carry the massive Scandinavian upstairs, though on one occasion, after Christian had come back from the Gare du Nord with the visible evidence that the Northern Star was not only shining, but was in, I discovered on reaching Kopp's that they had *both* collapsed, Christian on the first landing, the girl on the fourth. This time I called in Mme Thomas as well as her husband.

Under this sort of regime, though our eating improved, and was no longer confined to the contents of the Copenhagen Mail, regular work and, above all, writing, are almost impossible. Christian's Danish nineteenth-century radical poet, a Scandinavian *quarante-huitard* (and the Centenary was approaching), who had himself been in Paris and who was the ostensible reason for my friend's presence there, had to remain increasingly unchronicled. I think Christian only managed a couple of visits to the Archives de la Police, which, it is true, were situated on the sixth floor, at the very top of the Police Judiciaire. He did manage to obtain a Press card, as unpaid reporter of *Land og Volk*, but his reports on the French political scene at the beginning of the period of the Cold War were both intermittent and, I suspect, doctrinally unsound. The *hébertistes*, although they received my solicitous company for a few hours each afternoon – provided I did not call in *chez Thomas* at midday – completely failed to occupy my evenings, nights, or mornings.

Then came a treble change. Christian and the Italian girl got married at the *mairie du VIe*, M. Thomas and I acting as bridegroom's witnesses, Mme Thomas as the bride's. We had the wedding lunch in the Thomas' kitchen; the *appariteurs* were there, the lady with the white stockings fell under the table after singing 'Les Blés d'Or'. The Thomas found the couple a room and tiny kitchen further down the street. Shortly after, I too was able to depart from *chez Kopp*, though every now and then, when passing by the top end of the rue Monsieur-le-Prince, I would look in on the glaucous-eyed Alsatian, who noted with visible astonishment – for he was an observant man, as people in his trade have to be – my improved physical appearance and even evidence of a regular routine. 'Bonjour, Monsieur Cobb.' 'Bonjour, Monsieur Kopp.' I was not sad to have left my box-like room – it was the best thing that had happened to me since my demobilization – but I was quite sad when, one day, I saw a sign up over the Hôtel-Restaurant marked on the glass door *chez Kopp: Changement de Propriétaire*. And there have been a great many of those since.

At much the same time, for reasons I never fully understood – I think it had something to do with the increased charges of a *patente* – the Thomas sold up their business, M. Thomas becoming a taxi-driver. He remained independent, however, owning his own car and observing his own hours. They continued to live in the street; and occasionally I would be greeted by the stocky Alsatian, as he waited, wearing his perpetual cap, at the rank by the *Métro* station. The *vins charbons* had a brief metamorphosis as a *crêperie bretonne*, before its final degradation as a fashionable bar selling whisky, with high stools and concealed lights, and with the most unfunny name in neon lights, *Au Trou du Cul*. It was the sort of place patronized by young technocrats from la Résidence Ris-Orangis or la Défense, who came there with their wives and colleagues, on Friday and Saturday nights, blocking the pavements with their insolent cars, and waking up the whole neighbourhood with their row when they started up their vehicles at two or three in the morning. The rue Monsieur-le-Prince had started moving into the Fifth Republic even before France itself, and the process has been going on, at an increasing momentum, ever since. The female couple moved down the road to the Bar Condé on the corner of the rue de Condé. But there was no singing there. I do not know what became of the *appariteurs* and the two or three *retraités* who had formed part of the regular clientele *chez Thomas*.

I found my new room almost by accident, soon after it had been vacated by an American girl. It was still quite small, and was of peculiar shape, the wall on the right curving in at a slight bulge, so that it was not quite rectangular. I had been given the choice of this or a larger room next to it, further towards the centre of the flat, and had opted for the smaller room, partly because I liked to work in a confined space, partly because it enjoyed greater privacy, being at the end of a long, narrow corridor, and separated only by the kitchen next door from the back entrance. It was on the fifth floor of an *hôtel particulier* – *Cour et Jardin*, the latter approached by a double staircase leading from the courtyard to the principal ground-floor apartment – built in the 1770s, by a Parisian architect, for his own use and for letting out. Later I discovered that the house was classified *monument historique*, though I lived in it for a number of years before acquiring this information.

The house was next to the fine eighteenth-century barracks of the *garde républicaine* serving the Palais du Luxembourg; and I was sometimes woken up by the rolling of drums and by snatches of some fast marching tune. The room had a very high ceiling, and a french window down to the level of the parquet floor protected by a low railing. It faced north, towards the Seine, and on to a cobbled, resonant and, in the summer, wonderfully quiet and cool courtyard, surrounded with pots and climbing plants. The only sun that I ever got was from the bright reflections, at sunset on summer evenings, from the windows of the flat directly opposite. I had a sizeable table, facing the window; and at my back stood an old-fashioned marble fireplace (of the sort that one felt might at any moment emit a Magritte-like locomotive, with steam coming out of its stack) surmounted by a tall gilded mirror fitted into the wall, which gave the impression of depth, adding what seemed like an anteroom. A small bed, over which hung three bookshelves, and a narrow wardrobe which I could reach with my feet when in bed, occupied all the left side of the room, so that I could open the door inwards from my bed. To the right there was a condemned door in a recess, leading to a larger room, occupied for much of my time by a medical student and his current girl or girls – at one stage there were two of them, who generally alternated, but who, on one noisy occasion, arrived in succession.

Sitting up in bed, I could see into the room on the other side of the courtyard, which was the bedroom of one of the children of a barrister. And I could also observe the barrister's wife or the maid, busy in the kitchen next to it. In the spring I could see the house martins, caught by the early morning sun, as they wheeled round the roof, as if hesitating to fly right through my open window. Late at night, from the deep well of the sonorous courtyard, I could hear, in my half-sleep, the muffled request, in male or female voice, and sometimes, impatiently, in both: *Cordon, s'il vous plaît*, as from a distant cavern, and there would follow the far-away clang of the enormous dark green *porte cochère*, that was decorated on the outside with the heads of emblematic lions, their tongues hanging out, holding in their jaws two large brass rings. At various times in the night, one could just pick up the insistent peep-peep of the police alarm standing on the corner by the PTT, just off the rue de Vaugirard – a reassuring sound, because it made one appreciate the strength and size of the *porte cochère* and the silent fortress of the closed house.

The weekday morning sounds were equally predictable, and, therefore, likewise reassuring: at 5, the furtive, but purposeful, and vaguely obscene scraping in the bins, by, or so I assumed, a *chiffonnier* or a tramp in search of scraps of food, cheese rinds, or rags; at 5.30, the wheezing of a car that would never start in one go, the property of someone living at the very top, in one of the maids' bedrooms; at 6.30, the clatter of the dustbins, and the confused shouts of the dustmen; at 7.30, the bugles from the barracks. Sunday would be marked by a still silence, as though all movement in the city had stopped, save for the cries of the house martins and the insistent cooing of pigeons, followed, at 8, by the metallic boom of the bells of Saint-Sulpice, and if the wind were from the north those, more majestic, of Notre-Dame. There was a particular quality about the Sunday stillness. And, all through the night and the very early morning, one could hear the slow, rather hesitant clock striking out the hours, as if uncertain of the exact count, from the façade of the Luxembourg. In the 1950s, any time between midnight and 3 a.m., but never *before* midnight or *after* 3, one could pick out the dull thud of explosions, sometimes so close as to allow for the sound of tinkling glass, and sometimes far away, little more than a slight beat. And, according to the volume of sound, one would try to estimate the probable location of the latest *plastiquage*, for the OAS were nothing if not regular with their bombs.

At 7.45 in the morning, with the utmost regularity (Sunday excepted), the Bouvier brothers, Philippe and Alain, would start quarrelling, in the red-tiled kitchen next door, their voices rising in a competitive crescendo, right in my back as I lay in bed, like two parakeets, as they prepared, in a clatter of pans, what passed for their breakfast: *je t'ai dit mille et mille fois, Alain, de ne pas mettre la soucoupe par terre – Philippe, j'en ai assez, tu es sale, tu es dégueulasse – Alain, tu as laissé le gaz allumé* (this shouted up the corridor) – *Philippe, tu as oublié de vider les ordures, c'était ton tour – Non, c'était le tien –* they went at it hammer and tongs, the morning seeming to bring out in each the maximum of acrimony, as they screamed at one another, in total indifference to their listening audience (myself, fully exposed to their high-pitched denunciations, the medical student and his girl still able to pick out each word, through the thickness of two walls, so totally wrapped up were they in their daily dialogue of mutual accusation) before going off separately, Philippe, on his Vespa, to his chemical laboratory, Alain, on foot, to the Faculty of Medicine. After they had gone, still arguing all the way down the corridor, the front door of the flat angrily slammed behind them, the flat would fall silent, save for the occasional *coup de balai* from the next room, when, rarely, one of the medical student's girls was taken with the domestic urge. If they ever made love in the morning, they were certainly very quiet about it. But sometimes there would be stifled laughter, and I would wonder if they were laughing at the latest Philippe versus Alain dialogue. When we met in the corridor or on the staircase the student and I used to exchange our impressions of the two brothers, whom he was in the habit of describing as *complètement cinglés, quoi. Mabouls.*

If one of his girls was, now and then, shocked into action by the general disorder, this was a preoccupation that appeared to be totally remote to the bachelor brothers. For with their bachelorhood – and, when I went there, in 1948, Philippe must have been about twenty-four, Alain possibly eighteen or nineteen – went a magnificent *laisser-aller*, an amiable disorder. Judging from my nearby observation of the kitchen, they never washed a plate or a glass; there were, however, several complete *services de table*, through which they were apparently working, at the rate of a whole set a month, which would then be piled up dirty and perilously on any flat surface remaining, or on the tiled kitchen floor, so that to get out of the back door I had to wend my way through a series of Leaning Towers of Pisa consisting of plates and bowls, most of them of very handsome design. There were the remains of a motor-cycle in the hall, and Alain was in the habit of mending his bicycle in what had, judging from the disposition of the furniture, been the drawing-room before the war. Philippe slept on a camp-bed in what had been his father's study, which he had converted into a home laboratory, and from which, on Sundays, emerged sudden explosions, followed by screams of dispute from the far end of the flat. The dining-room table had been converted for ping-pong, a game that seemed to have been favoured by the brothers as a further occasion for high-pitched acrimony. And, apart from the mounting towers of plates, the kitchen was generally cluttered with orange boxes of over-ripe fruit and rotting vegetables that Philippe went out to buy, once or twice a week, very early in the morning, from les Halles. Some, I think, also came from bins, for, according to the red-haired Breton *concierge*, the furtive 5 a.m. shuffling sound had been produced on at least one occasion by Philippe, as he examined, with his laboratory patience and prehensile dexterity, the remains rejected by the other *locataires*. She attributed such behaviour both to the bizarrerie of the two young men – *voyez-vous, M. Cobb, ils sont un peu sauvages* – and to the experiences that they had shared during the years of the Occupation. Certainly, from my point of view, they were ideal landlords, leaving me to my own devices, and receiving with amused amazement my request to borrow a step-ladder, propped up against the jumble in the corridor, so that I could whitewash the ceiling of my room, which was scattering plaster confetti on to the bed. They were equally tolerant of my regular efforts to polish the parquet floor of my room.

In the morning, at 7.30, Philippe, in virtue of *le droit d'aînesse* always slightly ahead of the more lackadaisical Alain, could be heard coming with his characteristic slow, uneven footsteps down the long corridor which, running from the ex-dining/ping-pong room to the kitchen and passing by my door, was crammed with boxes and parcels packed up in 1940 and never since undone, and containing, from a gingerly conducted survey that I had made during the brothers' vacation one summer, dresses, women's underwear, hats, sheets, and linen. He still had a bad limp which, like the parcels and boxes, dated back to the *Exode* of 1940, when at fourteen, with his mother and Alain, then aged nine, he had been machine-gunned in the shins by German planes on the road west, somewhere near le Mans. Alain had escaped unhurt; their mother had been killed, and Philippe had had to go to the mortuary at le Mans to identify her body. He had somehow eventually hobbled back to Paris, against the prevailing stream of refugees, holding his brother's hand. During the Occupation, the two boys had grown up untended in the unheated flat, Philippe coping as best he could, though Marie, the family's former maid, was able to keep an occasional eye on the motherless household from the flat opposite, where she was in service to the barrister. I think Philippe's slow, timid gravity and perpetual sadness – his very pale blue eyes seldom lit up to any sign of merriment – must have dated from these terrible childhood experiences. Alain, on the other hand, had been preserved from them, his brother having somehow succeeded in concealing from him at the time the sight of their mother's body and the immediate and devastating fact of her death in the long corn, beside the summer road that in normal years would have led to holidays at the seaside. In most ways, Philippe had had to take on the double role of elder brother and of guardian, their father apparently having completely opted out, living from 1940 in his native Geneva – he belonged to an old HSP family of the rue des Granges – and only rarely coming to Paris. Something of Philippe's resentment at the responsibilities thus thrust upon him could be detected in the fact that he had opted for French nationality – that of his dead mother, a Teissier du Cros, again an old Protestant family, from the Gard – and that he constantly referred to *les Helvètes* with the sort of derision that so many French people generally reserve for *les bons Belges*. Indeed, the nearest he ever got to being light-hearted was when he was imitating *l'accent genevois* and making rude references to *le jet d'eau, vous savez, Monsieur, c'est le plus haut du monde*. Possibly for similar, though unstated, reasons, the brothers had become Catholic converts. Though they had cousins in Paris, they rarely saw them, and appeared to have cut themselves off from all human contacts save that of Marie.

Whether from choice, indifference, or meanness – and Philippe certainly was never prepared to throw anything away, even bringing home half-dead flowers that he had picked up in the street, or that he had bought at a cut price from the genial Algerian who had a flower stall on the corner of the rue de Seine and the rue des Quatre-Vents – the brothers lived in great discomfort, amidst the wreckage of the family furniture, camping in what, before 1940, must have been a comfortable and well-appointed flat. They slept without sheets and pyjamas, using old cushions from the salon as pillows and their overcoats as dressing-gowns. The central heating was turned on for only about a month, in January, and the water-heater for the bathroom every Sunday. When I acquired an oil-heater, *chez le Roumain* (I think in fact he was merely a gypsy), the *marchand de couleurs* in the rue des Quatre-Vents, Philippe was at pains to point out the heavy expenses in fuel which I would incur, and when I bought pillows and sheets from the BHV, they were both clearly disappointed that the legend of English toughness, drilled into them by their Protestant relatives, was not being borne out. Daninos, with his totally unconvincing *le Major Thompson*, was their *maître* in matters English; and I did not seem to fit the model.

Strangely, the telephone had survived from the pre-war period, or possibly Philippe had been unwilling to go to the expense of having it removed. Neither of the brothers ever used it; indeed, as far as I could make out, there was no one to whom they could have telephoned. Philippe had pinned up beside it a piece of paper divided into two columns, headed M. *Gaudeix* and M. *Cobb*, so that the medical student and I could mark down our daily calls. It was an easy number to remember, as it spelled out three Revolutions: DANton 71, 48.

The telephone arrangement was typical of everything else. It was as if we had entered into private treaties with the brothers, and, as long as these were observed – though they were unstated – they did not interfere. When, for instance, one of them met a partially clothed girl coming out of the lavatory, which was right at the end of the corridor, with a tiny window opening on to the back staircase, he would lean up against the wall, often provoking a minor cascade of parcels and boxes and battered suitcases, so as to let her pass, saying politely *Passez, Mademoiselle*. Yet they were not unobservant, nor devoid of malice, commenting, every now and then, with amused cynicism, on the latest state of play of my neighbour's love life. Otherwise, they were not interested, provided, however, that the girls came and went by the back door and the less prestigious, though still very handsome, back staircase, perhaps an unconscious twentieth-century transposition of the eighteenth-century theme of *Cour et Jardin*. As far as we were all concerned, however, we were all confined to the side of the *Cour*. Sometimes, through the french windows of the Klébers' *salon d'apparat*, approached by double steps, the stopping place once for approaching coaches and cabriolets, I could just make out a fountain covered in moss, an ivy-covered wall, and a small bit of grass, with a stone sphinx in the middle; but, for all I was concerned, it might have been painted on. In twenty years, I never set foot in *le jardin secret*.

Now I had a base from which, every now and then, to start off on the next stage in my *tour de France*, and to which to return, with enjoyment and reassurance, as to a place that I could domesticate, with a row of red and pink geraniums on the window-ledge that I could see from down below and that somehow proclaimed the fact of my residence – and not just a temporary residence either, but a long-term proposition; and with pictures and plates on what little wall space remained available, a vase made by a potter from les Bornes, near Bourges, on the mantelpiece, the flowers in it doubled by the tall mirror, a small shelf to the right of my table bought from *la maison du raffia (objets du Madagascar)* in the rue Danton. In the stillness of the daytime courtyard – as still as a night in Langres – with the children at school, the brothers at work, I could type without interruption, till lunch at four, dinner at nine.

And, from 1949, when I wrote my first article, till the early 1960s, my works in French would steadily accumulate on the Greek black and red bedcover: articles for provincial reviews, a small book from *les Albums du Crocodile*, published from the profits of patent medicines (Rhône-Poulenc), another published in Toulouse, a steady mobilization of Revolutionary Armies, the ever-present *problème des subsistances*, the pages concerning the years heavy in disaster and hopelessness: Years II, III, and IV, lying so lightly on my bed. At the end of each day that I did not visit the Archives, I would witness, with great satisfaction, the mounting pile of typed pages with footnotes trailing at the end of them like peacocks' tails.

I had occasional visitors; and, at one time, I had to make room, among the clutter of papers on the bed, for a dark freckled girl, the daughter of a doctor who practised somewhere near Enghien, and whose family came from the pretty town of Noyers in the Yonne, who came to me twice a week for English lessons. And it was here, too, at my table, that I received once a week Russian lessons from Mme Melgounoff, widow of a Socialist Revolutionary. When I went out, I would stop at the *loge* for a chat with the red-haired Breton *concierge*, who kept me informed of the activities of all the *locataires*. *Ah, Monsieur Cobb, toujours le mot pour rire*. She thought I was a wag; and she found the stories about the Bouvier brothers a source of endless entertainment. They were both rather frightened of her, mainly, I suppose, because they were terrified of being engaged in conversation by *anyone* outside the immediate circle of the flat. The *concierge* did not need to inform me about the habits of the *propriétaire*, Mlle de Montigny, an aristocratic lady from Mayenne, whose family had owned the whole house for a good many years; for I could time myself from her nocturnal wanderings: till midnight the *Relais de l'Odéon*, after midnight, till 2 or 3 in the morning, the *tabac* at the top of the rue de Tournon, where she would sit for hours, watching the bridge-players. We would exchange brief greetings, like travellers on secret missions who knew each other's business, but do not wish to seem too inquiring. It was, however, from her that I acquired much of my knowledge of the Bouvier family background. There are two things above all that make one feel one *belongs* in a community or quarter: familiarity with the *concierge* and acceptance by the *propriétaire*, for both represent *la longue durée*, time past, the assurance of a future succession of months and years, just as the silence of a Paris Sunday admits one, *de plein pied*, to the intimacy of a city, on the day on which its inhabitants, dissolving into family units, allow themselves a respite, to breathe, to dawdle, to look around, to sniff the air and look out for the buds in the Luxembourg – 'later than last year'. There was even reassurance in the morning concert of *piailleries* of the Bouvier brothers from the kitchen, an exchange governed as much by the *Trois Règles* as a play by Racine, and that, I felt, did not exclude affection and mutual dependence. After all, the tune and the invective had hardly changed at all for over fifteen years; and there seemed no reason to think it ever would, so closely bound up were Philippe and Alain in the closed, private world of their shared eccentricities, shared discomforts, and shared distrust of the outside (though I suspect Alain did in fact have friends among his fellow medical students, and that he hesitated to bring them home on account of his brother). I was so completely happy, in my quiet fortress, in the stillness and cool resonance of the courtyard, the *porte cochère* shutting out almost all sound of traffic and dispute as effectively as if we had been surrounded by a moat, or walking on one of my usual itineraries to this or that archive, that I would talk to myself out loud, mostly in French, for I had few occasions to use English, save when writing to my mother.

Yet, despite the moat, despite so many precautions, we were, all three of us, being threatened from close quarters; and the end came in a completely unexpected manner. The spartan habits of the brothers had been observed for some time from across the street, which, at the top end of the rue de Tournon, fans out as it climbs towards the Senate, increasing the gulf between the odds and the evens, and thus rendering, one would have thought, No 12 even more impenetrable to the gaze of the curious. Directly opposite us, in adjoining bedrooms, at the top of a hotel, there lived two sisters, the one good-natured, jolly and perhaps rather foolish – later she married a publican from Guildford, and settled in the Army Belt – the other younger, a bit sharp, not without calculation and, with a widowed mother whose mind tended to wander, certainly avid for security. I do not know at what stage Monique had begun to take an interest in Philippe's daily routine. I suspect that she must have used binoculars or a telescope, for from what her sister was later to tell me it was clear that, before even meeting him, she had been aware of the exact disposition of the furniture, parts of cycles, laboratory equipment, and sundry junk in the brothers' two adjoining bedrooms, the four long windows of which faced east directly across the street. The prospect, one would have thought, would not have been particularly tempting to anyone outside the second-hand furniture trade, though it might have intrigued a Simenon, as a literary problem setting out a series of clues requiring an answer. To the casual observer, it would merely have spelt out indifference and neglect; to a female observer, no doubt, the clear evidence of the absence of femininity. And to her, indeed, the sheer enormity of the disorder might even have acted as a sort of difficult

challenge. The curious thing was that Monique's window had in fact
une vue plongeante on to *Alain*'s room, so that, in logic, it would have
been the prime object of her solicitous scrutiny. Yet – and this is no
doubt where both Simenon and his *alter ego*, Maigret, would have
gone wrong – it was the room slightly on a tangent, the one on to which
she could only command a *regard de biais*, so that at least a quarter of
the room, including the camp-bed, would, like the other side of the
moon, ever remain shut off from view, that seemed almost from the
start to have commanded most of her attention. All of this must of
course be pure guesswork, though it was to be apparent that from a
very early stage Monique had, as it were, *jeté son dévolu sur Philippe*,
or had at least made him the prime object of her daily window-watching. In a conventional sense, he might have been described as better-
looking than Alain, who did not possess his rather gloomy distinction
and his washed-out blue eyes; and the limp may have aroused further
interest in his watcher. Or Monique, a provincial girl (I think from the
Charente; it seems likely, for the dead father had been in the French
Merchant Navy, and like so many of those who had made their career
plying between Bordeaux and Pointe-Noire, he had eventually suc-
cumbed to the massive abuse of *pastis*) and with attitudes that were
decidedly petit-bourgeois, may merely have decided that the elder
brother was the more viable proposition. But it would be indecent to
pursue the matter further. The fact is that she set her sights, literally,
on Philippe, though, for some weeks, or possibly two months, he was
sublimely unaware of this.

Monique at this time was out of work, or was in between two jobs.
This probably accounted for the beginning of her window-watching,
for it would have been inadvisable for a girl on her own – and she was
attractive – to have gone and sat in the Luxembourg. Furthermore, she
would have been alone most of the day, for her sister was on full-time
hospital work. This was important, for there was no great love between
the two girls, and had her sister been present in the day, she would soon
have become aware of her preoccupation with *en face*, and would have
been likely to have pressed her as to its purpose. As it was, she could
assume her watch unobserved and unsuspected. The initial stages were
simple enough, for there was no difficulty about establishing Philippe's
weekday time-table, punctual as he was to a degree of fanaticism: open

the *porte cochère* on to the street at 8.10 sharp, lift his Vespa over the bottom of the little door released by an electric catch – then off to the right, *pétardant*, past the Police alarm box and the PTT, turning left up the rue de Médicis, skirting the Luxembourg, at which stage he would be lost to her radar screen as he bowled along in the direction of his laboratory in the *banlieue-sud*. Then back, on the dot of 5.50, coming in low under her window. Child's play.

Her next move was to establish the pattern of *Alain's* daily (and nightly) movements, and this entailed greater difficulties, for he was not such a man of habit, often stayed late in bed, and his working hours varied according as to whether he was going to the Faculty or was on hospital duty. For if, as at some stage she had decided, she were to speak to Philippe – *aborder* is more eloquent, with its naval connotations – it would have to be in Alain's absence. And the fact that the young doctor was sometimes on night shifts, like her own sister, once ascertained, could be usefully mobilized for her campaign.

I suppose that Monique next made a series of discreet inquiries in the local shops. If she went to the *tabac*, she would have come away *bredouille*, for, like a number of the old-established inhabitants of the street, the brothers never used it: the *patronne* had collaborated 'horizontally' with *ces MM. de la Luftwaffe*, established in the Luxembourg, during the Occupation. I doubt in fact if *any* of the shops would have been very helpful, as the brothers hardly ever bought anything, and when they bought food, it was directly from les Halles, which were cheaper. And they certainly never went to cafés or restaurants. The sheer paucity of information may even have stimulated her interest in two people who, while living in a quarter, hardly seemed to belong to it. She would have had too much sense, on the other hand, to have made a direct approach to the *concierge*, and she could not at this stage have known about Marie and her former connections with the family. If she had had an ally in the PTT on the corner – a post office that once won the *Figaro* prize for the rudest *bureau de poste* in the whole of Paris – she would merely have discovered that the brothers received hardly any mail at all, save a monthly letter from Geneva, and a monthly *avis* from the *Comptes-Chèques-Postaux* of the rue des Favorites. In fact, I simply do not know what her next move would have been.

The one after – or the one *two* after – won my admiration for its ingenuity and cunning. One morning I received the visit of the elder sister. She introduced herself, saying that she lived opposite, worked as a nurse, was engaged to an Englishman in *le Surrey*, and what was it like living in England? Was *le Surrey* fun? Where could she take a crash-course in English? Would I translate a letter she had just had from *son Anglais*? And I started with this. There was no doubt about the English publican's interest, and I could see why. She was a buxom, pleasant girl, with an inviting frontage, pretty, bold brown eyes, and a very warm smile. She would look well behind a bar (where no doubt she still is). I liked her, and we talked away most of the morning. She wanted to know what I did, who lived in the flat, who owned it, and I told her. She let out that she had heard about my existence from her younger sister, but that she had come of her own accord, thinking I might be able to help. I said I would be delighted, and indeed saw her several more times, took her out for drinks, met her decidedly odd mother and eventually the publican, a moustached tweedy fellow without a word of French but as open and jolly as she was. I do not think she had, on this occasion, been the conscious instrument of her sister's curiosity; and as in appearance I am unmistakably English (*Monsieur Cobb, vous portez votre passeport sur la figure*) Monique would have had no difficulty in discovering that there was an Englishman living in No 12, though she could not have known on what floor.

I suppose from then on it must have been plain sailing. My own guess is that she must indeed have *abordé* Philippe one evening, as he was lifting the Vespa over the little door. It is of course just possible, for no man can ever judge another man in matters of this kind, that it was Philippe who had taken the initiative, and had actually spoken to the pretty dark girl whom he had seen on a number of occasions in the street. My first, and shattering, intimation of change was a ring on the front door one evening, quite late, 9.30 or so, when, a rare thing indeed, Philippe had gone out – Alain was on a night shift at Broussais – and there was this dark girl standing there. *Philippe est là?* she asked, and I said that he wasn't. *Il m'a dit de l'attendre*, so after some hesitation I showed her into what had once been the *salon*. I had no idea who she was, and did not connect her with my *anglomane* visitor of a few days before. But there was no doubt about the proprietorial tone of her inquiry.

After that, things moved fast. Philippe and Monique got married, Alain took up a locum in Tahiti, spent a year there, then came back briefly to clear up, returning to Papeete to set up in permanent practice. Later he married a Tahitian. That was the end of the *piailleries* from the kitchen. It was also the end of the disorder. The first danger signs came when Monique, who was *rangeuse*, and given to little yellow receptacles purchased from the basement of the BHV, set to work on the corridor. The numerous relics of the late Mme Bouvier disappeared in a day. Then it was the turn of the hall: the motor-cycle was all at once gone, to be replaced by arrangements in shells, and hanging lamps. The lavatory came next, the ping-pong table was reconverted, the kitchen was cleared. The medical student was the first to go; and I knew I was only living on borrowed time. There was no row, no scene. I was even told that I could keep the room to work in in the day. But what was the point of that? It would only make things seem sadder. I did not actually *leave*. I took things away bit by bit, but never *everything*, feeling that after twenty-one years the room and I had still some right to one another. I daresay my books are still there. Philippe is, or was quite recently. But all alone. Monique and the children went elsewhere, after a divorce. The *concierge* – not the red-haired Bretonne, who went west (I mean literally) – told one of the shopkeepers that M. Philippe had taken to talking to himself and seemed more remote than ever. I notice, each time I go past, that the four tall windows facing on to the street constantly have their white wooden shutters closed, as though Philippe had now gone a stage further and shut out the light of day. But it was good while it lasted, and I had a good run for my money.

4

Itineraries[*]

IN MY years in Paris, especially after the war, there was a fairly regular weekly pattern of itineraries within the city, or beyond it, suggestive of a certain restlessness and an innate loneliness. Yet I also valued
that loneliness, because it, too, brought the contrary promises of the
familiar and the unknown. I became habituated to a sort of cuckoo
existence, sampling, especially on Sundays, other people's houses: 103
avenue de Paris, Dourdan, a house always full of children, with a wild
garden and many swings and hiding-places, a see-saw, rope ladders to
get high up into the big trees, there were a couple of ash and an oak.
The house was next to a formal, regimented municipal park in the seventeenth-century French manner, as if in reproach to the happy untidi-
ness of the tulgy playground on the other side of the stone wall. The
house belonged to a local historian, M. Émile Auvray, who had
written a history of the Revolution in Dourdan and who had taught
for many years at the local *Collège*. I had got to know him through
the French Revolution which, in the past, had often served me well in
this respect.

M. Auvray was one of a number of *érudits locaux* I had met as a
result of common historical interests. What distinguished M. Auvray
from his fellow local historians was the fact that he didn't have a nose,
he had lost it at some earlier stage, I never discovered how, he just had
nostrils. One soon got used to the absence of the nose. He would meet

---

[*] A longer revision of this chapter was first published in *Something To Hold Onto*
(1988).

me at the station, his white hair waving in the breeze – Dourdan is on the edge of the Beauce – and smiling; we would walk to the house below the curling line of the ramparts. There would just be time for *apéritifs*, of which there would be a wide choice, in the garden, with M. Auvray's daughter and her husband, Théo, when he was on leave from the Côte-d'Ivoire. Mme Auvray, busy in the kitchen, would not emerge till lunch was ready. This was always an enormous affair, five courses, many plates, many glasses, laid out in splendour in the dining-room. After lunch, an energetic walk in the broom-covered chalky hills, as an addition to the *digestifs*, then back to the house for the six o'clock *apéritifs*, followed by a cold supper in the little room on the other side of the corridor from the dark, well-shuttered dining-room, which was not yet in use, the table still bearing evidence to the luncheon battlefield. I think this must have been the only time in the week in which the room opposite was used for meals. Piles of schoolbooks, exercise books, colouring books, children's comics, and back numbers of fashion magazines would be temporarily expelled from the table to make room for the plates and bottles. Apart from being cold, supper could compete, in respect of volume and variety, on pretty even terms with lunch. After supper, and generally with very little time to spare, M. Auvray, walking as fast as his short legs would carry him, would accompany me back to the station, taking the road below the curling ramparts, for the last train back to Paris. I generally fell asleep on the train, but always managed to wake up at my stop, Saint-Michel.

Nothing could beat a Dourdan Sunday: I liked the journey there, the little stations with increasingly pretty rural-sounding names once one was beyond the rather sinister Juvisy, I liked my little noseless friend (who made up in assertiveness – he didn't like being contradicted, especially on points of fact, and his son-in-law took a mischievous delight in contradicting him – for his small stature), I liked his wife – they were both from the Pas-de-Calais and had retained the harsh accent of their common origins – their rather solemn daughter, a teacher (almost inevitably), their easygoing son-in-law, and their wonderfully energetic children. I think of Dourdan every time I cross the quay by the entrance to the underground station Saint-Michel; but I have never returned there. It seemed best not to risk it. The house might have been pulled down, the roof leaked badly, the garden could have been tidied up, the trees might have come down in a gale, or strangers might have moved in. It was best not to know what had happened.

For other Sundays, for a period of eight to ten years, there was a grey stucco villa called something like *Villa Minouchette* – I know it was a diminutive and I am sure it was engagingly ridiculous, it also had a bizarre number, 19 *ter* – in a quiet avenue of le Vésinet. The avenue led to a little municipal park that was called *Les Ibis*. In the park there were fifteen or sixteen stone cranes perched on their concrete legs amidst foliage on a series of artificial islands linked by Japanese-style miniature bridges in cement made to look like rough wood. The islands were dotted, in studied irregularity, in an oblong lake with a concrete bottom. I suppose the cranes had been erected to lend substance to the name given to the park. The park was approached by a small *rond point* constructed around a stone statue, on a plinth, of an enormous stag proudly raising his cement antlers and staring haughtily down the avenue, with his back to the park. On the edge of the park there was a huge white and green house in the Moorish manner with little metal minarets, the home of a chocolate millionaire. The whole effect, I thought, made up most convincing Queneau country. But my friends did not read Queneau, they did not read novels, they thought they were frivolous, and certainly not conducive to militancy.

Minouchette was the improbable home of Lucien and Natasha Weitz (*née* Mjakotina), a Franco-Russian couple who personified the equally improbable match of an improvident and gesticulatory cosmopolitanism and a prudent, not to say mean, French petit-bourgeois provincialism. The neighbourhood, the villa itself (straight out of the early twenties), and its name all seemed an odd choice for a couple who continued to talk revolution (both at once), from morning to night, right through meals, through walks in *Les Ibis* (where Natasha would hold forth in her guttural and strangely accented French, waving her arms to give dramatic effect to a tirade, as if she had been trying to win over the stone cranes). But, in fact, the choice had not been theirs. The villa had been built by Lucien's father, a pale, rather colourless blond man, always dressed in a grey suit and brown bedroom slippers, with a grey cap on his head, a retired grocer from somewhere in Lower Normandy who was still living with them when I first got to know them and who would munch quietly, but doggedly

– he had rather loose-fitting dentures – through the mealtime double perorations, without ever raising his head from his plate. Another resident at that time was Natasha's aunt Vera, the widow of a Tsarist naval officer, a staunch supporter of the old monarchy (her father, she would proudly declare, in halting French, had been *baisé par le Tsar*, a turn of phrase that always drew a laugh from the children) and a regular attender at the cathedral in the rue Daru. The villa was not very large, but somehow they had managed to cram everybody in. Lucien and Natasha had five children, four boys and a girl. The boys slept in unmade beds in one room, they never used sheets; the girl, Anna-Claire, had a room of her own. Lucien's father occupied the best room of the house – it was, after all, *his* house – it had a balcony looking out on a small orchard and the unkempt garden; but he never sat out on the balcony, and he had quite lost interest in the garden. The elderly aunt had a small, dark room on the ground floor; in it there was a black-faced icon with a red lamp burning in front of it. Lucien and Natasha slept in a room over Lucien's study and facing on to the avenue.

Lucien and Natasha represented, in their joint effort – it was difficult to decide who was the sillier of the two, though I think I would have put my money on the Russian – what must have been a pretty comprehensive encyclopaedia of political failure. There was something almost admirable in their consistent ability to back losers. Natasha may have inherited it, for her father, before and after the revolution, had been a leading figure among the Socialist Revolutionaries. Perhaps she had won over Lucien from the start. When they had first met, in Paris, in the early twenties, they had militated with *le capitaine* Treint; from Treint, they had switched to Boris Souvarine. They had naturally opposed Thorez from the start; no name was more hated, *Villa Minouchette*, than *le Fils du Peuple*, the Great Betrayer. They had drifted for a time on the vague borders of Trotskyism. Then they had rallied to Marceau Pivert, just at a time when he had begun losing out to the majority line represented, within the SFIO, by Léon Blum. By the time I had come to know them, they were probably the last two surviving *pivertistes*. In the late thirties Lucien had been organizer and secretary of the Fédération de la Jeunesse Socialiste de la Seine, a group that had been rejected, as being out of step, by the national organization. Natasha and Lucien seemed to give flesh – not much flesh in the case of the former, she was very thin and angular – and blood to the word *minoritaires*. I suppose it was a form of pride, of having been right all along. I believe that, left to his own devices, Lucien might occasionally have strayed in the direction of the big battalions; but with Natasha constantly at his side, as a sort of high priestess of political purity, there would be little danger of his ever coming out on the winning side. By the time I had got to know them in the early 1950s, they had revised their view of Léon Blum, even expressing a lingering affection for *le Grand Léon*, whose public career had by then ended in political failure. The new demon figure was Guy Mollet, the man who had got the better of Blum. A regular visitor to the villa was Georges Boris, who had been Blum's *chef de cabinet* at the time of the formation of the Popular Front Government; Boris had sunk almost without a trace in the post-war political scene. For a couple who lived for politics – they certainly did not live off them – there was something almost touching in their unerring ability to get everything wrong. I think they regarded political success as the mark of Cain. After the Liberation of North Africa, Lucien had become the first – and last – editor of *Alger Soir*, a left-wing daily at once rejected by the PCA, by the more moderate Algerian nationalists, the followers of Messali Haj, and the majority of the *pieds noirs*. The paper had soon folded for lack of readers. He attributed the collapse of this no doubt worthy enterprise to the obscene alliance of the Algerian Communist Party and of the various settlers' pressure groups.

Once back in France, he had found employment as advertising editor of *La Revue des Mines*, the official trade journal of *Les Charbonnages de France* and of the mining engineers. When it was pointed out to him that this was an odd position for a convinced revolutionary, with twenty years of (mostly futile) militancy behind him, he would argue that capitalism could best be destroyed from within.

Sometime in the 1930s, he had attended a Fabian conference held in Balliol. This might have been a one-off event. But there was something badly out of focus about a Frenchman who then had made a habit of attending this sort of thing annually. At the first of these gatherings, he had been introduced to G.D.H. Cole, who had made a great fuss of him – I imagine Lucien was his only French disciple – and whom he visited on all his subsequent pilgrimages across the Channel. He took a touching pride in his friendship with the Sage of the Banbury Road, and he kept all the group photographs of these summer gatherings on the lawn of the Garden Quad. In all of these, one could spot him, fingering his pipe, seated in the front row; in two of them, he was even placed on the left of the great man himself. I think he regarded the photos as a series of sporting trophies of his political purity.

Lucien was a self-educated, self-satisfied *primaire*, lacking in imagination, prone to boasting in an effort to impress the first comer. He did not really exist in his own right, his main importance was to have been the husband of Natasha (perhaps he was vaguely aware of this himself, for, in the course of the summer following her death, while on holiday in the Cévennes, he was given to holding forth to total strangers, most of them Protestants from Nîmes, who would listen in polite bewilderment, about what a remarkable wife he had had. These embarrassing effusions would generally take place after lunch, on the terrace of the local hôtel-restaurant, and would be followed by the widower's copious and noisy tears). The effort may have been too much for him, for six months or so after her death, once back in le Vésinet, he fell quite comfortably into an incurably petit-bourgeois way of life, setting up with a nondescript woman of Belgian origin, who looked after his creature comforts – like his father, he now took to wearing carpet-slippers throughout the day – and who had long set her eye on the villa for herself and her illegitimate son: she got it in the end, the reward of patience and of sitting it out. The flow of visitors to the house dried up almost at once. Lucien in the absence of Natasha was not a person one would go out of one's way to know. This was something that, in Natasha's lifetime, had been quite clearly perceived by the four sons and the daughter of the couple.

It was not difficult to see why the boys should have taken their cue from their mother; Lucien was a dull fellow, always convinced of his own wisdom. He was quick to lose his temper when neither his wife nor his sons showed any willingness to listen to him. His own success in life had been to marry Natasha (described to me, not very tactfully, as I hastened to suggest to them, at the time of Natasha's funeral – we were on our way to the *Columbarium* of the Père Lachaise – as *cette étrangère*, by Lucien's Norman relatives). It had been a very strange choice on her part, as she had previously moved in Surrealist circles, and had been associated closely – even intimately – with a whole series of prominent figures of the French and the cosmopolitan Left. Souvarine had been more than an ideological attraction, and, at some later stage, she had lived with the historian Jean Dautry, at a time when he had been excluded, for some heresy or other, from the French Communist Party (later, having toed the line, he was allowed back in). Then I think there had been an interlude with Trotsky's son. Perhaps Lucien had eventually won the day simply because he had been so ordinary; his very ordinariness would have prevented him from ever competing on a footing of equality with his wonderfully flamboyant wife.

It was not very hard to take to Natasha, she was completely uncalculating, totally generous, and, often in spite of herself, great fun. There could be no doubt about her entertainment value, though to have been exposed to her regularly, day after day, night after night, might have been rather exhausting. I was only a Sunday visitor, and by no means on every Sunday, so I could measure out with some care my own degree of exposure to her performances. I am sure that she reserved the best of these for her enlarged, and, no doubt, more appreciative, Sunday audiences, and it is possible that, during the week, she actually took a bit of time off from dramatics, doing less walking up and down, and even sitting at table and eating, during meals, or what passed for meals. I had the freedom – as, indeed, I did with my friends in Dourdan – of being able to come and go as I pleased. (There is every advantage in being a *visitor* to a house – a role I seem consistently to have occupied in much of the present account – rather than in being *visited* in one's own, a passive position much more exposed and over which one has less control, and one that, as a general rule of life, I have always tried my best to avoid. There is a wonderful feeling of security in the knowledge not only that there is a convenient point of exit readily available: 'don't bother to get up, I know the way, I'll let myself out', but that one can choose one's own time to use it. It was also a role well suited to my own favourite stance, and one that I still endeavour to preserve, as an observer prudently placed somewhere on the sidelines, rather than as a participant in the thick of things and becoming too closely involved; one can observe – and listen – best from a little distance.) Confined within fortnightly and three-weekly intervals, there could be no doubt about Natasha's entertainment value, and she often came out with statements so utterly extravagant that they sent me into fits. She didn't mind being laughed at, taking it, I think, as a compliment.

I felt that there was even something to be said for Lucien; he was at least a convinced anglophile, even if that took the form of being an admirer of G.D.H. Cole and of attending annual Fabian conferences, sitting on the ground, cross-legged, or with knees up in the Garden Quad of Balliol: one should not be too demanding, French anglophiles, of whatever political persuasion, are rare enough. And I became very fond of some of the children, especially Anna-Claire, who had plenty of common sense, and of Roland, the third brother, who had absolutely none, and who was the only member of the family to have no intellectual pretensions whatsoever and to show no interest in politics of any kind.

In Paris my itineraries, both in the time I was living there throughout the year, and as recalled in a tenacious memory, were also closely linked to the *Métro*, a network that imposes its own entirely familiar succession of names and that one ends up greeting like old friends. Just as, by pushing a coloured button on one of the more elaborate *plans du Métro*, one lights up a whole line – Vincennes–Pont de Neuilly, Porte d'Orléans–Porte de Clignancourt, I wish I could remember the twin of Balard – in a series of shining yellow dots, so for me, over the years, certain stops would light up with the expectancy of familiarity, the strong likelihood of certain encounters, the sure guarantee of friendship, affection and greeting, the promise of someone to listen to and who would make me, and others, laugh: TERNES: the stately, exquisitely polite M. Alexandre – held locally in such high esteem as to be denied the banality of a surname – *vieille France* in person, with his gold-topped stick, his red *rosette* showing up on his rather shiny blue suit, standing at the counter, Café-Tabac des Acacias, in the street of the same name; one could not count absolutely on his presence at his generally recognized post, there were periods of months when he would not be seen, absent *en villégiature*, as he expressed it delicately, and no one would have had the bad taste to press him on the locality of his rural retreat; then he would be back again, his normal very high colour somewhat paled, taking up the thread of the conversation in his *ancien régime* French where he had left off six months or a year previously. His Months in the Country never amounted to *more* than a year. And outside, and visible from the café, *la grosse Fernande* – the name seemed somehow to designate her outsize appearance and boisterous character, so much so that I cannot imagine a Fernande who was thin, small, discreet, or silent – a big girl of outstanding vulgarity, speaking the Parisian of la Chapelle, always in good humour, and endowed with a capacity to fart very loudly to order, on her assigned beat, whatever the weather. But sometimes she would come into the café, out of the rain, closing her dripping violet and yellow umbrella, ordering for herself a *vittel-fraise*, and followed by her self-made deep blasts of thunder, as she exchanged cheerful remarks in doubtful taste with the regular customers of this well-placed outpost (the café was on a corner, facing on to the rue des Acacias and the avenue des Ternes, a double observatory of the Parisian night). Fernande, too, had her periods of absence, *en villégiature* I think in a different place from that favoured by M. Alexandre; but both seemed to have been creatures of habit. Fernande always came back apparently refreshed, her high spirits and her exuberant vulgarity undimmed.

OBLIGADO (as it then was, it is now ARGENTINE): my friend, Maurice Chauvirey, wearing his specially made cats'-fur waistcoat (the winters of 1946 and of 1947 carrying the memory of savage cold, the wind from the east sweeping down the avenue de la Grande Armée, providing the chilling advance columns of the expected Cossacks, wrapped up in furs, mounted on their little horses, and heading fast and purposefully westwards, in the direction of Neuilly; the wind seemed to announce the imminence of their arrival, but they never came, neither that winter, nor the next one, nor the one after that) and his brown hat, set at a jaunty, impudent angle, that he kept on even indoors, to cover his large, very round, very bald, very red head. Maurice, a comparative newcomer to the quartier des Ternes – prosperity in the black market had brought him here in the last year of the Occupation – had introduced me to *la grosse Fernande*, pinching her ample and resonant bottom, to a number of her colleagues, and to the courteous M. Alexandre.

FRANKLIN-D-ROOSEVELT: the assurance of a double welcome, the illusion, too, of a family responsibility – it may indeed have contained quite a few elements of reality, so regular were my evening visits, and so deeply was I taken into the confidence of both: the twelve-year-old Irène, a pretty, very intelligent child, with very dark hair, setting off her pale skin, and very black eyes, the whites of which were unusually large and expressive and which she was able to roll, apparently at will, to give herself a comic appearance: half-Greek, half-Welsh, and her mother, Mme Thomas, wholly Greek. Irène and her mother lived in a large single-room studio flat, with a tiny kitchen and bathroom off it, and which faced away from the avenue, on to the backs of other blocks of 1930s construction. Mother and daughter spoke French together, as well as to me. Irène's father had met her mother, then still a schoolgirl, in 1919 in Constantinople, where he had been teaching English. Before that he had been in the Army, but Mme Thomas had been uncertain in what rank, she had thought he had been an officer, but I had my doubts. Anyhow, he had done quite well for himself, marrying into an affluent family of local Greeks, the Papandopouloses; on the subject of his own family background in South Wales he had apparently been rather reticent. At some stage, they had come to France with their small daughter. The father had been shot by the Germans, near Grenoble, in 1943, accused of having spied for the British – later, the War Office was to claim no knowledge either of him or of the organization on behalf of which he had claimed to have worked, and had refused to grant his widow a pension. I was told about all this very early on, when I had first got to know Mme Thomas and Irène, in 1945 or 1946, and had done what I could, which had not been very much. She told me that she had never known what her husband had been up to from 1940 to 1943. He seemed to have been a pretty bad husband, and he had never been very truthful: that she had found at a very early stage of their marriage.

Mme Thomas looked permanently worried; worry rather suited her, giving her a wistful look and a timid, uncertain, apologetic smile. There was a thin tracery of worry around her eyes. She did not look as if she could cope. Indeed, she appeared so lost, bewildered and defenceless that the people at the embassy – she and Irène were British subjects – took pity on her, finding her a secretarial post with

NATO, then still in Paris, housed in huts below the Palais de Chaillot. In any case, she was not as defenceless and as lonely as the apparent existence of the bereaved couple, widowed mother and orphaned daughter, living in a single room – albeit a very big one, well-heated and well-appointed, in a building facing on to the old avenue Victor-Emmanuel III – might have at first suggested to the casual visitor. The Papandopoulos clan was present in strength. Mlle Cara, Mme Thomas's aunt, who taught the piano to young ladies from the XVIe, and who had been a pupil of the celebrated Gieseking – Mlle Cara told me that he had been celebrated – lived in the studio flat on the other side of the first-floor landing. I had known Mlle Cara before the war, when she had shared a small flat near Saint-Augustin with a German lady, Mlle Goetz, who had been my German teacher. During the Occupation, Mlle Cara had been denounced, but, having been forewarned by a friendly *commissaire de police*, she had been able to go into hiding. She thought she might have been denounced by Mlle Goetz, who, in 1941, had managed to obtain sole possession of the studio flat on the avenue Victor-Emmanuel III. On returning to Paris for the first time in October 1944, I had called on Mlle Cara, who had told me all about my former German teacher and what she, Edith Goetz, had been up to, and who had introduced me to her niece and her great-niece, living just opposite. So I could indeed claim to have been an old friend of the family. Mme Thomas's mother, her two sisters, and her brother, Thalis, were also living in Paris, in a large apartment, rue Lafayette.

On Thursday afternoons, I was in the habit of taking Irène to the Bois or to the Luxembourg, then to a *pâtisserie*. I much enjoyed these excursions, they gave me the illusion, without the wear and tear of the real thing, of parenthood; it was quite fun to be a Thursday afternoon father, and Irène was very good company, prattling on about her friends at school, and keeping me up with the latest school slang. Apart from Thursdays, I often went there on a Saturday and on Sunday. In the evening I would stay on at the studio until it was time for Irène and her mother to be going to bed. I would leave just as they were letting down a collapsible bed that fitted into a sort of cupboard in the wall. This was always the signal for me to depart. I would head back to FRANKLIN-D-ROOSEVELT with a comfortable family feeling. But I lost touch with mother and daughter and the big studio when Irène was fifteen. The two of them moved after that to a small flat in the wastes around the École Militaire. Several years later, Irène married the manager of the Hôtel du Pont-Royal (the bar of which was a favourite meeting-place for Gallimard authors). Irène had done very well for herself, and her mother was very pleased. There was a big wedding at the Lutheran church of les Billettes. I was glad at least that my small companion on the walks in the Bois or the Luxembourg had married a Protestant. So, I gathered, were the Papandopouloses.

To return to the *Métro* and its itineraries there was also, for instance, the long pull, with one change, via MICHEL-ANGE-MOLITOR, from ODÉON to MARCEL-SEMBAT, that, for several years, gave a clear identity to Sunday morning, culminating in the little, two-storeyed, so very provincial, grey house, at the top end of the avenue Jean-Jaurès, the home of *Le Vieux Maître*, the historian, Georges Lefebvre, whom Soboul and I were in the habit of visiting the first Sunday of each month, arriving at the hour of eleven, and leaving at half-past twelve, after having been offered two or three glasses of bitter Noilly-Prat. If our *directeur de thèses* expressed guarded – it would never have been anything more than that, he was not given to excess – approval of what we claimed to have achieved since our previous visit, I would reward myself by having lunch on my own in a small *restaurant d'habitués* a few doors up from the house on the same side of the avenue Jean-Jaurès. It made a nice change from Dourdan or le Vésinet. I liked regular itineraries, but the art was to vary them a bit.

One could never associate the *Métro* with threat, not then anyhow, it represented the map, just below the surface, sometimes high above the roof-tops, of journeys, regularly undertaken, in the knowledge of a welcome at the far end, then of the return, among a few sleepy passengers, to the comfort and safety of bed. As one emerged below the aggressive and posturing statue of Danton – *de l'audace, encore de l'audace*, and all that – it was indeed the sense of returning home, to base. Danton was like a familiar lighthouse, a symbol of peace, the promise of sleep. How often would I emerge there, just before the *Métro* closed for the night, in the late 1940s and the early 1950s, having travelled back from Mme Thomas's, changing at CONCORDE! There would be other regular destinations, on the outward journey: PORTE DE

CHARENTON, PORTE DE VERSAILLES, BALARD, PORTE D'ORLÉANS, indeed most places save PIGALLE or BLANCHE. The poesy of the *Métro* draws heavily both on its familiarity and its banality, its ordinariness: it is hard to take FILLES DU CALVAIRE seriously, SÈVRES-BABYLONE poses no threat, SOLFERINO, CHAMBRE DES DÉPUTÉS, as seen from below ground, are entirely unprestigious. LOURMEL, despite its vague promise of aristocratic distinction, is seen only in passing; it is somewhere I have never got out at. MALESHERBES, on the other hand, offers the prospect of comfortable wealth, slow-moving, roomy lifts and carpeted stairs, of medical reassurance (especially during my hepatic period of the early 1950s when I used to consult a liver specialist there: he was much more interested in Marat, a doctor of sorts, than in my liver) and of very good China tea with a retired cavalry general, who was also a historian and an antique-dealer, and who lived in a flat crammed with medieval ecclesiastical statues, reredoses and pictures, rue Jacques-Bingen, opposite the Soviet Trade Mission.

STRASBOURG-SAINT-DENIS represents the promise of the end of the month Friday girls, indeed, of one particular girl, nicknamed *Gaby la Landaise* (like M. Alexandre, she seems to have gone through life, in her case, brief, without the benefit of a surname), the object of my evening visits on the last Friday of the month, when I had been paid: Hôtel du Centre, on the corner of the porte Saint-Denis and the rue d'Aboukir. I liked Gaby, a good-looking girl with high cheek-bones and a delicate bone structure, well-spoken, intelligent, and amusing; and I was always prepared to wait till she was free, *l'affaire d'un instant*, the *patronne* would assure me. I did not have to tell whom I was waiting for. I called on Gaby I suppose something like twelve or thirteen Fridays, anyhow, just over a year. Then, one Friday, I asked the *patronne* if I would have long to wait; she said that I would indeed. Gaby was no longer there, nor anywhere. The week before, she had shot herself, placing a revolver in her mouth, in one of the sparse bedrooms on the fifth floor, No 78. There had been trouble with her man. She seemed genuinely upset, commenting that Gaby had been a well-educated girl, more than her *certificat d'études primaires*, perhaps even a *bachelière*, that she came from a very good home, and that her parents had a large shop – a grocery – in Dax. Gaby was only twenty-seven when she shot herself. Over the last forty years, she has often been in my thoughts, and I can still recall the unusual, rather striking lines of her face. She was amusing and observant and always seemed good-humoured. I think I most liked talking to her, we would start up much at the point at which we had left off, a month before. It seemed such a brutally short life. That was the end of STRASBOURG-SAINT-DENIS as far as my monthly Friday visits were concerned. After that, I moved further west, to RUE-MONTMARTRE or RICHELIEU-DROUOT (VAVIN or the appropriately named GAÎTÉ might offer similar services, there was something to be said for varying the Banks).

So, on the whole, the *carte du Métro* represents, or used to represent, an ever-reliable map of reassurance, familiarity, and often, as in the case of GAÎTÉ, appropriateness: GLACIÈRE really is what it says it is, NATIONALE, as one would except of that adjective, is scruffy, run-down and dreary, even if the old, sculpted, filigreed carriages of the *Nord-Sud* (so much in that name, too, a monument to Paris – 1900) have been replaced, and ORLÉANS–CLIGNANCOURT has become *inodore*, and the little *Dubo, Dubon, Dubonnet* man, in his bowler, raising his glass and emptying it *d'un seul trait*, has long since disappeared from the tunnels. How suitable that the evocation of the *Métro* should have played such a large part in the literature of exile, during the Occupation years, in the pages of the London monthly, *La France Libre*! How appropriate, too, that, in his recollections of a very deprived childhood in the XIIIe *arrondissement*, the populist writer and *argotier*, Alphonse Boudard, should have associated the *Métro* with his generally unsuccessful pursuit, as a pimply sixteen-year-old, of girls encountered in the favourable conditions, below ground, of the evening rush-hour: ('She got out at PLACE D'ITALIE, unfortunately she took the corridor DIRECTION ÉTOILE, and I was heading NATION'), the surest enthronement in individual memory.

Regular itineraries then represent the fragile barriers erected by the timid and the fearful, people like myself, in a modest endeavour to keep at bay the relentlessness of public events, and the orthodoxies of totalitarianism. I have become as much attached to the *carte du Métro*, within its old boundaries, because it is a map that has managed somehow to freeze, to immobilize, the continuity from the last years of the Third Republic, through the triumphant Occupation years (1943 being the apotheosis), to the present time, as I was, in the 1950s and the 1960s, to the two *ficelles* that connected la Croix-Rousse to les Terreaux and that lent a deceptively reassuring topography to *l'affaire de Caluire*, the arrest of Jean Moulin and of *le général* Delestraint, in 1943. Had not one of the participants at that fatal meeting taken the more eastern *ficelle* up the hill? I think it could have been the same almost anywhere, and not just in Paris or Lyon. When, for instance, I recall Columbia, South Carolina, what identifies the place as far as I am concerned, is a steep, sunny step down from the terrace of an ice-cream parlour and a small bar and eatery, down to the level of the street that formed part of the little shopping complex of Five Points. I grew attached to the steep step because I knew that it was there, and that I had to negotiate it with caution. It became as much part of a personal local topography as the six steps leading down from the level of the quay of the Saône, near the pont la Feuillée, quartier Saint-Paul, in Lyon, to the cafés, the restaurants, the little shops and the houses on the street that are several feet lower than the road itself. I recall in particular a restaurant, narrow and deep, from the vantage point of which one could only see the passing traffic: lorries, cars, buses, motor-cycles halfway up, their tops concealed, giving the little restaurant an agreeably subterranean feeling, as if it had been constantly in the process of sinking further and further into the ground.

There are many other places: Rouen, Roubaix, le Havre, Dieppe, Marseille, Brussels, that I have likewise succeeded in disciplining to topographies of reassurance and predictability. Oxford, however, has eluded me. Not so Cambridge, a place I associate with bitterly cold and misty February mornings and many cyclists, darting in both directions down the narrow lanes between close-packed colleges and the Regent House, their numbers and their urgency increasing on the stroke of the hour – nine or ten o'clock (from Trinity, from King's, from the University church, from Caius) – as I make my weekly way towards the ring road, to my lecture-room in West Road, meeting, at the level of the English Faculty, crocodiles of little boys in caps and blazers, as they head in the opposite direction. The numbers and the urgency of the cyclists gave me the agreeable impression that I was indeed walking and breathing to Cambridge Full Term time: but a Cambridge permanently stuck in February and March mornings, the cyclists with their breath visible in the sharp air, the big, ghostly trees

festooned with white. The place had admitted me because I stuck to a
regular schedule and because I was heading in much the same direction
as perhaps half of the eager armies of cyclists, their bells tinkling, their
baskets full of books and notes. So I was part of the general rhythm of
work. I found this both exciting and satisfying because, previously, I
had only observed Cambridge as a visitor, and now I was a participant.
Perhaps, too, almost by accident, I had stumbled on one of the secrets
of that university town, its uniqueness a rhythm of movement much
more generalized than that imposed by a slower-moving, more lethar-
gic, more college-bound Oxford, the awareness that, just before the
stroke of each hour, young people crossed the town to attend first one
lecture, then another, then a third. I liked thus to feel part of the
general movement, caught up in it, carried along by it, in exactly the
same way as I had early become habituated to the bizarre Aberystwyth
custom of 'kicking bar'. I suppose I would have achieved full native
status if I too had been on a bicycle, and not on foot. As a mere pedestrian, I did not entirely belong; and I could not help admiring the skill
of the cyclists in avoiding one another while not observing any discipline of right or left in the narrow alleyways as they pedalled so
determinedly in the one direction or the other, weaving effortlessly
between bollards and through narrow gates and passageways, and thus
establishing their own full *droits de cité* in a university town which is
also still a market town and the centre for a well-defined and very
beautiful agricultural region.

I suppose there is some sort of hidden chemistry about towns, capitals, ports, provincial centres. In Paris I used to feel it the most (it has
largely gone now, for there is no chemistry at all about *voies piétonnes*,
the mark of death for a once-living, unassuming street, about a
dehumanized rue Quincampoix, a cloître Saint-Merri given over to the
antics of jugglers and guitar-players, a rue Mouffetard invaded by
strolling players, pseudo-mummers and strident orchestras, as they
compete successfully with the organ of Saint-Médard). But I have felt
it almost as much in Roubaix, coming towards the centre from
Wasquehal and the canal; in Brussels, when approaching the *Ville
Haute*; in Lyon, always climbing up steps, or coming down them, a city
of innumerable *montées* and offering many unexpected perspectives
over red-tiled roofs cascading unevenly far below; in Marseille, coming

down from Endoum, or amidst the noise and bustle of the rue des Phocéens, an intimate thoroughfare in which the present-day *Phocéens* appear still to thrive; in Rouen, quartier Martainville; or Eau-de-Robec, a city which reveals most on its fringes, and least in its centre: the impersonal rue Thiers, the equally impersonal rue Jeanne-d'Arc; in Dieppe, in the narrow, secret streets of tall, gaunt houses in small grey bricks, behind the quays, and hidden by them: l'Enfer; even in the apparently unpromising le Havre, once one has climbed up to the heights of Sanvic or Graville. And there are traces of it still, though less vivacious, less varied, less pungent, less noisy, more anonymous, more restrained, than at the time of his schooldays as an *interne* in the Lycée Clemenceau, in the 1920s, of Julien Gracq's Nantes, a city then traversed, cut in two (as it still was when I went there in the 1950s) by the main line from Paris to Quimper, as described, in his recent masterpiece, *La Forme d'une ville*.

5

The Streets of Paris*

PARIS IS a manageable place; its frontiers are clearly marked, there is no doubt as to where it begins and where it ends, though, porte des Lilas, porte de Montreuil, porte de Versailles, there is a fairly wide intermediate zone. It is above all manageable physically, in that it can be walked from end to end, east to west, Vincennes to Neuilly; from north to south, Clignancourt to Orléans, though I have never in fact done either in one go. I have, however, walked through the night from Viroflay to Odéon, passing the longest DÉFENSE D'AFFICHER I have ever encountered, the apparently interminable wall of the Renault car factory in Billancourt; and, at regular intervals, between one and three in the morning, the whole length of the rue de Vaugirard whether from Issy-les-Moulineaux or the Lycée Michelet, in Vanves, past *Convention* and *boutons et jours*, to the corner of the rue de Tournon facing the Senate. Other nights have taken me from the centre of Montrouge again to the rue de Tournon. I have come down from the top of the rue de Ménilmontant, through the rue Oberkampf, and past the *Café du Centenaire* (which no longer exists, as if the memory of 1789 had been officially erased, the café now being replaced by a Wimpy Bar) and down through the Gravilliers, again to the rue de Tournon. Having fallen asleep in the *métro*, at the *Nation* terminus, when I eventually woke up, I found myself in complete darkness, at the end of a tunnel. Having reached the platform, I was finally able to find my way up a fire-escape, making my way home, a little before dawn,

* This chapter originally formed part of the Introduction to *The Streets of Paris* (1980).

down the whole dreary length of the boulevard Voltaire; and the walk from the rue d'Argentine (ex-Obligado) to the VIe was a more regular nightly occurrence. Whether from choice or necessity – no money for a ticket, or the last *métro* gone – there are very few Paris itineraries that, at one time or another, I have *not* had to walk. This has stood me in good stead, for Paris *should* be walked, because much of it, the most secret, the most modest, the most bizarre, the tiniest, is only discoverable by the pedestrian who is prepared to push behind the boulevards and the long straight streets of the Second Empire and the early confident years of the Third Republic. It is as if a different city, made up of tiny courtyards and diminutive houses, were prepared to reveal its unpretentious and endearing proportions only to the walker, still clinging to early nineteenth-century forms of transport and the itineraries imposed by the amount that two legs can tackle. Certainly cars have – should have – no place either in the impasse Cœur de Vey (XIVe) or in the passage Dieu (XXe), and only the owners and workers of the *Établissements Dupont*, the makers of luxury cigarette-lighters, are likely to have been aware of the existence of the tiny rue Dieu (Xe). The numerous *passages* of the quartier Saint-Lazare, the quartier de la Bourse, off the rue Mazagran, and other parts of central Paris can only be negotiated on foot. Aragon wrote *Le Paysan de Paris*, while still a young man, with his feet. Most of this sort of Paris is invisible to those too who rely on public transport (though the *Métro aérien*, between *Nationale* and *Glacière*, between *la Motte-Picquet* and *Bir Hakeim* or in some of its northern loops above *la Chapelle* may offer many suggestive, tempting, if fleeting views of third- and fourth-floor interiors: bedrooms, kitchens, figures silhouetted at night against drawn blinds, while the vast cutaways at the approaches to the Gare du Nord and Saint-Lazare present a whole range of windows, some with washing, windows that are only discoverable from the line) because so much of the city is closed off in courtyards, down alleyways, or beyond narrow *entrées*. A great deal of the city is still, as it was in the eighteenth century, an enfilade of tall green *portes cochères*, ornamented with heavy brass knockers, lions' heads, their golden tongues hanging out; and even now it is a place that secretes hundreds of hidden gardens, the foliage of which is sometimes visible from the street, peering over a wall, but many of which may be spied only once in a lifetime, thanks to the chance opening of an eighteenth-century double-door, approached by two sets of curling steps – *le perron* – *côté cour*, in a former *hôtel particulier*. For twenty years I lived in a room facing on to the courtyard of 12 rue de Tournon, a house built in 1778, and only once did I get a clear view of the tiny garden that lay beyond the main ground-floor apartment. Of course I was never able actually to set foot in it, so that it acquired the great desirability of inaccessibility and mystery, like the garden of a convent.

It is what lies *beyond* the *porte cochère*, or past the narrow entry into a deep rectangular courtyard that is so often the most rewarding, and the most unexpected. *Escalier D, au fond de la cour, fabrique de banjos, Escalier J, au fond de la cour à gauche, mécanicien* as well as providing a necessary indication to the complication of Parisian addresses in these enclosed places that can still be described as survivals of eighteenth-century *Cours des Miracles*, especially in the older central, east-central, and north-eastern districts (Hébert's newspaper, *Le Père Duchesne*, lay in the cour de la rue Neuve-l'Égalité, a courtyard which still exists off what is now – conquest having come in between – la rue d'Aboukir), should be taken as a slogan, and as an invitation, as challenging as an unexpected *fonds d'archives* is to the historian, to anyone who wants to get to know the city and to push beyond the formal façades of the *grands boulevards*, triumphal arches and the geometrical perspectives of streets, arcades and buildings designed for collective show and for the glorification of State power. *Les Mystères de Paris* lurk in dank, leprous places, and Haussmann knew what he was doing when he ordered the levelling of the Butte-des-Moulins to make way for the avenue de l'Opéra, and cut through the maze of the old *cité*, rue de Jérusalem, the lair of the *tapis francs*, to construct, in their place, an enormous neo-Gothic Palais de Justice, the triumph of Authority over Individualism. At least that is how I see it, that is the angle of vision that gives me most satisfaction. Just as I like my history to look inwards, from light into semi-darkness, from the street into the interior, if possible even to cross the threshold and negotiate the dark staircase, enjoying on the hand the smooth curling wood of the banister, just as I want my historical itineraries to be capable of reconstruction in terms of both walking distance and regular habit – to and from work, the different itineraries of leisure or of the seasons, and again the different *promenades de dimanche* – all of which will contribute to a sense of reassurance, because of predictability and continuity (because *discontinuity* in history is utterly alarming), so I feel that Paris should be both walkable and walked, if the limitless variety, the unexpectedness, the provincialism, the rusticity, the touching eccentricity, and the often tiny scale of the place are to be appreciated.

Of course, Paris, like any big city, represents a very large number of choices, ranging from the show spots, the garish quarters of vice and pleasure, to the stuffy, selfish, self-satisfied wastes of the avenue Henri-Martin. Most have something to offer, including the churches and the historic buildings. But the Paris I prefer is that of the minute, intimate, or semi-intimate domestic scale, not that of the village – for there cannot be a village in the absence of a church, and churches I have excluded,* as I have other historic edifices – but at least a couple of streets, whether dormant and semi-rural, or busy with small shops and barrows, cafés, and people carrying black shopping bags. Generally it is not very hard for the man on foot to discover, though he needs to step behind the scenes, behind those stern and unremitting friezes of tall uniform houses, drilled to Haussmann specifications, six or seven storeys, *chambres mansardées* at the top to accommodate the maids, bulbous, tummied balconies, sometimes supported by allegorical beasts or female sphinxes wearing breastplates and terminating halfway down, in sad grey stone or yellowish brick – Second Empire, Third Republic, or late 1920-style *habitations à bon marché* in yellow with green or blue lozenge motifs – the jumble of small houses, sheds, workshops, *impasses*, *passages*, former stables, of only two or three storeys, as if shy of visitors, and anxious to conceal their still rural proportions, their peeling plaster, the fading advertisements on their cutoff sides, or the still just visible lettering of a trade or of an inviting restaurant or café-title, their unassuming traces of care and intimacy: cages of canaries, potted plants, hanging up outside at head level, the communal tap in the form of an iron dolphin, dilapidated shutters, a profusion of chimneys and stove-pipes, the wiring and the pipes, shivering and gurgling, and both appearing highly dangerous, curling like

*Cobb was referring to the text and photographs of his book, *The Streets of Paris*.

jungle vegetation – stifling green *lianes* of suppurating sweat – around entry walls and up dim staircases, as if living off the damp stone and attempting to strangle the building and its tenants, a cluster of letter-boxes, double-surnamed (husband and wife), some in spidery hand-writing, some with printed visiting cards and *titres* (even little crosses for the *Légion*, palms, lyres, and so on), the complicated plans at the entrance to the *loge* representing the names and locations of the various *locataires*, and the entries to staircases which run through the first part of the alphabet, *Escalier A*, *Escalier K* (I have even seen an *Escalier M*, but an *Escalier W* has eluded me).

This book then depicts, in visual terms that are as minute as tech-nique will allow, a Paris that is both half-hidden, and, because it is unpretentious and takes up a great deal of space with its low-lying buildings and long yards, increasingly threatened. I make no apology for the multiplicity of pictures of courtyards, for I think that they offer one of the most abiding charms of the city; they also condition the friendly sociability of their inhabitants, the washing lines shared, the children watched from a score of inward-looking windows and stair-ways, their pets roaming at will, a stream of soapy water running through the central channel (*rigole*) of the paved yard. With almost the sole exception of the rue du Faubourg-Saint-Martin – one of the oldest streets in Paris, and, until Haussmann, with its twin, the rue du Faubourg-Saint-Denis, the principal north–south axis of the city – I have had no difficulty in avoiding the main arteries and the wide boule-vards, choosing, on the contrary, side-streets that are still paved and down which will run streams of water, at the bid of the long brooms of uniformed municipal employees concerned with *la voierie*. On such streets, as well as on busier ones such as the rue de Ménilmontant, the intention has been to take in at least one example of every common trade and of every type of small shop: *couleurs* (they smell nice and they are pretty), *vins, alimentation, vins-charbons, coiffure, laverie, blanchisserie-pressing, fumisterie, coutellerie, serrurerie, boulangerie-pâtisserie, enseignes, papeterie, électricité, mercerie, boutons et jours, cordonnerie, boucherie, médailles et décorations, tailleur, imprimerie, mécanique, tôlerie, chauffage, ambulances, doreur, relieur, remaillage, tampons, jouets, farces et attrapes, postiches, ceintures, soutiens-gorge, gaines, vieux papiers, bouchons, métaux et chiffons,* small workshops, cafés, bars, restaurants. The only trade that managed to elude us was that of the *pompes funèbres*, death having long since escaped from the modest proportions of the small shop; and, despite much study of the names in the *loges* of *concierges*, we were unable to discover a single *Madame Irma*, fakir, or *cartomancienne*. Perhaps we should have looked in the XIIe.

In short, a place of human proportions and in which most people can give names and greetings to most people, in which a couple of men, or a couple of women, will linger, holding their black *cabas*, with leeks and carrots sticking out of them, to exchange a few words, after making a purchase, in which there is time to linger, and in which the shopkeeper, behind his counter, will take a professional pride in his ability to hold the attention of the prospective customer:

Bonjour, madame, beau temps, n'est-ce pas? Dame! voilà bientôt l'été. Pour une miniature ou pour une photographie? Photographie. Et quel format? Vous ne le savez pas? L'avez-vous avec vous, cette photo? Non? Alors, chère madame, comment voulez-vous que je vous vende un cadre? Vous voulez le choisir, comme ça? Au jugé? Quelle grave erreur, madame . . . Je ne fais pas du travail d'amateur . . . Ce serait un crime de mettre dans n'importe quoi l'image d'un être cher . . . Votre fils? Vous voyez . . . Treize ans? Et il sait déjà ce qu'il veut faire? Ah! ingénieur. C'est un beau métier . . .

Queneau's photographer has all the time in the world, as well as a remarkable *baratin*. The sales talk is as important as the sale. This is not the sort of Paris in which impatient people will rush blindly from or into a *bouche de Métro*, their eyes turned inwards, on the unseeing journey to work or back home. On the contrary, it is a leisured place, walkable in all its limits, and in which there is the opportunity to dawdle, to stop, to see, to notice small changes and to have one's attention caught by a drawn blind, by a closed shutter, by a shop-door without its handle, by the small square of a white notice, *fermé pour cause de décès*, or *fermé jusqu'au 1er septembre*, by a sign-painter painting out a familiar name, by a child's face at a window, by a geranium in flower.

Two of the areas included, the Xe and the XXe, represented, in the roundabout itinerary covered on foot, the passing of a complete day, at least during the hours of October light, from 7-ish to 6.30, so that it might be possible to follow the activities of a quarter and the movements of its inhabitants through the day and at least from hour to hour, and preferably from a fixed and unobtrusive vantage point. In the Xe, the footbridge over the canal offered us, over several hours, the view from the captain's bridge, both waterwards and quayside-wards, and even beyond the quays, towards the interior. In the XXe, we did a full circle, ending up much where we had started from, rue des Amandiers. In both *arrondissements*, by the end of the time, we had begun recognizing people, and begun being recognized by them.

The two of us, the tripod and the photographic equipment, one of us ahead and scouting out courtyards and *entrées*, the names on *loges*, objects in windows, the other following on, burdened with a clutter of equipment, had become part of the familiar landscape. In these two areas of north-east Paris, at least, we were able to perceive what Jules Romains, in *Le 6 octobre*, has called *la respiration de la grande ville*, a living entity breathing through the hours of the day and the coming night. The other areas were covered over shorter periods of time, though we often stopped long enough to see the people who had gone in (a shop, a café, a restaurant, a park) coming out. We chose weekdays because we wanted a landscape with people, wanted too to be able to distinguish between a Wednesday and a Thursday, between mid-week and a Friday (when people have more money to spend); and so we avoided the unusual movements of a Saturday, or the Sunday stillness save in the neighbourhood of cemeteries. And we chose early October, not in deference to *Le 6 octobre* (itself, however, an excellent choice, just after *la rentrée*, with everyone back in the city and oysters on the stalls, a pre-1914 Thursday), but because the October light of the Île-de-France seemed especially favourable to what we had in mind. There would have been little point in operating in the dead month of August, *la morte saison* indeed, rows of closed shops, their shutters down; and winter would have been too uncomfortable for work carried out mainly outside, though occasionally under the cover of a glass roof, or a balcony, or in the entry of a staircase. We took a risk on the weather and were lucky. But then October is nearly always the best month in Paris; and those who have been away are glad to be back in the city – perhaps the only justification, as far as I can see, for the almost professional zeal that the French – the most stylized, elaborately dressed, elaborately equipped *vacanciers*, a nation in fact of Hulots, of any Europeans – devote to the serious, elaborate and tiresome business of summer holidays. In October, these at least are over, the *bronzage* has been completed, and everything is open again.

The responsibility for the *arrondissements* in part covered, and, more important, for those left out, lies entirely with the author. They represent in fact hardly a tenth of the total area of the city; and a similar topography, whether squat and low-lying, or climbing steeply northwards, and as friendly and as provincial, could certainly have been illustrated elsewhere: for instance in the adjoining XIXe, as much part of Belleville-Ménilmontant as the XXe – indeed, we strayed into it on more than one occasion, and as much part of Dabit's Paris of the twenties and thirties as the Xe and the XVIIIe; or in the quartier des Ternes, in and around the rue des Acacias and in the *villas* beyond the church of Saint-Ferdinand; or in the *Village Suisse*, near la Motte-Picquet-Grenelle, off the rue de Siam; or in and off the rue Saint-Charles; or in the rue des Favorites and the coaching-inns and former stables near the *Centre des Comptes-Chèques-Postaux* in the XVe; even in some shopping streets in les Batignolles, just off the boulevard Malesherbes; or in the hidden wastes and narrow streets off the boulevard de Picpus, in the XIIe. This is merely a selection, and one which will perhaps tempt others to look further, at least on the Right Bank.

The XVIe, the VIIIe, and most of the central areas excluded themselves. The old Halles is a sad desert; the Marais has become a museum, its original inhabitants dispersed to the *grande banlieue*, and replaced by middle-class intellectuals, their wives dressed like Gipsy-Rose-Lees in expensive rags, and armed with *Le Nouvel-Observateur*, or by young technocratic couples, fresh from the *Grandes Écoles* or from the provinces. The quartier Saint-Merri has been frozen into a network of *voies piétonnes*, one of the surest ways of congealing a once-living quarter into the slow death of fashion, tourism, sex-shops, antique-shops and expensive *boutiques*; in the rue Quincampoix, the small cafés have given way to bars and couscous restaurants. The Île-Saint-Louis is for millionaires, its central street for picture-galleries. The Gravilliers and the Temple have indeed survived, but they have never had any large concentrations of nineteenth-century domestic architecture. The VIe has been lost beyond hope – the last hope was the old marché Saint-Germain; the librairie Clavreuil, in the rue Saint-André-des-Arts the only shop left of the street as it was in the 1930s, a last outpost of a once living quarter, quartier de Buci: *on est entouré d'étrangers*, comments sadly Clavreuil fils; the VIIe is similarly infected, the quartier Saint-Séverin is totally ruined.

I feel sentimental about the Xe because, like Louis Chevalier, who began to discover Paris in the company of the son of a *concierge*, boulevard Sébastopol, I began there, quartier Bonne-Nouvelle, in sight of the *Rex*, *Le Matin*, and the rue de la Lune, in 1935, my own *apprentissage de Paris* (and I could hardly have had a more Parisian apprenticeship, save in the XXe or the XIXe). But the Xe, especially in its eastern and north-eastern quarters, is also largely unspoilt and little known, once one leaves the *grands boulevards* and the two triumphal arches of the porte Saint-Denis and the porte Saint-Martin, for so long the official point of entry of victorious armies, not always French, and so part of public history and topography. The XXe was chosen because it is like no other quarter – save parts of the adjoining XIXe, likewise steep, and likewise sharing parts of Belleville – and because it is well aware of its uniquely cosmopolitan and popular identity. A great many people – from Dabit onwards – have written about *les gars de Belleville*, none better than Louis Chevalier in his *Les Parisiens*, but none, so far as I know, has illustrated this high citadel of *l'esprit parisien* (which, in the nineteenth century, emigrated northwards and up the hill, abandoning the rue Saint-Denis, described as the quintessence of Parisian cheek and Parisian irreverence by Mercier and Restif in the previous century). Since then, too, it has remained a citadel of mutual tolerance as between fellow Bellevillois and Bellevilloises, taking in wave after wave of immigration, first from the Massif Central and the Midi, then from the Jewish *Stetl* of Central and Eastern Europe, more recently, Algerians, Senegalese, Guinéens, Gabonais, much of francophone West Africa, so that, rue Ramponeau, a poster in Arabic script advertising an Egyptian film will lie side by side with a poster in Hebrew script announcing a religious festival (this is after all the terrain of Émile Ajar, of the childhood of a very alert boy, *la vie devant soi*). So the inclusion of Belleville-Ménilmontant needs no justification, the pictures of the up-and-down place speak eloquently for themselves. The XVIIIe tempted me by the sheer beauty of the name of the quarter, *la Goutte-d'Or*, and by the sinister reputation it acquired as a daily and nightly killing ground during the Algerian War. I wanted at last to explore the *casbah*; but I found much more than I had counted for: rural islands, a *villa*, sunny houses discovered up steep steps. For a year or more I gave English lessons to an Egyptian film producer – he made very bad films for the Cairo market – who lived above the cutting in the rue Geoffroy Saint-Hilaire, almost opposite Jussieu's cedar on its *butte*, and who used to take me to drink mint tea at the Mosque, so I came to appreciate the area of the Ve that extended from the rue Poliveau to the rue des Boulangers; and for several years I had eaten *chez Mimile*, above the place Lucien-Herr. Much of this part of the Ve has survived, though with many gaps, like bad teeth. Finally, the quartier de Gergovie, the only interesting area in the otherwise sadly banal and often rather mean and hopeless – what could be more wretched than the rue Gassendi – XIVe, seemed to call out pathetically for attention, before its small houses and amazing courtyards were smothered by the spreading horror of Maine-Montparnasse.

PART II

Angles of Vision

6

Pre-revolutionary Paris[*]

ALTHOUGH HIS family was of provincial origin – on the paternal side, they came from the *basoche* and the small nobility of Nemours – *l'abbé* Germain Brice could claim to have been Parisian born and bred. He was baptized in the capital about 1653, lived most of his life in the parish of Saint-Sulpice, and, in the context of the *Description*,[1] he might be described as a 'sulpico-imperialist', so convinced was he that this was the only quarter of Paris utterly worthy of careful development, strict legislation and the attention of gentlemen; and he died there in 1727, aged seventy-four.

There were nine editions of the *Description*, eight in Brice's lifetime; the ninth was published long after his death, in 1752, by *l'abbé* Pérau and Mariette, who completed the work and brought it up to date, as well as correcting a number of the original author's factual errors. The editor of the latest edition was thus well advised to have chosen this last version. It also has the important advantage of illustrating, almost house by house, street by street and quarter by quarter, the extensive building of town houses undertaken in the first half of the eighteenth century – that is, in the most hopeful and prosperous period of the *ancien régime*: that which followed the Peace of Utrecht and the death of Louis XIV. In this respect, as in so many others, the great divide is the year 1715. In the five years of intense speculation that followed, the

* Published in *Tour de France* (1976).
[1] Germain Brice, *Description de la ville de Paris et de tout ce qu'elle contient de plus remarquable*, edited by Pierre Codet (Geneva and Paris, 1972).

building of town houses, both on the part of the nobility, the *gens des finances* and the *parlementaires*, was given an intensive stimulus, while the Regent, by moving the seat of government from Versailles to the Palais-Royal, placed a further premium on the development of the rue Saint-Honoré, of the parish of Saint-Roch, of the faubourg Saint-Honoré and of the rue d'Antin. This set the trend of development westward, on both banks of the Seine, for the rest of the century. But the period of most rapid development was that covered in the ninth edition of the *Description*, between 1715 and 1752 (and the four following years, up to the outbreak of the Seven Years War, in 1756). As in so many other aspects of eighteenth-century life, the Seven Years War represented the other great divide. As Michel Gallet insists, it is from the 1760s rather than the actual accession of the young king, that the *style Louis XVI*, both in domestic architecture and furniture, can be dated. The war slowed up urban development in Paris for perhaps a decade, but there was a new spurt in the 1780s and this was maintained right up to the Revolution.

Apart from the rapid increase in the building of prestige town houses in the first half of the century, what emerges most forcefully from Brice's own account and that of his successors is the truly dramatic extent of the construction of religious houses: monasteries and convents, as well as of a few churches in the same period. Between 1716 and 1752, 22,000 new private houses had been built, 4,000 of them provided with a *porte cochère*, a clear indication of luxury growth. In the single parish of Saint-Germain-des-Prés, by 1752 there were thirty-six monasteries and convents, most of them built since 1715. Both these developments filled the good *abbé* and his successors with considerable alarm. The former, on the subject of the luxury growth of the rue d'Antin, was to evoke the fate of Thebes, Memphis and Babylon; 'un luxe immodéré' could, he thought, only lead to moral turpitude and to the eventual destruction of the metropolis. Mariette and Pérau were likewise moral physiocrats; and they further emphasized that the enormous extent of unproductive monastic buildings, all of them surrounded by huge gardens, could only increase the misery of the poor and contribute to the development of slum conditions in the surviving older quarters.

Brice, who owed much of his success to his position, from the 1680s, of Guide, Philosopher and Friend to the young Catholic princes of the Rhineland and of the other German states and to his profitable connections with the House of Saxony, wrote his *Description* with a very practical aim in view. It was his task not only to *décrasser*, to smarten up these young noblemen – and his clientele extended to the Lubomirski and the Radziwill families in the East – to teach them the rules of deportment, but also to provide them with competent riding masters; at the time of the Peace of Utrecht, there were seven riding schools in the faubourg Saint-Germain alone; by 1752, there were only three, a contraction perhaps due to the relative decline of the diplomatic position of France in Europe. Brice himself took them on in Divinity and Latin, as well as giving them a smattering of history (very much a smattering, for the early editions of the *Description* reveal the *abbé*'s own uncertain knowledge of pre-Valois France).

But his principal concern was to provide his pupils with a walking guide of Paris. It was perhaps the care with which this guide was arranged that accounted for its enormous success throughout the century; there was nothing to rival it till the publication of Mercier's *Le Tableau de Paris*, between 1782 and 1788, and Mercier was in any case more concerned with social observation than topography and the description of buildings and monuments. Brice gave his young German clientele the sort of minute, detailed, rather ponderous guide that the great Baedeker was to provide for their Wilhelminian compatriots in the nineteenth century.

For this purpose, he divided his guide into three main divisions: 'la Ville', 'l'Université', 'la Cité'. Within these broad categories, he established a series of walks, in logical sequence, street leading into street, and designed to take half a day each, with a pause for lunch, a meal well earned, if the itinerary had been strictly adhered to, for they were pretty hefty walks. Brice's young princelings must have been in tip-top physical condition: though, in the early eighteenth century, even the fat princes of the House of Hanover could no doubt be expected to cover plenty of ground on foot.

The walks start, logically, with the Louvre, the Tuileries, the quarters of Saint-Germain-l'Auxerrois, Saint-Honoré, the Butte Saint-Roch, already quite a heavy programme. Thence to the Halles, the rues Saint-Denis and Saint-Martin, Sainte-Avoie, the rues du Grand-

Chantier, Vieille du Temple, Saint-Louis, place Royale and neighbourhood, rue and faubourg Saint-Antoine, l'Arc de Triomphe (later the
place du Trône), the château de Vincennes, and back by Reuilly, the
Célestins, quartier Saint-Paul, Île Notre-Dame, to the Left Bank, porte
Saint-Bernard, Saint-Victor, Jardin Royal, the Gobelins and the
faubourg Saint-Marceau, a truly massive loop, the equivalent of a
couple of present-day *Métro* lines. The other walks take in the rest of
the Left Bank.

Brice provided a completely comprehensive tour of the city; and he
was not afraid of exposing his more delicate princelings to some of the
filthiest, most stinking and most overcrowded quarters of Paris; it was
not just a *Tournée des Grands Ducs* of the high spots, of the new
centres of luxury. Perhaps his walks were also to have a moral purpose.

Brice and his successors are much given to general statistical
information which, one can reasonably assume, was highly inaccurate
and was based on inspired guesswork on the part of the physiocratic
abbé, who had no doubt drawn some of his inspiration from Vauban.
Thus, in the 1752 edition, the authors, while taking into account the
effects both of war and dearth, especially in the first three decades of
the century – Brice in particular was well aware, as a churchman and
as a specialist of ecclesiastical painting, of the weight of the 1709
famine on Parisian popular memory – come out with the amazing
statement that the total population of the city at the time of publication was in the range of 800,000, including 150,000 servants. We do
know, with some accuracy, that on the eve of the Revolution Paris
counted between 600,000 to 750,000 inhabitants, domestic servants
forming about 13 per cent of the total; and we can also surmise that
the population of the city had been steadily increasing in the previous
twenty years, so that we can place the 1752 figure in the same category
of hit-or-miss fantasy which lay behind a great many of Mercier's
statements in the 1780s. Mercier, for instance, was never at a loss to
quote a figure; 232 middle-class girls a year, he confidently affirms, had
abortions in discreet *maisons de santé* in the early 1780s. Of course he
has no means of knowing. But he, like the 1752 authors, is writing for
a public that likes to be offered firm totals. Equally suspect is the
estimation of the horse population of Paris at 100,000 (one horse for
eight inhabitants, according to their own reckoning), though they may

be nearer the truth when they add that, of this total, 10,000 horses died or were killed each year. Perhaps the relative accuracy of such statistics is unimportant, for what matters is that they should have been accepted by contemporaries, just as it was widely believed by people like Brice that the population was declining in the first half of the century.

Brice is certainly on safer ground when enumerating the number of houses built since the Peace. These were, after all, visible, and we do know that he took a great deal of trouble to see for himself what was going on, just as he displayed a grimly ecclesiastical persistence in attempting to force open recalcitrant doors, in order to scout out the pictures and works of art in the possession of named patrons and connoisseurs. He was not easily turned away, and, when he was, the owner received a vengeful reference in the book, as if he had sinned personally against the *abbé*'s princely cares. We can then accept his successors' figures for the number of street lamps, quarter by quarter. *La lanterne*, at this time, had not acquired its sinister significance of 1789. The record goes to the prosperous rue Saint-Martin, the very quintessence of Paris civility, of 'l'esprit parisien', with a total of 415: next come Saint-Germain-des-Prés (396), the Marais (361), the Palais-Royal (341), Saint-Antoine (333). At the other end of the scale, we find Sainte-Opportune (152), Saint-Jacques-de-la-Boucherie (183) and les Halles (142).

Generally speaking, the more recently built quarters, those containing the greatest number of *hôtels*, are better lit. In other words, street lighting was directed primarily towards the defence of property and the safety of the upper classes, while quarters like Sainte-Avoie and the Gravilliers could be left to the twilight of poverty, disease and stench. (The *abbé* and his successors classify both parishes and churches in terms of smell; before 1714, Brice states, the faubourg Saint-Honoré had been neglected for building purposes, owing to the stink of the great sewer and the prevalence of disease, while he displays the enthusiasm of an estate agent in vaunting the fine air of Saint-Germain-des-Prés; Saint-Merri, along with some of the other finest Gothic churches still surviving, is dismissed as 'dirty, ill-lit and stinking', Brice adding that the Paris churches as a whole are the dirtiest in Europe – but he had never been to Poland or the Russian Empire.) The figures for street lighting in 1752 are confirmed, for the revolutionary period, in the late General Herlaut's famous thesis, written while on the General Staff during the First World War, on *L'Éclairage à Paris pendant la Révolution*.

In his industrious enumeration of pictures, works of art, buildings worthy of attention, church architecture and charitable institutions, Brice comes in the way of a great deal of information which must be of the greatest value to the social historian, even though the *Description* has been used the most extensively by art historians and specialists of the history of architecture. Urban history is a whole and Brice is an integral part of it. Writing both during the terrible crises of the late seventeenth century and, again, shortly after the famine of 1709 and, in his eighth edition, just after the disastrous rains of the spring and summer of 1725, this tutor to the sons of the German nobility proves himself to be acutely aware of the calendar of popular fears as well as of that of disease and recurrent epidemics. The extension of the Hôpital Saint-Louis, he informs us, was provoked by an unprecedented outbreak of scurvy, following the 1709 crisis, and he mentions the two votive pictures of the two de Troys, father and son, kept in the church of Sainte-Geneviève, the one depicting the blessed fall of rain, following a long period of drought in 1709, the other the equally blessed break in the rain clouds in 1725, both attributed to the direct intervention of Sainte-Geneviève. Both pictures were brought out in the annual procession for that specifically Paris saint. However irreligious the eighteenth century may have been at its higher levels, the merciful changes of the season are still the object of popular thanksgiving.

Equally, he notes, on the second Saturday of each month, the cult of the Virgin will bring a record congregation to the image of Notre-Dame-du-Mont-Carmel, in the church of the Carmes. Elsewhere he comments on the subject of the church of le Petit-Saint-Antoine ('obscure et malpropre'), on the disappearance of some of the most feared diseases of the poor. 'Cet hôpital' (attached to the church of the same name)

étoit destiné pour une espèce de maladie épidémique, nommée *le mal de Saint-Antoine*, laquelle a duré en France l'espace de 4 ou 5 siècles, mais qui a cessé comme plusieurs autres incommodités populaires: entre autres *les*

Ardens, la Ladrerie, le Pic Saint-Fiacre, le mal de Saint Marcon & de Saint-Main, & plusieurs autres, les quelles ne sont plus connues, que par la lecture des vieux auteurs.

He repeatedly insists on the difficulty of supplying such an immense population with an adequate water supply – a problem of which present-day planners of 'le Grand Paris' are only too well aware – and refers to the poor quality of the water at the disposal of the inhabitants of Saint-Antoine. A convinced urbanist himself, he frequently complains of the lack of light and the recurrence of accidents caused by such massive obstructions as the Grand Châtelet and the Bastille ('cette masse énorme de bâtiments gothiques enfermée d'un fossé profond gâte étrangement tout ce quartier, en coupant l'alignement de la rue Saint-Antoine, du côté de la Ville & du côté du Faubourg'). The *abbé* would have been the first to applaud 14 July 1789.

He provides further information on the subject of fairs, popular morality, circulation and retribution. As from 1705, the Foire Saint-Laurent would open on 24 July, going on to Michaelmas. The Foire de Saint-Germain ran from 3 February to Holy Week, much too long in the opinion of Brice, who lived in the area, as it provided a magnet to gambling, fisticuffs, drunkenness and turbulence, especially at dusk. A crime very common among building labourers was the theft of lead off the roofs of buildings in construction, one 'roofer' throwing the stolen lead down to his accomplice, waiting in a neighbouring courtyard (*la cour* thus offered advantages other than those of prestige).

Of all the streets in Paris, that of Saint-Jacques and its prolongation in the Faubourg witnessed the heaviest circulation of people, horses and goods, with forty wine-carts a day penetrating Paris from the south. The rue Saint-Antoine, on the other hand, had above all a representational role, in the calendar of the monarchy; it was the route of all state entries, while ambassadors, about to present their credentials, were given a sovereign's escort at its eastern end. The execution of counterfeiters and forgers, the sometimes learned *abbé* notes, often took place near a place called la Croix du Tiroir, rue Saint-Honoré, because it was near the old Mint (the beautiful *monnaie* on the quays was built long after Brice's death).

There was a time and a place for everyone and for everything in this traditionalist world, a world always best described by churchmen. There was a place even for repentant prostitutes with the 'communauté de Saint-Valère', rue de Grenelle, founded in 1706; while unemployed female servants were looked after, for periods of three days, at the Hôpital Sainte-Catherine; in return, they had to wash and bury the city's daily supply of unclaimed dead. There was a time for singing, and the place was the chapel of the Filles de l'Assomption, renowned for the quality of their voices, who would draw vast congregations during Holy Week.

As a churchman, and with his intimate knowledge of the calendar of saints popular with Parisians, Brice can often reach down to a level of popular *mores* denied to a middle-class observer like Mercier. Indeed, his book offers a striking contrast between the fixity, the immutability of popular habit and fears, and the immense and painful changes being wrought by the ruthless expansion of the city westwards and by the equally heartless demolition of whole quarters in the interests of alignment and to display the newly acquired wealth in 'la grande parade' of the *gens des finances* and war speculators. Perhaps nowhere is incipient class conflict more apparent and more bitter than in the beautiful, but ostentatious architecture of the new town houses. Brice himself felt this, when he mused uneasily on the fate of Babylon and Palmyra. It is even more apparent in M. Gallet's book.[1]

Only an art historian or an architectural expert could form an opinion of Brice's ability as a scholar and a connoisseur. Certainly he had the modesty to accept the criticisms of his contemporaries when he made factual errors. He had a genuine admiration for early church Gothic, though he complained that most of the Paris churches were dark and gloomy. But he had little taste for the later stages of Gothic and regarded Saint-Étienne-du-Mont as an architectural monstrosity. His taste tells us more about his attitudes as a moderate Gallican than as a critic. He much disapproved, for instance, of the ostentation of Jesuit churches, which he contrasted with the primitive simplicity of pure Gallican tradition, and it is quite apparent that his poor opinion of Jesuit architecture would have been extended to the Society itself.

[1] Michel Gallet, *Paris Domestic Architecture of the Eighteenth Century* (London, 1972).

He was in this respect very much of an eighteenth-century *abbé*, as he was also in his dislike of monastic extensions and his belief that the contemplative orders served no useful social functions; he did, however, have plenty to say in praise of the nuns who were in hospital orders.

Perhaps the main impression one retains from his book is one of sadness at so much wanton destruction, at the loss of so many masterpieces. From his account, it is apparent that the dreadful Haussmann was not the only culprit. Brice mentions a number of churches that had been pulled down in the early years of the eighteenth century, and, if he had been Lieutenant de Police, and not just a comfortable and easygoing tutor to well-born, if not well-bred, young Rhinelanders, Poles and Saxons, it is clear that he would have used his powers to remove several public buildings, either because he thought that they were ugly, or because they blocked the road, caused accidents, cast shadows over the neighbourhood, or, crime of crimes, broke the alignment of a recently planned street.

M. Gallet is at present Deputy Keeper of the Musée Carnavalet. No one could have been better qualified to write a study of Paris domestic architecture in the course of the eighteenth century, and his knowledge both of the new town houses and palaces, of the architects, engravers, carpenters, painters, jewellers, goldsmiths and craftsmen who embellished them is prodigious. His book, as well as containing a very large number of very beautiful plates, plans and drawings (some of which are now at Waddesdon), offers a list of leading architects, with their biographical details. The study (very well translated), which has never been published in French, is an indispensable guide to anyone interested in this fascinating and, often, saddening subject.

But it is much more than a chronicle of changing tastes and styles. Like Brice, M. Gallet has a great deal to say which will be of value to the social historian, on such subjects as the architecture of libertinage, the architecture of class and the physical environment of masters and servants. He quotes a little-known novel of Bastide, *La Petite Maison*, which illustrates better even than *Les Liaisons dangereuses* an architectural fantasy favoured by late eighteenth-century society; the hero, the Marquis de Trémicour, seeking to impress 'la belle Mélite', takes her to a small *pavillon* that he has had constructed in a park, not far from Paris. Preceded by a Negro page, who lights the chandeliers and clusters of candles in their path – the Marquis has arranged for the visit to take place after nightfall – the girl's wonderment increases with the discovery of each new marvel: *trompe-l'œil* on the wall of the dining-room, a hunting scene that climbs up with the grand staircase, ingenious mechanical devices at each storey, hangings in blue, woodwork in pale yellow, the larger rooms in white and gold, a profusion of monkeys, nymphs, dolphins, cenotaphs, pagodas, cherubs, waterfalls and grottoes among the decorative motifs, the visit increasing in inventiveness with each room, to culminate in the sheer amazement of the exquisite bedroom, its walls painted, according to the recommendations of *l'abbé* Le Camus, the recognized authority in the matter, in blue (as conducive to rest and sleep).

The Negro, after withdrawing the candles, disappears through a hidden door that responds to the pressure of a secret spring, taking the back staircase to his quarters, either on the ground floor (which is cold) or over the stables. Left alone with the Marquis, Mélite, overcome with gratitude, admiration and wonderment, succumbs in his arms. Architecture in the service of Seduction. Is not the whole theme of abduction, the *enlèvement*, in fact an architectural exploration? Is not the division between *côté cour* and *côté jardin* not merely a search for privacy, an affirmation of prestige and a stage convention? Is it not also an aid to abduction? *La belle* waits with a candle at one in the morning, *côté jardin*, a Picard servant produces a ladder, while liveried servants light the way with flaming torches, a closed carriage is waiting at the corner of the street, driven by a coachman with his face covered. The next morning, *la belle* wakes up in some 'pavillon de Hanovre', finds herself facing on to a walled park, with sphinxes vaguely seen in the morning mist. Watteau was perhaps more of a social realist than has generally been imagined.

One is surprised at the absence of architectural metaphors in the seduction scenes in *Les Liaisons*. But Sophie knew the advantages to be derived from lunges in the direction of the bell-pull. Laclos was an artillery officer not an architect, and he conducted seduction, as he might have done a siege, in military terms. The second staircase might be used to keep the servants away from their masters; but it could also come in useful, as in the case of *Manon*. The increasingly elaborate mechanical devices adopted in the course of the century were not only designed to keep the servants at a distance; they too could be instruments of seduction. M. Gallet has hit upon an interesting theme.

He also helps us to understand the intense resentments of the enormous armies of servants. 'The ground floors were cold in winter. In the Palais-Royal and the Hôtel de Noailles, we find them almost entirely reserved for pages, gentlemen in waiting and servants.' Liveried servants, secretaries, and so on, were generally lodged in rooms of six to eight beds above a stable of thirty horses; it is doubtful whether even resident chaplains would have been much better housed. Equally, the cruel meanness of the mezzanine, as opposed to the splendour of the *Ier*, in any ordinary eighteenth-century town house, further emphasized class divisions in terms of location. The mezzanine, like the servants' room over the stables, was no doubt a school for revolutionary militancy. And, as mechanical devices became more and more ingenious, personal contacts between master and servant became rarer. The servant's work might thus be lessened, but his resentment correspondingly increased.

In another sense, too, late eighteenth-century architectural styles might be said to have contributed to class antagonisms. 'The detached block of the Italian villa', writes M. Gallet of the 1780s,

> succeeded the secluded precinct of the hôtel court. It was a supreme irony that, at this moment when aristocratic society stood at the edge of the abyss applauding *Figaro*, it exposed itself to the full glare of the Third Estate.

A very good point. The aristocratic connoisseur was furthermore beginning to live in a late eighteenth-century fantasy world; 'Cottages, dungeons, pagodas, cenotaphs aroused in him a longing for distant lands and recollections of times past. In forlorn caverns echoed the lugubrious murmur of falling water . . .' Dickens would, rightly, have made much of this sort of thing. Alongside this bizarre fantasy, we may note the funereal mood of the engravers Delafosse and Desprez, around 1785.

The Revolution did not bring to a halt all building. 'La maison Batave', an exercise in community building, near the Halles, was completed in 1792, while the amazing Le Doux, a revolutionary before the

Revolution, built a few of the houses that had been commissioned by the American, Hosten. But the Revolution itself constructed its monuments only in cardboard and plaster. They were indeed little more than stage properties, just as David was little more than a stage designer. The beauty of French domestic architecture, which reached its most perfect expression in the 'pavillon de Hanovre', in Le Doux's stupendous Hôtel Thélusson and in the exquisite Hôtel d'Orrouer early in the period (1733), was never fully recovered, save for a few exceptions under the Empire. For the revolutionaries, beauty was a trifle, a luxury, a form of social arrogance, an assertion of inequality. They were of course right, but at what a cost! The degradation of so many of the *hôtels* described and depicted in *Paris Domestic Architecture of the Eighteenth Century* began in 1792 or 1793, when they fell into the hands of speculators or, worse still, of Ministries.

Haussmann did his best to complete the process, and conservation, when it came, generally came too late, though Paris has still got more to offer, in terms of eighteenth-century domestic architecture, than any other city in Europe. M. Gallet's book can thus be used as a guide, as Brice's was, as well as an architectural dictionary.

Architecture, it is true, was again to be placed in the service of Seduction, but hardly in the style of 'la petite maison'. Nothing could have been more hideous than the stuffy, overcrowded town houses of mid-nineteenth-century *cocottes* and *poules de luxe*. Fantasy was lavishly employed, especially in the mechanical devices and in the local colour of the celebrated 122, of Third Republic fame; but it was not a fantasy of a sort to dazzle 'la belle Mélite'. Most Paris brothels tended to look like public lavatories – English ones, not French ones – the Sphinx, like a swimming-bath in the Egyptian style. Their disappearance cannot be accounted an architectural loss, though it is undoubtedly a cultural one.

7

Central Paris[*]

THIS[1] IS a very important book, a pioneering work in urban history. It might be objected by some that it is a study of Paris in the absence of the Parisians: and it is true that Anthony Sutcliffe is a very far cry from Professor Louis Chevalier, especially as the latter is seen in his recent work *Les Parisiens*, which attempts with great effectiveness to relate the Parisian to the particular environment of his quarter or his suburb, as well as of his place of work, and to locate both in time as well as in space. Louis Chevalier is indeed far more aware of the continuity of Paris history than Dr Sutcliffe, whose principal point of departure – and it is a very important one – is a royal edict of 1783 limiting the maximum height of buildings. Dr Sutcliffe is more exclusively concerned with the physical environment and its evolution than with the people who are subjected to that environment. His approach is purely factual and is massively statistical. So this is no romantic study of *vieilles pierres*, in the manner of Georges Lenôtre. But that is one of the book's many merits: the author is not out to expatiate on the picturesque aspects of Saint-Merri, Saint-Gervais or Sainte-Avoie, because he knows that the 'picturesqueness' so often hides, both from the passing tourist and the middle-class preservationist living well away to the west, the permanent realities like tuberculosis, as well as the mounting discomfort of overcrowding and dilapidation. He knows what historical interest, and the fascinating jumble of ancient, narrow-

* Published in *Tour de France* (1976).
[1] Anthony Sutcliffe, *The Autumn of Central Paris* (London, 1971).

fronted plaster houses, may mean in terms of human misery to their inhabitants, often crowded a whole family to a room. The people who live in the rue Volta, the only street in Paris with fifteenth-century half-timbered houses, would not feel themselves particularly privileged.

Indeed, as a result above all of the demolitions carried out by Haussmann, and of the rare demolitions that have followed 1870, slum conditions in the central areas of Paris have steadily worsened. Haussmann thought in terms of prestige and accessibility: he was concerned to show off certain public buildings – both old and new – to advantage, by isolating them. But he gave little thought to the human consequences of his demolitions and failed to provide any cheap adequate accommodation for those who were driven out. When new accommodation was provided, under the Second Empire and the Third Republic, it generally satisfied the needs of a different clientele, the blocks being divided into apartments and the rents generally being beyond the reach of the former inhabitants. Furthermore, the limit on height meant that the new buildings would actually take a smaller number of householders than those that had been destroyed. The result was that the surviving areas were further invaded by refugees from neighbouring quarters. The victims of the demolitions in the rue de Rivoli moved east, from the Ier, to crowd into the IIIe and the IVe.

This has been the general pattern – at least in the IIIe and IVe – over the last hundred years, though as far as the Marais is concerned there is at present a likelihood of increasing middle-class investment and residential settlement in what appears to be in the process of becoming as much a Museumville as the Vieux-Montmartre, the place de l'Estrapade, or the quartier Saint-Paul in Lyon. In all such instances there are three possible choices: complete demolition, with the destruction of all traces of a historical past unique not so much in terms of individual buildings as of a whole quarter; the degeneration of a quarter into a total slum; or massive preservation, in the form of a Malraux-type *frigorification*, accompanied by the usual face-lifting, cleaning of façades and so on, with the retention at least of the outward aspects of the quarter – minus its normal inhabitants, driven elsewhere, into suburban *bidonvilles*, or into the Buffet-like spiky horrors of Arcueil and *la grande banlieue*. Saint-Paul, la Croix-Rousse, le Vieux-Genève, Carouge have become *quartiers d'agrément*, inhabited by well-to-do intellectuals and professional people, who, having moved into some of the quarters of nineteenth-century revolutionary ferment, can sometimes enjoy the sensation of being revolutionaries themselves.

It is an extraordinary story that Dr Sutcliffe has to tell. Paris, unique among capitals, has succeeded in preserving in its centre – or in what was its centre up to the 1840s and 1850s – something like 70 per cent of buildings dating back to the reign of Louis XVI or even earlier. The author is concerned only with the four central *arrondissements*: had he extended his survey to the Left Bank, the picture would not have been very different. The east centre on the Right Bank – the IIIe and IVe – was largely overlooked by Haussmann, as already under-privileged and slightly peripheral. Apart from that, its survival was a result of neglect, lack of municipal funds, medical advances, the fractionalization of properties (most landlords would own only one or two houses, and the properties themselves tended to be on a very narrow frontage, but extended back in depth – both factors that would make large-scale expropriation or purchase or area-planning extremely difficult), low rents or controlled rents in the period between the wars and, in the ten years following the Liberation, the persistence of artisan forms of trade and industry, and the accidents of two wars, both ruinous to the finances of the Hôtel-de-Ville, without being in any way destructive of its buildings. The active intervention of the preservationists came very late and counted in fact for very little. The Commission du Vieux-Paris was, one suspects, a good alibi for Hôtel-de-Ville negligence: few of its members appear ever to have resided in the quarters that they wished to preserve. In any case, under constant pressure from the elected representatives of the outer *arrondissements*, especially under the Third Republic, there was very little that the Hôtel-de-Ville could do about the IIIe and IVe even if it had wanted to. The author makes the useful point that authoritarian regimes like the Second Empire and the Fifth Republic are better equipped to undertake large-scale town-planning than a democratic regime in which the representatives of the four inner *arrondissements* had to compete with those of the other sixteen for the allocation of such limited funds as were available. Under the Third Republic, the VIIIe, the XVIe, the

XVIIe and, to some extent, the VIIe were always likely to get more than their fair share for public works, improvement and construction.

By the 1930s, it had become apparent that tuberculosis could be held in check by purely medical means, without the massive clearance of the areas over which it had had the most persistent hold in the course of the previous century; at this time it was, in any case, a much greater threat in the suburbs. So, apart from the partial demolition of Sainte-Avoie, the IIIe and IVe were left almost entirely alone. Saint-Merri, which had the highest death rate from tuberculosis in 1923 (and which had been the principal centre of the cholera epidemic of 1832) is still with us; and so are Saint-Gervais, Saint-Nicolas-des-Champs and the Blancs-Manteaux. It was a victory for preservation achieved by default in the absence of any other plan. The fate of the Ier is still in the balance, though it now seems likely that the rue Saint-Denis will be preserved along most of its length. Some *hôtels de passe* in which the very lowest grades of Paris prostitution plied for so long (right round the clock, night and day) are in the process of becoming *hôtels de tourisme*; many more have been sold to speculators, concerned to convert them into middle-class apartments; and the Halles district, emptied of those directly employed in the provisioning trade, is destined to be redeveloped as a middle-class residential zone or as some grandiose *cité des arts*, set aside to lodge eminent intellectuals from abroad, while the original inhabitants are driven eastwards, or into the suburbs, near the new Halles. The attraction of a central location near the river and of a quarter with such strong historical associations – Mercier, in the 1780s, described the rue Saint-Denis as 'la plus commerçante de Paris'; Louis Chevalier claims that, up till the Revolution, *l'esprit de la rue Saint-Denis* constituted the quintessence of Paris wit and irreverence – seems likely to guarantee its physical survival, though under entirely new management.

In the IIIe at least, a certain number of skilled artisans and small tradesmen in *articles de Paris* have been able to hang on, and both the IIIe and the IVe still have their contingents of Polish Jewish immigrants, of Algerians and Portuguese, though in declining numbers. Jewish immigration from the East has almost dried up, and the mass of Algerian and Portuguese labour has moved to the appalling *bidonvilles* of the periphery.

In short, though the outward aspects of the Right Bank centre have been preserved almost intact, in human terms this eminently Parisian complex is in the process of complete destruction. This is especially true of the Ier, the population of which has been steadily declining over the last hundred years. A social evolution so complete cannot fail to alter the character of Paris as a whole, by destroying the neighbourliness of the *quartier*, the village mentality of those who live above their place of work, depriving the city of much of the wit, the individualism and the independence of the small artisan and of the violence and joyful sexuality of the old population of the Halles.

The Right Bank centre has, over the last eighty years, lost much of the importance which it previously derived from its central position within the city, and which was further underlined by the construction of the Samaritaine, the Belle Jardinière and the Bazar de l'Hôtel-de-Ville. The Cité itself was entirely destroyed by Haussmann, the worst of many acts of vandalism committed by the authoritarian and insensitive Alsatian (he tore down the church of Sainte-Marine, knocked down the choir of Saint-Leu and was about to set to on the Arènes de Lutèce, in the Ve, when the fall of the Empire saved, *in extremis*, that monument of Roman Paris). The Palais-Royal began its long agony in the 1840s; what had been the centre of the world in the 1780s, under the Directory, and even in 1815, has now become an arcade of seedy shops – medals, ribbons and postage stamps – and a playground for children. Even Colette was unable to give lustre to that sad relic.

One of the most interesting sections of this valuable book is in fact the discussion concerning the gradual displacement of the centre of Paris, over a period of 170 years. In the late eighteenth century, there could be no doubt as to the preponderance of what now constitutes the Ier. The Palais-Royal was the social centre of the city, with the rue Saint-Honoré firmly established as the most fashionable shopping area. The decline of the rue Saint-Honoré parallels that of the Palais-Royal: in the 1840s and 1850s, the luxury trade began to move westwards, to the rue du Faubourg-Saint-Honoré. After the Revolution, there was also a residential move to the north-west, to the Chaussée-d'Antin, as bankers and moneyed people tended to clear out of the violent areas of the centre and the east centre, where they had found *sans-culottes* and worse living, literally, on top of them. Even Réveillon went west. But the most important displacement came under Haussmann: with the Gare Saint-Lazare early established as the most important station for the suburban traffic, and with the cutting of the avenue de l'Opéra (it was not, however, completed till 1876, in time for the Exposition) the development of trade, banking and every form of economic activity became emphatically centred on the VIIIe, in the area between the new Opéra, Saint-Lazare, the Chaussée-d'Antin and the boulevard des Italiens. This transformation was deliberately accelerated by the construction of the rues Halévy and Auber, to facilitate access from Saint-Lazare to the Opéra and beyond. Saint-Lazare is probably still the main point of entry of the armies of the *banlieusards*, though Louis Chevalier, writing of the early 1960s, makes similar claims for the bus and *Métro* stations of Vincennes; but most of those who arrive from the east likewise work in the VIIIe.

The growing predominance of the Opéra and the *grands boulevards* was further favoured, and has since been perpetuated, by the construction, in the 1890s, of the Paris *Métro*. The lines, constructed just below the surface – the Paris subsoil, with its honeycomb of quarries and the prevalence of sandstone that easily crumbled, was felt, by the early *Métro* engineers, to be unsuitable for the construction of a deep, tubular system, on the London model – followed the rectangle of Haussmann's wide new thoroughfares and of the older boulevards. The Châtelet station, it is true, was a focal point for north–south and east–west traffic, but it did not have the importance of the Opéra, the meeting-place of four lines. The *Métro* system continued to favour the IIe (one line followed the course of the rue Réaumur, serving the Bourse and the Sentier quarters) and, to some extent, the Ier (Vincennes–Étoile, the first line to be constructed, was a recognition of its still important geographical location, though it was probably more designed to favour the development of the Concorde, Madeleine and Rond-Point areas) and further contributed to the isolation of the IIe and the IVe. The area between the rue des Archives and the Bastille is served by no stations, except for Arts-et-Métiers at the northern end, and Saint-Paul at the southern.

While well-to-do residents continued to move, under the impetus of Haussmann, first to the plaine Monceau, then to the Champs-Élysées and beyond, towards the Bois, establishing the VIIIe, XVIe and XVIIe (in parts) as the most desirable areas for middle-class residence, the Champs-Élysées was never a serious contestant to the IIe and VIIIe as the true centres of Paris. As Chevalier has suggested, the Champs-Élysées enjoyed only a brief preponderance, in the 1920s, as the centre of fashion and of the developing film industry. Only one newspaper ever moved there; and since the 1930s, it has steadily declined as a centre of taste. Only emperors, kings and *chefs d'état* ever reach Paris by the Gare du Bois de Boulogne, taken out of its dust-covers every decade or so for such occasions. The quartier de Gaulle is too peripheral to attract to it the principal activities of Paris, though it is discreet enough to serve as a rendezvous – rue d'Argentine, rue des Acacias – for the *deussaquatrier*, the successor to the *cinqaseptier* (*Je te trouverai, chérie, sous de Gaulle*). Nothing, it would seem, is likely to dislodge the VIIIe from its dominating position.

The decline of the east centre is, then, the main theme of this fascinating book. The author dates it from the Revolution; and in this he may be wrong, for the movement from the Marais had already begun with the development of the faubourg Saint-Germain. Certainly the violence of the Revolution hastened the move westward, but the ultimate condemnation of the area came with Haussmann.

As wealth, trade and industry moved out, an increasingly depressed proletariat moved in. At the best of times, the two *arrondissements* were bordered, to their east, by the alarming and envious armies of the *classes dangereuses* – it was a short step from the rue de Lappe to the quartier Saint-Paul – and the area behind the Hôtel-de-Ville became, in the nineteenth century, the principal centre for lodging-houses, particularly for building workers who, although they were hired there, can never have found much employment in a part of Paris in which scarcely any building at all took place between the 1780s and the 1970s. It escaped the building boom of the 1900s. An original French proletariat from the Limousin and the Massif Central, entering by the Gare de Lyon or Austerlitz, just across the river, as well as refugees from the Cité, was later joined, at the time of the pogroms, by poor Jews from the Russian Empire – the Marché du Temple had in fact been a preserve of Jewish furriers since the eighteenth century – and later still by Algerians. With each new wave, overcrowding got worse, and the houses became more dilapidated. It was only due to the fact that they had been so well-built in the sixteenth to eighteenth centuries that so few actually collapsed into the street, though a number had to be propped up on wooden staves. The author gives the east centre a long respite – at least to the end of the century.

But it is a future without a function, save possibly as a magnet to tourism. The presence of the vast complex of the Archives Nationales is hardly likely to revitalize a quarter: rather does it accentuate its decrepitude. It also symbolizes a phenomenon frequently commented on by the author: the steady increase in the average age of the inhabitants of the IIIe in the course of the last eighty years. The presence, too, of the Mont-de-Piété is perhaps even more symbolic of parasitism, decline and a run-down poverty. The *Spectacles du Marais*, organized with great pomp, and to the sound of many trumpets, by André Malraux in the mid-1960s, brought the inhabitants of the XVIe and the XVIIe, the intellectuals of the XIVe, to the courtyards of the Palais Soubise, the Hôtel de Rohan, the Hôtel Lamoignan, the Hôtel de Beauvais, to listen to concerts or plays; but they did not linger. Nor did their affluence. *Son et Lumière* did nothing for the inhabitants, save to deprive them of sleep. It would take a greater magician even than Malraux to bring a new sense of identity to the once magnificent east centre. It is a sad story; but, if Sedan had not come so providentially when it did, it could possibly have been even sadder. The empty shell of what had constituted the more basic elements of the *sans-culotterie* has survived almost intact – Jacques Roux could find his way round his parish, almost house by house, even if most of his parishioners of recent years would turn out to be Muslims – while the Éditions Spartacus, of Trotskyite inspiration, can propose to the middle-class revolutionary a complete tour of *le Paris révolutionnaire* almost entirely within the confines of the two *arrondissements*. The Marais has much to offer almost anyone save its inhabitants.

Dr Sutcliffe does not, as I say, sufficiently take into account the continuity of Paris history, quarter by quarter, save in respect of the survival of their buildings, nor indeed the continuity of that ancient theme: Paris versus France, the provinces versus Paris. He describes, for instance, the anti-Parisian federalism and the efforts at decentralization undertaken in the post-Liberation years and expressed most eloquently in Jean-François Gravier's *Paris et le désert français*, published in 1947. But this kind of attack represents an ancient tradition of representative regimes, while authoritarian ones are always likely to redress the balance in favour of the seat of government.

Historians of the eighteenth and nineteenth centuries will be struck by other forms of continuity that emerge from his study, particularly, of the east centre. Eighty years after the Revolution, the average size of a workshop here was a master and eight or nine journeymen; many of these workshops were in huts encrusted on the side of former mansions and situated in courtyards of buildings, the dilapidation of many of which had been accelerated by the Revolution, when, as a result of the sale of *biens nationaux*, most of them came up for auction, to be snatched up by speculators or fragmented by a score or more of independent artisans. Thus, in the 1850s and the 1880s, not only were the cadres of a *sans-culotte* way of life still standing: the *sans-culottes* themselves were still there, or at least their social equivalent. Saint-Merri had witnessed outbreaks of cholera in 1832, 1849, 1854 and 1865; it topped the list for deaths from tuberculosis throughout the 1920s; it had been under special surveillance, both from the Lieutenant de Police and the Bureau de Santé, in the last years of the *ancien régime*; and it figures as a plague spot in a number of *Traités de Police* published in the 1780s and the 1820s. More astounding, the author records an outbreak of the plague in the Clignancourt area in 1925.

Many of the features that he claims as characteristic of the two *arrondissements* of the east centre in the first half of the nineteenth century have been described, in detail, by Mercier, writing in the 1780s, and by Restif, in the 1790s. His neglect of both authors gives his book a certain lack of depth, while he certainly overestimates what he describes as 'the industrial expansion' of the eighteenth century. For, one suspects, in the east centre, people have lived six or seven to a room for a number of centuries.

In the early years of this century, and again in the 1920s, the Hôtel-de-Ville made desultory efforts to provide both cheap and hygienic housing for the lower income-groups, in the *habitations à bon marché*: but these were mostly built on the periphery or in Montrouge. Nothing of the sort was done for the inhabitants of the IIIe and the IVe. Many of them were foreigners, others recent arrivals from the provinces, others again had moved in from other areas recently demolished. Very few of them worked either for the State or for large enterprises. The only effort on their behalf was a massive clearance of the riverside section of the IVe, started under Vichy (a regime which, despite its many political turpitudes, seems to have had quite a good record in the matter of public health; the *chantiers de la jeunesse*, whatever the intention of their creation in the form of character-breeding and the development of leadership instincts, probably saved many former slum children from tuberculosis) and completed under the Fourth Republic. The effect of this, as of all previous demolitions, was to make the conditions in the surviving areas even worse. The author concludes soberly, on the subject of the physical survival of the east centre: 'Whether or not this can be regarded as a satisfactory state of affairs depends on whether one can reconcile the survival of one of the oldest and most fascinating city centres of Europe with the tribulations of many of those who have to live and work there.'

8

The Period Paris of René Clair[*]

HISTORIANS AND examiners, for professional or educational reasons, will favour one set of great divides; private individuals, when concerned with the remembered past, will opt for a variety of others, depending on age, experience, and national origin. For myself, recalled French history will fall into two quite distinct periods, with a gap in the middle: 1935 to 1939, and 1944 to 1958. During the 'years between' I was absent from France; and, after 1958, as far as I was concerned, nothing could ever be quite the same again. I have returned frequently to France since then, but more and more as an observer, who was beginning to lose his way in unfamiliar territory, and who was no longer able to read the new signposts or even always to understand the new language. I know few French people under thirty-five; and those I do know are the children or grandchildren of friends. Nor am I by any means alone in dating the transformation of Paris, from what it was, to what, unhappily, it now is, from 1958.

In my personal textbook of contemporary French history, the opening year would be 1935, for that was when I first went to Paris; but I do not think it has any other significance. The real dividing line, for the later history of the Third Republic, would be 1934. There is no need to emphasize the political importance of *6* and *12 février*; but the great divide is provided by the *affaire Stavisky*.

It is not just a matter of public history; it is also the gap between a Republic that was still curiously light-hearted, even in its amiable

* This essay first appeared in *People and Places* (1985).

cynicism and humorous, but shameless self-examination, and a
Republic that was becoming sombre, divisive and increasingly frightened. M. Alexandre belongs to the sunnier side of that gap; and his
mysterious death in Chamonix is the end of something more than the
fantastic life of a generous, pleasure-loving, fashionable Russian
adventurer. There was a *style Stavisky* which was also that of a period.

Put in another way, it might be said that I had come in at the tail-end
of the last great period of French *insouciance*. The death of Serge-
Alexandre was like the untimely and quite unsuitable end to a party. I
was in time for the overlap: the mystery surrounding the death of the
conseiller Prince, his body discovered on the line from Paris to Lyon,
at the evocative la Combe-aux-Fées. Another event of the previous
year, the assassination of Alexander of Yugoslavia and Louis Barthou,
had much less impact in Paris; what most people seem to have retained
from it was that it had happened in Marseille, and on the Canebière to
boot. An almost loving indulgence in the ever-widening ripples of the
affaire Stavisky seemed to represent a lingering, sentimental attachment to a period of relative optimism, as well as to the desire to exclude
anything from outside that might jar a comforting sense of continuity.
Even *Le Canard* was both more light-hearted and much more amusing
in 1935 than it would be in the following four years. The departure of
Jean Galtier-Boissière may have had something to do with this change
of tone.

Of course, much of the *insouciance* was mere affectation. The first
half of the 1930s were years of bitter social conflict and often brutal
police repression. Nevertheless, 1934 *does* seem a watershed. There
was nothing frivolous about 1936, although 1937, *l'année Expo*, did
indeed have hints of a partial return to fantasy. Much of the fantasy
was provided by the Exhibition itself, particularly by the twin spectacle offered by the German and Soviet pavilions, as they faced one
another, over a narrow channel, in competing ugliness. But a direct
outcome of the *Expo* was the *affaire Weidmann*, a one-man, artisanal,
precursor of the massacres to come. Weidmann murdered only half a
dozen people or so, nearly all of whom he had met – for they were a
disparate lot: a taxi-driver, a seedy commercial traveller, a *demi-
mondaine*, an American ballet-dancer – while acting as a guide at the
German pavilion. When the young German was finally arrested at the

famous villa – *faux manoir normand* – in la Celle-Saint-Cloud the house was found to contain all the clothing, handbags, shoes, luggage, jewellery and so on of the meaningless victims: even the red and black G7 taxi, with an R numberplate, was in the garage. The *affaire*, as it gradually unwound, was rightly seen as an unscheduled prolongation of the *Expo*; and many people at the time consoled themselves with the hope that *tant que durera l'Expo, il n'y aura pas de guerre*. It was a pity that it could not have been carried over into the following year; but this Weidmann, right up to the time of his public execution in Versailles, succeeded in doing. With Weidmann gone, there was the chaos of the mobilization of 1938 and the ugly panic of the Parisian well-to-do.

In their portrayals of Paris and its inhabitants, René Clair and Georges Simenon stand on different sides of the 1934 divide, the *cinéaste* on the sunny one, the Belgian writer on one almost wholly sombre. But it is not just a matter of chronology; Maigret had made his first appearance in 1929; but he seems almost to have gone out of business in the second half of the 1930s; and unlike Queneau's Valentin, he even missed the opportunity of taking a look at *l'Expo*, perhaps because his creator was inside it, as an exhibit. The difference is both in temperament and in the choice of an observatory. Clair is always light-hearted, tender, sentimental, full of fun, wonderfully inventive, and wholly optimistic; he is also in a hurry, and his characters have to move very fast; there is not time for philosophizing. They are also always redeemable, even bank managers, industrialists and politicians, even *Immortels*; and bearded senators may all at once be taken with the itch to sing and dance. There is always a way out: prison, or the open road; suicide may be contemplated, even attempted, but a girl in a short black velvet dress, a *bandeau* and enormous made-up eyes will arrive just in time. It will end in song; even *concierges* and villainous-looking *surineurs* will join in. Taxi-drivers are light-hearted poets of the night, even the *agents*, buttoned to the neck, like presidential chauffeurs, eternally waving their hands outwards to the cameras, at the assassination of Doumer or at that of Alexander, even *agents* are *bon-enfant*. Nothing could be farther removed from the self-searching, the sense of guilt and failure that seem to dog most of Simenon's people.

147

For the urban décor, there are five constant favoured components: the attic with a skylight, offering easy access to the roof, the chaotic, jagged geography of roof-top Paris, chimneys and stove-pipes, chasms and drops, the staircase climbing to the seventh floor, the café, blazing with lights, open all night, and the dark street, its *pavé* gleaming liquidly like dark treacle. Clair is *the* poet of the Paris night: a bluish sensuous night of dark velvet, carrying a whiff of powder and the promise of adventure, indeed, a perfectly convincing evocation of the Parisian night of the 1930s, at a period when the night was still democratic and *à la portée de tout le monde*: areas of impenetrable black, picked out by the yellowish headlights of the black and red G7 taxis, contrasting with the brilliant milky-white lights of a café: curtainless windows, dimly lit, silhouetting a woman undressing, and adding a further shade of yellow. A café in which *le père la Tulipe* and *Jojo la Terreur* might encounter, at the bar, a *noceur*, in white tie, a runaway accountant, or a lovesick *monsieur décoré*, not a flight of fantasy, but an accurate representation of a limitless sociability that did exist, especially between midnight and four in the morning, in the 1930s, and that even partially revived in the 1940s.

Nor is the *chambre de bonne* or the studio beneath the roof an object of poetical creation. In the 1930s, as they had been ever since 1914, rents were so low that the poor artist or the *grisette* could indeed live sparsely *sous les toits*, especially in a central *arrondissement*. And the *pneumatique does* arrive within two hours, the post *is* delivered on Sundays, the newspaper *does* come out on Sunday (but not on Monday), taxi-drivers *do* wear peaked caps, *mauvais garçons do* wear checked ones and black and white shoes, senators *are* fat and bearded, important personages *do* wear stocks, artists and *instituteurs do* wear *lavalières*, and Parisians of both sexes *are* more likely to be dark than fair, so that their eyes will dilate in the light and dark of the city night, their brilliantined hair will glisten under the white lights. It is still best to keep away from the *Zone* at night. Nor is the Bastille yet entirely safe; and the rue de Lappe could still provide unpleasant surprises in 1930. The accordion and the *appareils à sous* still hold their own. Clair's villains, decked out in conventional *mauvais garçon* rig, all appear to be French; indeed, they readily talk Parisian, like everyone else, including the elderly *boulevardier* or the *aristo en rupture de ban*.

Perhaps we are indeed still a little ahead of the Corsicans, well ahead of the Tunisians; the Yugoslavs have not even been thought of.

There are students; but they are in the conventional Murger tradition: artistic, but unrecognized, torn between two girls, or sharing a girl with their best friend. They live on the top, in conventional fear of the *concierge*, who, when things are really bad, proves indulgent and even generous. Professional people are professionally dressed: hard collars, dark hats, black overcoats, spats. The PJ wear long belted macs and grey hats with dark bands; elderly and sweet-natured *poivrotes* wear black straw hats with artificial violets; *bistrotiers* are moustached, and wear caps and aprons, they have curly dark hair, a variety of trades still sport peaked caps. All the men, and most of the younger women are constantly lighting up – an action that illuminates their faces in the dark – and they have cigarettes hanging from the bottom lip while they talk. Small boys wear smocks and berets. Fringe characters – their identity and occupation not at once revealed – will wear berets too; in Clair, the beret gives nothing away, and it is of the modest variety, not the fascist floppy kind. There are more berets about in Clair than in the second half of the 1930s, far more again than in the 1940s. Indeed it might be argued that the death of the beret coincides with that of a Paris of human proportions.

For the abiding attraction of René Clair is not merely a matter of nostalgia, though there must always be plenty of that, because he *is* a period piece. He evokes the easy, unsuspecting sociability of a city the inhabitants of which share a common slang and most basic assumptions, and enjoy a wide area of mutual encounter: the café, the street, the market, the staircase, the shop. No one is especially afraid of anyone else; and nearly all can converse in an imaginative and briefly expressed irreverence. The common ideology is scepticism, softened by friendship, understanding and habit. There is also plenty of love, spring-like and unashamed, infectious and encouraged. The function of the newspaper is to carry *petites annonces* and the *chronique judiciaire*, as well as news of Longchamp and Vincennes, to furnish a covering to the floor during house-painting (and a friendly *peintre en bâtiment*, wearing a newspaper in the manner of the Carpenter, will help out, in return for some other service) and to envelop meat and vegetables. The function of the *hauts personnages* is to be ridiculous; but if they step down from their plinth, they will be forgiven. Urban society is geared to the modest aspirations of routine and habit of individuals and individualists; the enemy is loneliness, and the remedy is companionability and verbal exchange. French is for speaking. Everyone is really all right, if approached in the right way. The burglar has his job to carry on just like anyone else, the counterfeiter is an artist who has retained an artist's pride in the quality of his production, even the *gigolo* is perhaps more comical than cruel.

It is, of course, also *le monde à l'envers*; for, in Clair, there is nearly always more satisfaction in coming down than in going up. The room is only at the top physically and there is a sort of release in the gambler cleared out, in the cashier who has gone off with the cash, in the banker who has taken to the quays or the Halles, in the industrialist who has headed for the open road. The only allowable success is in love; and if you do win the lottery, you give it all away, remembering all your friends and neighbours, organizing a splendid repast, champagne, *vins de choix*, in which all, even the *agent* and the *entrepreneur des pompes funèbres*, will readily join in.

Join in what? A celebration, even a way of life aimed at the satisfaction of simple enjoyment, conversation, food and drink, the spring, sunshine, and of course, the cadre, the *only* cadre for personal and collective fulfilment, PARIS. Clair's Paris no doubt sometimes *sent le carton-pâte*, quite a number of his streets look as if they had been put up in Épinay (they had), the roofs and shop-fronts especially often seem overdone. Yet they *are* recognizable. Of course Clair is an artist and an urban poet, of course his films are delightfully light-hearted fantasies. But there is much more to him than that. He is as convincing a witness of place and period as Carco or MacOrlan. But surely, it will be objected, people cannot all have been so *nice*? Well, I think, on the whole, they *were*. We are now a very long way from the 1930s. Clair's attics are now converted into studio apartments for university teachers, antique-dealers (who never feature in Clair's films, in which we only encounter modest and picturesque *brocanteurs*), technocrats, *énarques*, the staircase has been deadened by carpeting, the doors do not open readily and are protected by electrical alarm devices, even the *concierge* has been disposed of. Many of the shops have gone, most of the cafés have been replaced by bars.

Paris by night is no longer a reality lived by its inhabitants, no longer a place for the lonely, in which they may feel drawn by the inviting blaze of a café; it has been reduced to a jaded round of tourist night spots. Much of the city is dead at night; some of it is dangerous as well. Clair's characters have mostly been expelled from the city, following the unfreezing of rents, the destruction of the Halles and of enormous areas of the IVe, to Rungis and elsewhere, taking with them a friendliness and a ready irreverence now only available in daytime, and already running out on the *métro-express* in the early evenings. It is no longer a place where people of all conditions may meet regularly, informally, in the endless excitement of the chance encounter. Where would they meet? There is no longer any common ground, and much of the old centre has become a single-class stronghold, shuttered, selfish, uninviting. Those cafés that have not become bars, have been converted into branch offices of banks. The long yellow-lit windows of Clair's films, silhouetting a young man in shirt sleeves or a young woman in a summer dress, no longer have anyone leaning out to take in the street, for there is nothing to take in, just a dark trench, between rows of silent cars parked on the pavement; and the yellow light has been replaced by a discreet table-lamp, *la lumière tamisée*, the shouts across the street have given way to the filtered sound of elaborate record-players. Paris has largely lost its human dimensions; René Clair's Paris really *did* exist; but it doesn't any more.

9

Maigret's Paris[*]

THE BEST historian of Paris, if he ever set his mind to it, would be the *afficheur*, the man who climbs his ladder to stick up, with the indifference of the technician, billposters, advertisements for patent medicines, announcements of public sales by auction, decrees of general mobilization, electoral declarations and political denunciations, on the considerable amount of space still left available after the passing of a much repeated law of July 1889: *Défense d'afficher* – Stick no bills. The damp, blistered sides of Paris houses have screamed with the strident history of the capital for at least two centuries: red on black, black on yellow, black on white, blue on white, in butterfly variations of anger, denunciation, self-justification, promise, threat, command, information or cajolery. The pursuit of the Parisian has to be spread as widely as that: it cannot be confined only to the Archives and the works of reference; he is to be followed, for example, in two centuries of novels, from Restif and Mercier, through Maupassant and Darien, to Charles-Louis Philippe, Dabit, Fallet, Guimard, Aragon, Albertine Sarrazin, Queneau and Simenon.

Le 6 octobre, the first volume of the immense *Les Hommes de bonne volonté* of Jules Romains, opens with an evocation of the approach to the capital, as an express train runs screamingly through the suburbs: the chaotic mass of disparate villas of Villiers-le-Sec, the damp, black tenements of Aubervilliers and Pantin, capitals of tuberculosis, a green bus seen on a small square, a 30-foot face a greenish grey, staring out

---

[*] Published in *Tour de France* (1976).

of the murk, the huge advertisements painted on the cut-off sides of steep houses – *Suze, le jambon Olida, Porto Antonat* – the approach to the Gare de l'Est.

Simenon, too, is constantly and attractively reminding one that history should be walked, seen, smelt, eavesdropped, as well as read; he seems to say that the historian must go into the streets, into the crowded restaurant, to the central criminal courts, to the *correctionnelles* (the French equivalent of magistrates' courts), to the market, to the café beside the canal Saint-Martin, a favourite hunting ground, to the jumble of marshalling yards beyond the Batignolles, to the backyards of the semi-derelict workshops of the rue Saint-Charles, to the river ports of Bercy and Charenton, as well as to the library. There is a real Maigret quadrilateral in Paris: it's bounded by the rue des Archives, rue de Turenne, place des Vosges, rue du Roi de Sicile, quartier Saint-Paul, rue Vieille du Temple, making up the old faubourg Saint-Antoine and the Marais, on the Right Bank, beyond the Hôtel-de-Ville. This is where he likes to place his lonely, secret little people, because he knows it is, or was, a *quartier de petits gens* and of Jewish immigrants. He is as fond of it as of Maubert-Mouffetard, on the Left Bank, in the Ve *arrondissement*, the ancient centre of poverty and of the Paris tramp; as fond of it as he is of the XIIe, in the wastes of the avenue Voltaire, to the east of the Marais, or the lock at Conflans, the place where the Oise joins the Seine.

It is a geography savoured by Maigret, because he dislikes desk work and is endlessly excited by the prospect of smelling out the ambience of a quarter never previously visited, or neglected for many years. And it is pleasant for the reader, who is thus taken well off the routes of any guide, even those, underground and often invisible, of the recently published *Guide de Paris mystérieux*. Maigret is only grumblingly and briefly seen in the precincts of Saint-Germain. If it is to be night spots, he prefers Pigalle and the place Blanche. He's aware, very much aware, of Saint-Médard, the church at the bottom of the rue Mouffetard that has given its name to that crowded quarter, but he's not of most of the XIVe, on the southern fringe – he's not missing very much. Yet he's spotted the old carters' inns and the *restaurants des chauffeurs*, often with courtyards like country inns, that specialize in *bœuf gros sel*, with leeks and carrots, in or off the rue des Favorites, in the XVe. He has, on occasion, to penetrate the hostile steppes of the XVIe and the XVIIe, the citadels of the Parisian upper bourgeoisie, of bankers and industrialists and rising technocrats – the home, too, of young Maoists and of idolaters of Che – and go up in voluminous but slow-moving lifts, climb up heavily carpeted stairs, even show his card to discreet, shocked *concierges* – boulevard Malesherbes – boulevard de Courcelles . . . But he isn't happy there – at least not until he can get away from the wide avenues into some side-street, to find a small café opposite a *boulangerie*. The Ternes, the seamy side of the Étoile, is much more his style of things, and one can appreciate why: the rue des Acacias, with its individual houses, might be in provincial France. Maigret is admirably selective in his omissions. Pigalle, les Halles, the rue de Berri and the rue de Ponthieu, both off the Champs-Élysées – all these had to be in, but he manages very well without the Latin Quarter, and so can we.

The historian, at least, may well have been obliged to follow him to a place of work, the Archives de la Police, that he shares with the heavily-built, slow-moving Commissaire. And if some of the regular subjects of the historian are stowed away, in green boxes, at the top of the Police Judiciaire, the French equivalent of Scotland Yard, 36 quai des Orfèvres, he should have an eye too for those who are there in the flesh, handcuffed between two rugger-built inspectors, or sitting nervously on the green plush benches, in the corridor, on the first four floors (there's been an improvement in the furnishings since Maigret's time). For history is not only at the top, on the fifth floor, among the bombs and pistols and guillotine blades, alongside the fingerprint people: it's vertical too, so that the historian climbs through a sort of inverted order of crime and delinquency, mounting from murder and homicide, through embezzlement, to blackmail and counterfeiting. Perhaps, in fact, the order is purely the accident of a building bursting at the seams. But it's just as much the job of the historian as it is Maigret's to observe, and to explain, at least the changing pattern of clientele in the PJ's week, as seen from the corridors: Monday, *ces demoiselles*, a noisy, chattering, impudent, loud-mouthed, humorous, chain-smoking, garish throng; Monday, too, is reception day for the hangers-on of that ancient trade – *souteneurs*, hotel-keepers and so on, though, now that the Halles have been moved out, there will be less of both than in the more conventional times of Maigret. On Wednesday, it's the turn of the counterfeiters, Section Financière, while the summer season, which thins out the usual presences in the hazy corridors, multiplies that of small, well-dressed, lithe, professional-looking men, their dark hats on their knees: cat-burglars and house-breakers for whom the holidays of most represent the working season of the few. Murderers, male and female, in *crimes passionnels*, may be seen emerging from the inspectors' rooms, hiding their eyes against the flash bulbs of the press, very early in the morning or very late at night – they're not day birds. Elderly couples in black, dressed like provincial employees or in the ancient suits of peasants, in their Sunday best, are the parents of the assassins or the assassinated; they have come up by the night train.

Saturday's haul includes young men in leather jackets, the uniform of the suburbs, who have invaded the city, on their strident two-cylinder red motor-bikes, and who, plying hilariously in gangs drawn from the same factory and the same barrack-like block of cheap flats, have been involved in punch-ups with middle-class students, in an effort to make pay night seem more memorable. Sunday is a quiet day in the PJ, but it isn't for the morgue: the hours between one and four on Sunday morning are favoured by participants in *crimes passionnels*. Infidelity is likeliest to be a weekend luxury, at least when found out, for there can be little check on the 2 to 4 p.m. variety – even murder takes time and has to be fitted into leisure. And for exactly opposite reasons, suicide will favour the same night hours of the beginning of the weekend when lonely people are loneliest.

Maigret's *enquêtes* have brought him awareness of another calendar – intimate, and perhaps dangerous, because too intimate – a calendar that marks the hours rather than the days, like that of public transport. He has an eye – and we with him – for the *gros Auvergnat* standing behind the bar in his blouse, washing out glasses, as well as for his customers, as they succeed one another during the day and – near les Halles, porte de la Villette and rue Brancion – during the night, for cattle and horse-slaughtering observes no repose. An eye for the 7.45 employees, *pousse-café*, the nine o'clock painters, building workers, glaziers – in their white smocks and paper hats – *un petit blanc sec*; for the 11 o'clock *commis voyageurs*, *représentants*, *un petit blanc sec*; the

midday-to-one rush of ricard, pernod, chablis, beaujolais, the afternoon solitary marc or calvados, the furtive *martini sec* offered by the
customers, *après consommation* in a neighbouring hotel room, to
the prostitute, who has time on her hands, 4 p.m.; the 6 o'clock rush,
the *apéritif* regiment, the evening card-players (a dying race in Paris if
not in Simenon's west of France), the solitary 3 a.m. on repeated marcs,
the Sunday-morning queues at the PMU, the cafés that contain authorized municipal betting shops, the *gros rouge* of the all-night horse-
slaughterers. It is a drinker's day, round the clock, as complete as that
described, nearly two hundred years earlier, by Mercier.

Maigret is a historian of habit, of the *déjà vu*, like any good policeman; he is a historian of the predictable; and even in the 1940s, 1950s
and 1960s, one still feels that he is an observer of the 1930s, whether in
Paris or in the provinces. He is also a historian of class. He is at once
at home with the *concierge* (as befits a policeman) with whom he is so
much in accordance: his own father was a gamekeeper and likewise a
faithful retainer of the well-to-do and the high-born. He is basically
loyal: he has much in common with the bank clerk, the shopkeeper,
with the young provincial semi-failure in the Paris setting. He is not
wholly a townsman himself, still something of a peasant. He can smell
the impending rain – he is like the Breton greengrocer next to the
Maine-Montparnasse conurbation, an elderly lady who states that it
will be wet tomorrow, because the martins are flying low. Maigret, in
fact, is very much the archetypal Parisian of the eighteenth, nineteenth
and twentieth centuries, still half a countryman, with rural values, still
carrying the native province with him in the Paris streets. We are stuck
eternally in the Third Republic.

This is why Simenon is so reassuring to people of a certain generation. It's a cosy, slippered world. The *patron*, in his blue overalls, standing behind his aluminium bar, breathes heavily over the glasses as he
wipes them with the corner of his apron; *truands* – people who would
prefer to avoid social contacts with the police – head for discreet inns
on the Marne, to plan operations or to lie low; boxers past their prime
take to running bars in the neighbourhood of the Champs-Élysées,
their wives, one-time strippers, have gone to fat, go in for blue rinses
and are excellent cooks. Simenon, like Eugène Sue, has the secret of
eternal youth; both are profoundly counter-revolutionary writers. Sue

canalized popular violence into myth. Maigret explains away youthful revolt in pipe-puffing, paternalistic terms, an invisible tear in his eye, for he knows, while he waits for the inevitable eventual blubbering breakdown of the young man who, for hours, has been fighting so hard to keep it all back, that it has to come out in the end.

So Maigret is perhaps a bad social historian insofar as social history is the awareness of change as well as of continuity. But he is a very good popular historian insofar as popular history is the observation of habit, routine, assumption, banality, everydayness, seasonability, popular conservatism, especially in leisure, eating habits and clothing, the pattern of the week, that of the weekend, that of the *grandes vacances* (how he loves the empty Paris of mid-August, but how he curses, like any *aoûtien*, the fact that virtually every *crémerie*, every *boulangerie*, is shut!); he thinks nostalgically of a quiet, shady green spot down by the Loire, but he never goes; he is always about to retire.

The Parisian, both in Simenon and in real life, is an elusive being, hard to define in terms of place of birth. After the Second Empire, Paris might make fun of the southern accent, mock the gawky Auvergnat or the unlicked Lyonnais who put on black sleeves to protect his jacket, generalize about the alleged greed of Normans, laugh at the way Belgians spoke French, and refer to the simplicity of Breton girls. Such attitudes would often conceal the fact that the mockers themselves were of southern descent, had Auvergnat parents, had only recently arrived from Lyon, or, like Bel Ami, from Canteleu, on the heights above Rouen, had, on arrival, gone to the Hôtel des Nantais, reassured as they were meant to be. Even today there is no one more energetically Parisian than the young man who is making his way in the city, ensconced in those little tribal corners of *pays* that, time and again, Maigret succeeds in revealing: tiny ant-heaps hidden from the passing eye, the family relationships of which, a whole network between Paris and the native village, the attentive Commissaire has managed to unravel. When Gaby or Marcelle or Dédée or Micheline is found murdered, in a maid's bedroom in the VIe, she is likely to have come from Narbonne or Pézenas, la Rochelle, Roubaix, Quimper, Douai or Moulins, rather than from Pantin or Vanves-Malakoff on the frayed fringes of the city. Simenon is right to have made so much of the girl with the fibre suitcase as she nervously feels her way through a

Paris terminal. He is a novelist of loneliness and alienation, of the process of urbanization in individual terms.

Few writers could be more aware of the family: he is a twentieth-century *physiocrate* who implies that the country boy should have stayed at home and that the young girl, if only she had listened to her mother instead of doing a bolt up to Paris, would have come to no harm. His books are full of matriarchal figures, and most of those who come to a violent end, who are disgraced, abused, mocked or ruined, have stepped out of the family unit. The ties of family are so persistent that, after an absence of nearly thirty years, *la Tante* suddenly re-emerges, to take over what is left of a sinking ship. Perhaps what is most depressing, most petit-bourgeois, about Simenon is this insistent presence of aunts, cousins, sisters-in-law and grandparents.

Much of what he sees and writes is already an evocation of the past, but so long as Maigret is with us – and we cannot let him retire, much less die – there is still hope for the *pêcheur à la ligne*, for the Sunday painter, for those who like to drink standing up at the counter, for those who seek simple, modest, harmless enjoyments, for those who can smell spring in the air, for those who, like Maigret, are descendants of the proverbial Parisian *badaud* and who are inquisitive about small things. So ultimately our debt to Simenon is not only as an unconscious historian, but as a poet of a world of fraternity and simplicity already almost submerged, and remembered with nostalgic affection – the uncomplicated world of *le Grand Bob*, one of his most sympathetic characters, and of so many other weekenders on the Marne.

10

Brassai's Paris*

BRASSAI, the *Hibou Nocturne* of the velvet blue-black and brilliant, liquid white of the Paris nights of the thirties, was entirely fortunate in his period. It enabled him to command a wider, more varied spectrum than that offered by the much darker eighteenth-century night of Restif, the original Night Owl. The Hungarian photographer was working at a time – 1931–2, and so a Paris still recognizable in that of three years later, when I first went to the city – when the electric night had long replaced the softer gas night of the July Monarchy and the Second Empire. He is as skilled in looking out on to the street below, on to the bright lights of the fairground as seen from an upper window, as looking in, penetrating the much-used intimacy of a brothel bedroom on the fourth floor, or the still dangerous sociability of a ground-floor *bal musette* in the rue de Lappe, some of which were still the rendezvous of the really bad boys in the flat, long-peaked caps and with long points to their shirt collars, *cols Danton*. He is at his best as a miniaturist, with a wonderful eye for significant detail – detail that, at times, places his visual chronicle firmly in the early thirties, and that, at others, illustrates the remarkable continuity from the thirties to the late fifties, eliminating the Occupation years altogether, as if they had brought no significant changes at least in the outer aspect of things. The lurid pattern of a wallpaper, the texture of a bed-cover (which will not be removed), the simple, summary architecture of a *bidet*, the regulation fringed towel, handed over at the moment of payment for the

*This essay first appeared in *People and Places* (1985).

room in the brothel or *hôtel de passe*, hanging on the edge of the wash-basin, having served its purpose to clean up the man, following his brief moment of pleasure: the continuity of a reassuring sordidity.

The *lack* of continuity is more striking. Here are girls with carefully curled fringes of their very dark hair, four or five adjoining curls, like a row of cedillas facing the wrong way, the now lost, distant race of working-class and lower-middle-class Parisiennes of the 1930s, their eyes bright with excitement, drink and invitingness. The brilliantined and well-brushed hair of the men, the neat parting to the side, the men apparently as dark as the girls, like the characters in a René Clair film, speak as eloquently of the thirties as the curled fringes of the girls. Both seem somehow more French than the chlorophylic inhabitants of the *Hexagone* of the 1980s, as though, at that time, no blond French had existed. It may of course all be the effect of the night lights. The bad boys, too, look very bad indeed, as though they meant business with their *eustaches* – their knives – ready to hand, famished and rat-faced, as they stand, feet insolently splayed out, caps to one side, with their hands in their pockets. Equally menacing is the waiting group of *la bande du Grand Albert*, silhouetted against a brightly-lit long peeling wall somewhere near the porte d'Italie. All – fringed girls and stony-eyed men – have limp Gauloises hanging provocatively from their lower lips, as if further to emphasize their Frenchness. Here are the broad lapels of the jacket, in loud check, the made-up bow-tie over a pullover that comes up to the collar of the shirt, the bow-tie like a toy stuck on, a burly man, pleased with himself as he stands squarely at the counter of a café, *bal musette*, in the rue de Lappe. It was as if Brassai's characters, caught wide-eyed by his flash bulbs, were con-sciously acting being French. Were the French more French then? They were certainly more joyful, more uninhibited, more eccentric, less conformist.

The choice is as varied as was the intensive night-life of a still living, socially varied Paris. I particularly like the sailor and the petty-officer, with the fringed girl between them, and in front of them a rising pile of saucers. The girl is paying more attention to the sailor, turning towards him; the petty-officer is too far gone, he will never make it. Then there is an amazing lateral shot, through a glass panel, of a *bal musette*, an elderly man in a hat, such a one as could have been described in the happy thirties as a *noceur*, his mouth wide open, in laughter or in song, supporting himself on two girls, rather like the elderly gentleman described by Guilloux in his *Carnets*, who, when it was proposed that they make an outing to a brothel, says: 'Wait while I put on my Légion d'Honneur.' Among the strange creatures of the night collected by Brassai the strangest is *la môme Bijou*, rippling with cheap jewellery, rings and bangles, hatted, gloved, wearing a moulting fur, many scarves and floating draperies, a sort of dotty elegance gone to seed, her eyes bright and slightly mad, as she stares at the camera, holding a glass. She is said by some to have been the model for *la Folle de Chaillot*.

A police cycle patrol – *les hirondelles*, some of the police with 1914-style moustaches, accompanied by two burly inspectors, heavily muffled, their breath visible – are waiting expectantly at a brightly lit corner, staring into the night. On the facing page are five men of *la bande du Grand Albert* looking in the direction of the patrol.

Before and after: a couple, reflected in the long horizontal mirror beside the bed, the man still in tie and waistcoat, his hair unruffled, his jacket thrown carelessly over the chair, the woman partly beside him, both lying on a bed-cover decorated in a flower pattern, the clothing soon to be removed but not the bed-cover. Then the woman sitting on the *bidet*, her broad and sagging bottom protruding over the rim, as she washes herself in front, her feet in flowered high-heeled shoes, the man balanced on one leg while putting on his trousers. Stage three: the woman, still naked save for the shoes, her broad back marked by the red line left by her brassière, reflected in the mirror, the man, now in his shirt, adjusting his tie and brushing his hair in the mirror of the heavy wardrobe that, for some reason – for this was a place for unclothing, not for keeping clothes – so often cluttered the bedrooms of brothels and *hôtels de passe*.

There is a bizarre picture of three short girls lying on a couch, like dolls, their faces heavily made up, against a huge flowered wallpaper, two little dogs lying at their feet and looking like toys. The outside girl is wearing net stockings and black buckle shoes that accentuate her doll-like respectability. A well-dressed lady in a saucepan black straw hat is showing her hand to a voluminous *cartomancienne*, the tarot cards spread out fanwise on a table covered with a heavy cloth, against a corner background of wallpaper samurai. The grotesque gorilla-man, in a heavy plaid dressing-gown, bends over the little naked blond boy, Peterchen, in a Montmartre hotel bedroom that houses gymnasts and circus people. Or the benevolent, child-like face of the old tramp beneath his shapeless beret, heavily bearded, sitting holding his little black cat, his overcoat tattered at the cuffs and held together by a large safety-pin, on a winter night on the quays beneath the Pont-Neuf, his female companion lurking in the offing, having refused to be photographed. Brassai is as compassionate as he is observant; and he warms to the independent and rather well-spoken *clochard*, the denizen of a lost age, when the quays were still free of traffic and the home of tramps and lovers. But he can also be merciless, as when he portrays, twice, the triple-chinned *taulière*, queening it, in black dress and heavy necklace, over her own establishment: once, when she is seated playing cards with two of her girls, one looking very bored, and a customer, his hair brushed back; then when she is standing commandingly in front of a heavy mirror, her three chins sagging beneath her blotched face.

Brassai's album is a nostalgic one. It depicts a Paris still vibrant with life, throughout the night hours, and when it was still possible, at the café *Au Carrefour de Buci*, to meet *le père la Tulipe*, a misnomer, for, top-hatted, he sold violets, bought at the Halles, standing at the counter, from four every morning, for a round, or several rounds, of *canons*, most of which he was offered by customers grateful for his familiar presence.

As Louis Chevalier has written, and as Brassai might have said, something of the wonder and variety of the Paris of Balzac and Eugène Sue had survived into the thirties, and, indeed, beyond, into the early sixties, before the *Ville-Lumière* began on its slow death, early to bed, burglar-alarms set, all doors bolted and barred.

I I

Succès de vandale[*]

OF THE Western capitals in the past two world wars, Brussels and Paris were those that experienced the least destruction, either from artillery and aerial bombardment, or from rockets. On Good Friday 1917, the church of Saint-Gervais, in the Marais, received a direct hit, during Mass, from a shell from Big Bertha; and in the Second World War, the northern quarter of la Chapelle was heavily bombarded in the course of an RAF attack on the marshalling yards of the Gare du Nord. There was also considerable damage, just outside Paris, as a result of the bombing of the Renault works in Boulogne-Billancourt. Brussels got away with even less damage, though it was attacked by the Luftwaffe a few days after its liberation, in September 1944.

The damage which has been inflicted on these two cities is not, then, the result of enemy – or Allied – action. It is the result, almost always, of vandalism from within. In Brussels, *la ville haute*, once a delightful combination of seventeenth- and eighteenth-century domestic architecture, and also containing a few fine medieval churches, has largely been destroyed by the Common Market. The construction of the Gare Centrale and its link-up, by a central underground line, with the old stations of Nord and Midi has resulted in the disembowelment of the seventeenth-century quarter of the rue Haute and the rue Blaes, beyond the porte de Hal, on the rising ground leading to the rue Royale (among the buildings destroyed was the delightful Maison des Arquebusiers, an *haut-lieu* of Brussels municipal history); the pulling

---

[*] Published in *Tour de France* (1976).

down of what had been left of the quartier des Marolles after the redoubtable Polaert had gutted this heavily populated area, during the reign of Leopold II, when constructing the enormous Palais de Justice (no wonder that in Brussels patois 'espèce d'architecte' is the most unforgivable insult!); the isolation of the church of Saint-Hubert and that of Saint-Gudule, standing in a forlorn wilderness; and the disappearance of the old Mont-des-Arts, including the shop in which Paul Colin was assassinated by a Resistance fighter in 1943.

Les Marolles, both a home of linguistic oddities – *espèce de tonnenlinker*, and other combinations of French, Flemish and Bruxellois – and a wonderful maze of tiny, steep streets, the pavements of which would be covered, in the spring and summer, by card-players, is now merely a memory of a lost folklore, the one-time home of the *smokeleers* and of the Belgian capital's brighter pickpockets, counterfeiters, and specialists in false papers. The only comparable attack on a city's popular culture was the blowing up of the Vieux Port in Marseille; but at least that was carried out by the Germans. For the doubtful privilege of becoming the capital of Europe – or rather of 'Europe' – Brussels, or at least *la ville haute*, has paid the enormous price of an almost total loss of identity. The lovely Saint-Gudule, once surrounded by the harmony of such seventeenth-century town houses as the Hôtel d'Oursel, is now incongruously exposed to a faceless place de l'Europe. It would be interesting to hear the comments, in *la langue des marolles*, on the subject of such impudent vandalism.

Georges Pillement, a gallant old fighter, has a sadly similar story to tell on the subject of the wanton destruction of Paris over the past seventy-five years: similar, at least in the extent of the damage, and the persistence of short-sighted or deliberate vandalism. For, whereas in Brussels there has been a single culprit – 'Europe' – in Paris there have, over the years, been any number. M. Pillement, in his justifiably angry book,* lists the worst of them. They include the Banque de France, a persistent offender, in its constant need to expand its premises above and below ground; M. Cognacq, the founder of la Samaritaine; the neighbouring la Belle Jardinière; les Galéries Lafayette, to which the lovely Hôtel de la duchesse de Berry fell victim; l'Assistance Publique

---

* Georges Pillement, *Paris poubelle* (Paris, 1974).

(victim: Hôpital des Enfants Trouvés); Michel Debré, as Minister of Defence (the destroyer of the Temple de l'Amitié, 20 rue Jacob); the American beautician, Helena Rubinstein, who had a seventeenth-century town house on the Île Saint-Louis pulled down, in order to erect an apartment block; a whole line of Prefects; the Mont-de-Piété; the Army; the *sapeurs-pompiers*; the *gendarmerie*; the Ville de Paris itself, which ordered the demolition of a charming folly in Bercy, to make way for the extension of the Halle-aux-vins; the main Paris branch of an English bank, boulevard des Capucines, responsible for uprooting the delightful Pavillon de Hanovre, and exiling it incongruously to the far end of the parc de Sceaux; insurance companies; building societies; hospitals; the old Compagnie Nord-Sud which, when constructing its own underground line, insisted that the streets immediately above it should follow its track, in order to assure its regular custom, so that a whole section of the rue du Cherche-Midi was swept away to make room for the prolongation of the boulevard Raspail; building speculators in alliance with the *conseil municipal*; and, of course, more recently, especially under the Fifth Republic, the sort of technocrats who, too grand themselves ever to use public transport, have failed to modernize the TCRP, to add to the *Métro* lines, to provide mini-buses, and have thought exclusively of increasing the speed of circulation of private cars within the city, thus, in most cases, adding to the chaos, while cutting huge swathes through the centre. The name of the terrible Delouvrier at once comes to mind.

Though President de Gaulle took the initiative of having the Grand Trianon done up and made into an official residence, and though he himself at one time contemplated moving from the Élysée to the Pavillon du Roi in the fort de Vincennes, no doubt in order to emulate Saint Louis (his proposed move at least had the permanent advantage of giving the French war records extended premises), for a man so deeply concerned with the past, with the continuity of French history, he seems to have shown little interest in the efforts of such bodies as the Commission du Vieux-Paris to preserve as much as possible of that history on the ground. The period of his presidency was in fact one of extensive destruction. But if de Gaulle had allowed a lot to go because his angle of vision rarely reached down to the level of mere *buildings*, his successor, Georges Pompidou, was an active, indeed grandiose and visionary, vandal, who managed to achieve, in a quarter of the time, almost as much square-*kilométrage* of destruction as the Alsatian Attila, Baron Haussmann.

The foreign visitor, on seeing for the first time the vast area of destruction contained in the quadrilateral between the rue Beaubourg and the boulevard de Sébastopol, and extending down as far as the rue de la Verrerie, might assume that Paris, too, had experienced something on the scale of the Warsaw Rising. But he would be wrong, for this scene of devastation is what has been officially described as *le plateau Beaubourg*, and, unofficially, as *le trou Pompidou*, and a mighty *big* hole it is: the late President, an active patron of modern art in all its uglier forms, had set his eye on this area as a suitable place to erect a *centre des arts*, or a series of experimental theatres. There is nothing there at all at the moment; but the rue Quincampoix has been cut into three, the church of Saint-Merri stands almost alone, deprived of its natural *entourage* of old streets, and the old quartier Sainte-Avoie has almost entirely disappeared. Pompidou also had his plans for the quarter of les Halles and the rue Saint-Denis; he managed to get the markets down in his lifetime, with the result that the old market church of Saint-Eustache stands, like Saint-Merri, on the edge of a desert.

But at least the site is to be preserved, and the rue Saint-Denis has been saved. Had Pompidou lived even a little longer, there would probably have been little of historical Paris on either bank. As it is, apart from his *Grand Trou*, his principal monument will remain the gigantic buildings to be seen caught in the perspective of the Arc de Triomphe when viewed from the Carrousel. The election of M. Giscard d'Estaing has brought a welcome halt to the *zèle gaullo-destructeur* of the Hôtel-de-Ville and the Conseil de Paris. The new President has dropped the *voie-exprès Rive Gauche*, which would have ruined the little that has been left of the banks of the Seine and would have brought down, in a matter of years, Notre-Dame; and he has granted a reprieve to the Cité Fleurie.

As M. Pillement shows most convincingly, part of the trouble has always been that no single authority, at least since 9 Thermidor, has ever held responsibility for Paris as a whole, that the city, far from ever having had a single master, has always been saddled with a whole lot of them, most of them acting independently of one another.

In other French cities, a *maire* can do a power of good, or evil. Herriot in his very long reign in Lyon, Médecin in Nice, were active preservationists, whereas Mondon, the unspeakable *maire* of Metz, has managed to destroy most of the old city. In Paris, buildings are pulled down in a semi-secret manner, on the casual recommendation of a single authority, and even the eagle eye of a Georges Pillement or a Michel Fleury may miss some *ordonnance ministérielle* tucked away, and in small print, in the *Bulletin municipal*. In Paris, irreparable decisions are often taken in a furtive manner; *les démolisseurs*, like pickpockets, prefer to avoid publicity. To begin with, there are two Prefects, the territories of each of whom are not clearly defined. M. Pillement suggests that *hauts fonctionnaires*, at the summit of their careers, and for whom promotion to Paris will represent the ultimate reward, after many years sitting it out in Gap, or Mende – the Prefects have rarely been native-born Parisians (though the good Poubelle was); some have been Corsicans – are unlikely to feel strongly about a city in which they were not brought up. But the Prefects are far from enjoying a monopoly of destruction. Each Minister has been allowed his allocation of wreckage; and that of Environment, Alain Chalandon, managed to have pulled down 81–83 rue de la Verrerie, a *crime en longueur* to which we will return.

But the most persistent and joyful demolitionists have always been the official architects of the city – there would be a very strong case for introducing the Brussels insult to Paris – who, even in the days of horse traffic, thought less in terms of people, of beauty, of the past, than in those of the speed of circulation. Already, in the 1780s, the Lieutenant de Police is ordering the widening of this street or that, while limiting the height of houses, and a series of eighteenth-century royal *ordonnances* required that all half-timbered houses should be plastered over, with the result that buildings that had previously been perfectly solid became damp and often eventually collapsed into the street. This sort of thing has gone on ever since; straightening, widening, chopping off corners, making winding streets stand at attention, cutting swathes of wide avenues through the centre – the Commission des Arts of 1795 had already planned most of the horrors that were to follow over the next two centuries – uprooting trees, narrowing pavements, removing statues, and, more recently, honeycombing the city with shallow *park-*

ings souterrains, into which will no doubt soon crash the few churches and historic mansions allowed to survive. One should not be too prone to blame the Gaullists, though they have been especially active *démolomanes*. They have a long tradition to look back to.

Indeed, one of the few consoling features of this sad chronicle is that things might have been even worse. M. Pillement lists, with fascinated horror, some of the plans of 'improvement' that were not in fact carried out (the two world wars offered a welcome respite in this respect). From 1901 to 1914, a series of authorities examined lovingly an atrocious project to prolong the rue de Rennes – in its drab ugliness the joy of any town-planner – across the boulevard Saint-Germain, right up to the Seine. The rues de Seine and Mazarine would have gone, the rue Jacob been cut, the new street would have eaten up the rear courtyard of the Institut. Fortunately, for once, MM. les Académiciens served a purpose other than their own mutual admiration: they protested, they wanted to keep their rear entrance. In 1912, *on croit rêver*, there was a proposal to drive a road through the middle of the Palais-Royal, to speed the flow of north–south traffic. In 1916, thanks to the war, the lovely rue François-Miron was given a temporary reprieve. And because of shortage of labour and material and high building costs, there was a lull in pulling down from 1916 to 1920.

Early in the 1920s, Le Corbusier presented *his* plan for the quartier des Halles: it was all to come down, to be replaced by eight huge tower blocks facing on to the Seine. By some miracle, it was not adopted. But, frustrated in his attempt on Paris, the Swiss *démolomane* and collectivist was able to give his full measure much later, in Marseille. One should be thankful for some small mercies, and Paris was at least spared a Perret or a Le Corbusier.

For *Paris poubelle* makes extremely depressing reading, despite these occasional, almost accidental, reprieves. The 'improvers' regarded it as a great concession to the complaints of the preservationists if they allowed them, out of municipal funds, to take a photograph of some eighteenth-century marvel lined up for destruction. *Mais prenez donc une photo*; and an awful lot of the illustrations of this book originated in this way. Save during the two wars, the process of destruction has been continuous: construction of the ugly rue Dante (1899); destruction of the Maison de l'Arbre de Jessé (1900); of the Abbaye aux Bois (1901); of the Enfants Trouvés (1902); Hôtel de Chastellux (1903); the first assault on the rue Mouffetard (1904). 1906 was a bumper year for demolition, on both Banks. In 1907, the boulevard Raspail was extended. In 1908, the Tour Dagobert came down, in 1909, the Couvent des Dames Anglaises. The year 1911 saw the end of Sue's *tapis francs*, rue de la Grande Truanderie. In 1913, the quay facing on to the southern end of the Pont-Neuf was 'disengaged' (*dégager* is a favourite word with *les circulomanes*), the rue Dauphine and the rue de Nevers truncated, and a hideous circus in brick erected: if not the *worst* building in Paris, at least the most prominent bad one. The building boom started again in 1922. In the following year, Cognacq, the art collector, pulled down the lovely Hôtel de la Vieuville. The Hôtel Fersen went too in the 1920s. The last barracks of the Gardes Françaises, rue de Penthièvre, went in 1929.

Since the Liberation, the demolitionists have been busy mopping up the remains of the rue Mouffetard, tearing apart the whole quarter to make room for the rue Jean Calvin, suitably named, for it is a sad street. On the Right Bank, the area from the Seine to the level of the rue François-Miron has been razed.

The old headquarters of the *poste aux chevaux*, rue Pigalle, went in 1965. They have also had a go at the upper ends of the rue Saint-Jacques, and most of the rue de l'Ouest seems at present to be imminently threatened by the spread of the appalling Tour Maine-Montparnasse. Recently I called on a friend who lived, 83 rue de la Verrerie, in a wonderfully rambling *Cour des Miracles*, the remains of the old Hôtel des Voyageurs de la Ville de Reims, which contained, among other treasures, an outside wooden staircase dating from François I, and eighteenth-century staircases and floors in wood and diamond-shaped red tiles. All that remained of the house, and its neighbour, No 81, was a huge hole. Both houses had been placed on the protected list by the Commission des Sites. But the owners had allowed them to fall into such a state of disrepair that they had obtained a discreet order from M. Chalandon for their destruction. As M. Pillement remarks, this is a method of hastening demolition much favoured both by the public authorities and, sad to say, by the owners, including some who belong to very old families, anxious to obtain a maximum profit from the sale to property speculators of a *terrain* in central Paris.

M. Pillement himself, as an experienced observer of impending vandalism, has witnessed the progressive deterioration of many of the finest eighteenth-century *hôtels particuliers*, the removal of iron work, of *portes cochères*, and has, on many occasions, always unsuccessfully, attempted to warn the authorities responsible. The authorities have not wished to know. He even instances cases of buildings having not merely been neglected in this way, till they could reasonably be described as a public danger: he quotes cases of others that have been deliberately rendered unsafe by the removal of parts of the roof or of supporting props. His comments on the avidity of building speculators are in contrast to what he has seen happening in places like Prague or Warsaw, where every effort has been made to preserve as much as possible of the historic past of these ancient towns. Perhaps he is being too pessimistic, for, in Paris, there are a number of people as vigilant as himself: Hillairet, Dauvergne, Fleury, de Saint-Rémy, historians, antiquarians, archivists, actively concerned to bring to a halt seventy-five years of thoughtless destruction.

There have been, also, in recent years, some serious efforts at preservation. The case of the Marais has been much quoted, and it is certainly true that a number of *hôtels particuliers* have in fact been saved, cleaned up, their courtyards cleared of all manner of encumbrances – wooden sheds, glass roofs – as well as of the many activities and the many artisans that they housed. But this has been preservation at a very great cost. The houses of the Marais, with their many ancillary activities dispersed, have been frozen into the lifelessness of museums. The shells have been preserved, but there is nothing much inside. There was much greater excitement in discovering, behind the chaos of workshops, *baraques*, tin roofs, the vague outline of the Hôtel de Venise, or the Hôtel des Ambassades de Hollande, or the Hôtel Lamoignan, than in thus being directed, by a series of maps attached to the street lamps, to the now dead town houses of a quarter that has been completely museumified. Even so, this is perhaps preferable to complete destruction. And, in any case, no one has worried about the smaller dwelling-houses and the less fashionable streets.

Of these last, so many long since gone, M. Pillement writes with the nostalgia of an urban poet, as well as with the necessarily suspicious alertness of a witness very much aware of the equally vigilant contrary concern of public authorities and speculators in search of profitable destruction. He refers to the extinct rue de Venise, once the principal centre of tuberculosis: 'La nuit est venue; les pauvres maisons hydropiques . . . reniflent une dernière fois les relents de pommes, de poires ou de fraises que les vents traînent selon les saisons, et ferment les paupières.' And he evokes the neighbouring rue de la Reynie, also gone: 'Rue de la Reynie oncques voiture n'a jamais passé. Les corpulents marchent de biais, seuls les maigres vont à leur aise en collant les bras au corps' (though, in this category, the thin can still get down the rue de Nevers and the rue Visconti, near where Oscar Wilde died: I have never made out how he could even get into it). He is even more eloquent on the subject of the poor rue Brantôme: 'Nul passant ne s'y attarde pour déplorer sa trop régulière misère . . . Seul le vent y muse souvent, mais en vain, ce gros malin, essayant d'agiter les trois couleurs des drapeaux de zinc des lavoirs.' How right he is to compare these ancient, humble streets, to some poor old woman who has never had looks:

> La rue du Maure n'a jamais eu de jeunesse. Elle est née triste entre de hautes maisons. Elle a un coude charmant entre deux vieux murs. Elle est silencieuse, mais elle ne pense à rien. C'est le royaume du sommeil. Revenues du fin fond des faubourgs lointains les voitures à bras s'y endorment le soir, accablées de fatigue et de misère, leurs bras levés vers le ciel et un rayon de lune dans leur ventre creux . . .

The tin flags of the *lavoirs*, so unseasonable, for they at least can never merrily crack to the gusty wind, the handcarts of the *marchands de quatre saisons*, their arms raised in tired and hopeless protest – 'we have come from Vanves, from Montreuil, from Montrouge' – the odour of rotting fruit, brought on a timid wind, the cats that compete with the multicoloured posters to give a semblance of life and movement to these dark, damp cuttings: these are as evocative of a Paris that once was and is almost no more, as the hidden courtyards, the old hand pumps and fountains, or the mounting steps of Belleville. Alas, rue de Venise, *M. Pompidou est passé par là*.

M. Pillement has written a sad book, for it is the relentless inventory of so much beauty lost, and so often lost needlessly. He understands that a street, in its irregularity, is an entity that represents something, that contains a message hidden from the average *passant*, but perceptible to anyone with time, patience and imagination to spare. He talks primarily of what has gone. Fortunately, even after years of *gaullo-destructomanie*, there have subsisted plenty of obscure corners, deep courtyards, private *voies sans issue*, tiny shuttered *bicoques* almost entirely hidden in thick foliage, along an abandoned *ceinture*, green *volets* lit by hearts or diamonds, minuscule *vins charbons*, high front steps leading to street doors that have not been opened for a hundred years, blind windows, railings climbing beside an old winding staircase, the semi-secret, just visible, entry to an oddly rustic fairyland, the swing doors of a tiny hotel, rue de la Goutte-d'Or, full of menace, evocative of sordid violence, the artisanal architectural fantasies of the *facteur* Cheval: Gothic crenellations, terracotta *châteaux-forts* picked out in sea shells. Cranes and storks cut out in wood with metal beaks, old Abeille tins filled with scallop shells, laid out in complicated patterns; messages of love or insult on oozing, leprous Utrillo-like walls, forlorn cemeteries approachable through thick undergrowth, the sound of someone practising on a French horn, the bright medley of a *marchand de couleurs*, the gaudy ceramic bricks covering the wall of a *pensionnat*, Villa Poissonnière (*Voie Privée*), the chains blocking one entry of *bains publics*, the 1920-style advertisements on glass, in one of the closed *galéries*, beloved of Aragon, the tangled, romantic ironwork of these *ponts des suicidés*, the discreet unpretentious entry to the Morgue, the old-fashioned shop-front of the Maison Borniol, the leading entrepreneur in death, the many-headed golden horses of the *boucherie chevaline* opposite the horse slaughter-house, rue Brancion, the endless fantasy, excitement, naivety, inventiveness and individualism of *le Paris Insolite*, a Paris fortunately both too secret and too humble to attract the dangerous interest of a Pompidou or the avidity of a speculator.

12

The Assassination of Paris[*]

ARCHITECTS, TOWN planners, and specialists in traffic circulation are much more dangerous than sociologists, who, so often, have merely served to complicate what might have seemed self-evident and simple to the historian. The errors, assumptions, and miscalculations of the former are both durable and visible: solid contributions to human misery, whereas, while sociologists may attempt to bypass history, or to render it unintelligible and unreadable, they do not seek to destroy it altogether.

What virtually all architects and urbanists since Haussmann have had in common is a loathing for the past and an overriding desire to erase its visible presence. Like sociologists, they have little time for individuals and their trying, quirky, and unpredictable ways, tending to think only in terms of human destiny: so many units in the formation of a Grand Design (or a *Grand Ensemble*, to use a modish French expression), as if people, in rectangular blocks of a thousand, or ten thousand, were to be assimilated to a gigantic set of Lego. There is nothing more remote from humanity and more devoid of the human scale than an architect's model plan for a new urban development. Even the trees are puny and plastic, and of a sickly green (*chlorophile*); the cars, lined up in their *parkings souterrains*, are gaily coloured, but the people to be assigned to the new Alphavilles are not even dots.

One of the few, wry, consolations to be derived from Norma Evenson's well-researched and implacable record[†] of architectural

* This essay was published in *People and Places* (1985).
† *Paris: A century of change, 1878–1978* (Yale University Press, 1979).

insensitivity is the realization that the horrors that architects and planners were actually *able* to perpetrate were as nothing to those that they had *meditated* and that, for one reason or another – often a war, or an economic recession (both concealed blessings for the urban dweller) – they had not succeeded in getting away with. Consider Le Corbusier, in his forty-year campaign against the beauty and variety of Paris. How he *hates* the place! With what sovereign contempt does he treat its mindless inhabitants! Here he is already in 1925 obsessed with his *grande croisée*, a swath of huge expressways cutting through the centre of the city, east–west and north–south, marking Paris like a hot-cross bun. And here he is again back in the 1920s, with plans to uproot les Halles and most of the old street system between the rue de Richelieu and the rue Saint-Martin, and to erect on the vast quadrilateral of the old Right Bank thus devastated a series of tower blocks, the first of many versions of his alarmingly named *Ville Radieuse*. And here he is in 1931 proposing a grandiloquent entry into the projected *Voie Triomphale* (the triumph of inhumanity), either at the porte Maillot or the pont de Sèvres.

The implacable Helvetian is tireless in his assault on Paris, doggedly determined to line both banks of the river with an aligned barrier of dragon's teeth. What is the secret of his hatred of the place? Is it the rancorous provincialism of a twentieth-century Girondin? Anyhow, right up to his death, he submits plan after plan for the dehumanization of the city, and appears as constantly surprised by the rejection of his overtures. It must have been only a minor consolation to him to have been given a free hand in Marseille, or rather outside it, for the erection of what the locals at once nicknamed *la maison du fada* – the idiot's house.

What distinguishes Le Corbusier is the sheer persistence of his war against the French capital. As the years go by, and conceit and rancour take their toll, the black lines on his maps, criss-crossing the city at its very heart, get blacker and thicker and more impatient, the ordered rectangular cubes of high-rise blocks become heavier and more febrile. The main assault is still on the Seine and its vicinity; but, with each year, the pencil of potential destruction moves inward, mapping out further swaths of demolition, as he greedily eyes the tempting fruit of the once plague-ridden pockets of the city known as the *ilôts insalubres*: Saint-Merri, Sainte-Avoie, Saint-Gervais, Saint-Paul, the Gravilliers, and the promising space left by the destruction of the old fortifications on the northern rim of the city.

Others do not quite last the pace thus set. But the awful Eugène Hénard, working at the turn of the century at the municipal office in charge of public works, could tote up at least twenty-five years of anti-Parisian dream-drawings. By 1903, long before the Swiss *marchand de soleil*, he is already obsessed with a *grande croisée* of his own, provided, in this instance, by a widened rue de Richelieu, leading to an avenue de Richelieu on the Left Bank, forming the main north–south axis, and intersecting an enlarged avenue de l'Université. His east–west axis would have actually cut through the courtyard of the Palais-Royal, while a further swath, the avenue du Panthéon, would have obliterated the rue Mouffetard, which, being narrow, and warmly human, has attracted persistent assaults from several generations of planners. If Le Corbusier reserved his most persistent loathing for the old Right Bank centre, Hénard was primarily out to destroy the quartier Saint-Germain-des-Prés.

He was not alone in his distaste for the jumble of narrow streets stretching from the carrefour de Buci to the rue Mazarine, the rue Guénégaud and the rue de Nevers. The architect André Ménabréa, writing in 1932, looked forward to the razing of the whole area, in order, so he said, to erase the memory – somewhat remote – of the September Massacres of 1792, when, so he claimed, the rue de Tournon, the rue de Seine, the rue de l'Abbaye, and the rue de l'Échaudé had 'run with blood'. Why not, then, tear up the rue de la Grande Truanderie and the rue de la Mortellerie, because they commemorated long-forgotten killings and ancient violence? Why not raze the cloître Saint-Merri, because it too had been the scene of a more recent massacre?

Even as late as 1937, urbanists were still toying with plans to prolong the rue de Rennes (the most desolate, inhuman street in Paris) to the level of the Seine, either at the Pont-Neuf or at the pont des Arts, or at both, knocking off a wing or two of the Institut de France in the process (it was in the way). As in 1913, when similar proposals had been made, so in 1939 the advent of a providential war saved the integrity of the old Left Bank. The architects and planners and the technocrats of public health not only followed one another in their hatred of a human past and of a human street plan; they copied one another, from decade to decade, handing down, from 1900 to the 1960s, schemes for the assassination (an expression used by Professor Evenson) of les Halles, the clearance of the riverside areas to the east of the Hôtel-de-Ville, the brutal invasion of the tranquillity of the enclosed Palais-Royal – a safe paradise for lovers, *flâneurs*, and children – and the cutting of a huge swath through the quartier de Buci.

From 1900 to the 1960s, all such plans were dictated by a false priority, an obsession with the improvement of internal circulation, east–west and north–south, at the expense of a long-established human geography. Paris for the automobile, rather than Paris for the Parisians. This is what Paul Delouvrier, urbanist and prefect of the Seine, had in mind, in the typically pretentious phrase written in 1963: *Paris doit épouser son siècle.* One can see what this *mésalliance* signifies when one contemplates the fate of what had once been the Right Bank quays until they were converted into roadways.

So, indeed, it could have been much worse. The unfulfilled blueprints of destruction, the firm red lines of the planner's pencil are even more chilling than the visual – and aural – evidence of what has actually been achieved by the combination of urbanists, architects, and building speculators. Had M. Pompidou, who also liked to talk of Paris being forced to marry her century (which did not prevent him from living on the agreeable tip of the Île Saint-Louis), lasted a little longer, the canal Saint-Martin would have gone, covered over to carry a semicircular highway which would then have roared through the lower slopes of the Montagne-Sainte-Geneviève. And the quays of the Left Bank would have gone the way of those of the Right, and the Seine would have become as unapproachable as the majestic Hudson River. President Pompidou *did* get his *trou*, his hole, officially designated as *le plateau Beaubourg*; and he is commemorated by a strange building that rises above the modest levels of the old houses of Saint-Merri and Sainte-Avoie and that looks like a gigantic *paupiette de veau*, with all its innards displayed on the outside. Others have compared it to an enormous, multicoloured, and very venomous insect.

Most of the worst horrors, the vast mushroomed, domed follies of the 1960s, are well away from the centre. Except for the unfortunate people who must live or work there, no one needs to go anywhere near the convention centre and shopping complex at the porte Maillot, much less to the vast complex of high-rise apartments and office buildings at la Défense; the glass and concrete apartment blocks at the Front de Seine are only visible if one approaches Paris from Versailles by car. It is possible even to avoid the immense uniform towers of the new porte d'Italie; and only a few elderly enthusiasts of a little-known XIIIe will recall, with nostalgic affection, the small streets and courtyards, the low-lying houses, and the warm and varied sociability of the rue Nationale and the rue du Château des Rentiers, now mere names derisively harking back to a vanished topography that was still quite recently genuinely working-class and that tightly enclosed a shared fraternity and a confident *esprit de quartier* that was sure of its environment and was content to stay put. This was the Left Bank equivalent of Belleville and Ménilmontant and managed successfully to combine a population of XIIIe-born French – many of whom had only left the *arrondissement* to do their military service, and some of whom, among the older female inhabitants, had never crossed the river, indeed, had never *thought* of crossing the river – with sizeable groups of Algerian immigrant workers. Now the factories and workshops have gone, along with the two-storeyed houses; and so have those who worked in them. The new inhabitants of the vast porte d'Italie complex are young, middle-class couples, with no memories of the old XIIIe, and nothing to attach them to a recent, but vanished past.

The Boulevard Périphérique circles Paris with the constant roar of tyres, the screams of sirens, and the presence of sudden death. But, as its name implies, it is well outside the city proper, and may be only briefly glimpsed from the comfortable safety of suburban overhead railways like the *ligne de Sceaux*. The horrors of the huge high-rise complex of Maine-Montparnasse, constructed during the 1960s, and the Tour Zamansky, it is true, cannot be disguised: the one sticks up like a threat from another planet, at the end of a neat line of trees in the Luxembourg gardens, the latter dwarfs the beautiful proportions of the tip of the Île Saint-Louis. What, one wonders, did M. Pompidou make of *that*? The white hulk of the vast District de Paris building stares arrogantly across the river at the stilted cement and glass jungle of the Faculty of Science, as if defying the old-fashioned and familiar barges in between making their way to or from the equally familiar sand port of Paris.

But, since the 1950s, the greatest damage to Paris has not been architectural so much as human: a process that might be described as the de-Parisianization of Paris, as a result of the removal from the city of much of its traditional and characteristic population. Since the turn of the century, Professor Evenson tells us, the balance between Parisians and *banlieusards*, or suburbanites, has been steadily reversed. In 1901, the population of Paris stood at 2,700,000, that of the *banlieue* at 955,000. In the following year, nearly 200,000 people are stated to have been living in *meublés*, a form of cheap furnished flats that persisted through the 1930s and that survived at least into the early 1950s, enabling both the provincial newcomer and the foreigner to live comparatively cheaply in the city.

The exodus from the city seems to have begun in 1919, as a result of the introduction of the eight-hour day and the extension of the suburban railway network, and, between 1919 and 1939, by the formation of *cités jardins* on the model of the suburban English Garden City of Letchworth, designed by Ebenezer Howard. Because of the *octrois* – the toll houses on the outskirts of Paris where a tax was collected on goods entering the city – which were still in existence in the mid-thirties, food was cheaper beyond the municipal barriers, inducing many people to move just beyond them, into overcrowded *communes* such as Vanves, Pantin, Aubervilliers, Malakoff. In 1926, there had been as many as 40,000 people living in the old military zone beyond the obsolete fortifications built around the city in 1845; all these *zoniers* had been cleared out by 1932, when on the former *zone* were built a series of HBM blocks (*habitations à bon marché*, quite literally, cheap housing), apartments accommodating up to 120,000 people along the northern edge of the city.

By the previous year, 1931, the balance between Paris and the suburbs had narrowed to 2,900,000 and 2,100,000; and on the eve of the Second World War the two populations stood about equal. However, because of the enormous influx of young provincials to Paris following the Liberation, the figures were temporarily reversed; and during the terrible winter of 1953–4, many were found to be living in temporary edifices, minor *bidonvilles*, or shanty towns, within the limits of the city. Two years later, a quarter of a million families were officially listed as *mal-logés* within the Département de la Seine. In 1970, the population of Paris had declined to 2,600,000, that of the *banlieue* had reached 5,600,000. Since then, this trend has certainly been accelerated.

For instance, following the clearing of the Marais, and the redevelopment of the area as a predominantly middle-class quarter, 20,000 of the original inhabitants were resettled in the suburban *grands ensembles*, complexes of high-rise apartment buildings, schools, and shops built during the fifties and sixties. This process of alienation has been sensitively described by Simenon in his novel *Le Déménagement* – the 'move' from the warm and closely observed sociability of the rue de Turenne to the bleak anonymity of one of the *grands ensembles* south of Paris: Arcueil, Orsay, or Antony. One would be quite hard put to encounter, as one used to, Algerian workers in the small hotels of the rue du Roi-de-Sicile, or Yiddish- or Polish-speaking Jews in and around the rue des Rosiers at the present time; and both the small workshops that cluttered the courtyards of seventeenth-century town houses and palaces and the wholesale establishments, button manufacturers, shops selling *articles de Paris*, garment depots, and even the old clothes' trade, once the staple activities of the IVe, have almost disappeared from the quarter. A few kosher butchers and *one* kosher restaurant in the rue des Rosiers are the sole reminders of what had been until quite recently the oldest Jewish settlement in the city. A little further to the west, the rue des Lombards, the rue de la Verrerie, the rue Saint-Merri, and the rue Quincampoix, once the beat of the most antique prostitutes in Paris, since they became pedestrian precincts (*voies piétonnes*) have lost their *hôtels de passe* and their tiny cafés, and have gained – if that is a gain – couscous restaurants, antique shops, bars, and discos. The odd Algerian café may be found still surviving – but not for long – on rue François-Miron.

Of course, it would be hard to lament the clearance of the old plague spots, the *ilôts insalubres* of the IVe and the IIIe; and, architecturally, the church of Saint-Gervais, released from a clutter of low-roofed hutments, now stands out to full advantage, above its steps, while, with courtyards cleared of the many huts that had invaded them at the time of the Revolution, the *hôtels particuliers* of the Marais can be seen in something of their original splendour. From being an area of small manufacturers and independent artisans, the quarter has been transformed into a balanced mixture of museum and luxury middle-class residence. It is nearly all there to be seen and appreciated. But it is as well to remember that the transformation was made at enormous human cost. The Marais, as an area of social mixture and of varied occupation, is now dead. In 1979, walking to work along the quai Henri IV, I was stopped by a patrol of the CRS, the riot police, who had blocked off a rectangle of streets between Saint-Paul and the quays with four huge police vans, a punitive operation that lasted a whole morning, the aim of which was to clear three families of squatters, each consisting of a mother and two or three small children, from a group of houses designated for improvement, in the rue des Lions Saint-Paul. The Marais has been recovered as a tourists' paradise. But the quarter has lost all warmth and originality.

Long-established artisans, small shopkeepers, café-owners, coal-selling *bougnats*, the employees of the Sorbonne, taxi-drivers, typists, and white-collar workers living in hotels or *meublés* have likewise had to abandon the VIe and the Ve; and a present-day Jean Rhys would now be hard put to afford to spend even a single *night* in one of the small streets off the quai des Grands Augustins. There will be no more novelists of the VIe, for there is no life there any more to write about. The *arrondissement* received its official death warrant as a *quartier populaire* – or at least a *quartier mixte* – with the final destruction, after a long campaign carried out by the locals against the planners, of the old marché Saint-Germain. In June 1980, in the rue de Tournon, where I had lived for twenty years, and in the rue des Quatre-Vents, I could only find *one* tradesman, a *marchand de couleur*, who had been there since the Liberation. All the others had gone, their food shops and small restaurants replaced by boutiques and shops selling Asiatic knick-knacks.

In the neighbouring *arrondissement*, the rue Mouffetard (or what has been left of it), once the most popular market of the Left Bank, and a street of intense sociability, has been given over to tourism, bars, and pornography. Only a few old inn-signs – an oak, the Trois Sergents de la Rochelle – hang as sad, limp reminders of what had once been a triumphal gulley of small shops, barrows, overhanging clothes-lines, and popular eloquence. *Les gens de la Mouffe* have been spirited away, as on a magic carpet, to Sarcelles or to another of the New Towns of the Paris region. Only the big *gendarmerie* barracks and the convents and monasteries behind their tall green *portes cochères* are reminders of the odd mixture that had once constituted the peculiar flavour of the quartier Maubert-Mouffetard: monks and nuns, *gendarmes*, and a population of long-living small shopkeepers, many of them widows, according to Louis Chevalier the oldest female age group in the city. Their place has been taken by young *pied-noir* couples running pizza bars and by elegant antique-dealers.

Following the destruction of les Halles, the rue Saint-Denis, the most authentically Parisian of all streets, and for two hundred years the academy of *l'esprit parisien*, has likewise entirely lost its traditional population of people in the food and drink trades, of *les forts*, people who had been in the same work for generations – and of their concomitant: inexpensive prostitutes. What is left of the quarter is rapidly undergoing a total social transformation, similar to that of the IVe, the former *hôtels de passe* and *meublés* having been converted into high-priced middle-class residences. The old Ier *arrondissement* has by now lost all artisanal character so that the population of the central markets, as depicted successively by Zola, Georges Arnaud, and Simenon (in *La Mort d'Auguste*), would now seem as remote as the memory of the all-night café *Le Chien qui fume*, and the lecherous and potentially violent population, as depicted as late as 1966 by Louis Chevalier in *Les Parisiens*. Even the title of his book would now represent an archaism. The once noisy night streets are silent and almost empty, save perhaps for Gaëtan and Marie-Claire, exercising their poodle and out for a midnight stroll in order to purchase *Le Nouvel-Observateur* and *Charlie-Hébdo* at the nearby revolutionary book-shop-cum-pornography.

Of course, there are still pockets of *les petites gens*, of Parisians recognizable to Eugène Dabit and to Raymond Queneau and to other populist writers, in parts of the Xe and at the eastern end of the XIIe. But the Left Bank XIVe and XVe have been totally recolonized; and there is no longer any hint of the transport workers who once inhabited the rue des Favorites, off the *métro* Convention. The Javel quarter has, thanks to the Front de Seine, jumped up several classes as well as several levels. No place any more for the humble and eccentric characters of MacOrlan's *La Tradition de minuit*. The XIVe at the present day would suit Lenin and his petit-bourgeois tastes even better than it did when he was living in the rue Marie-Rose; and he would have as neighbours the widest possible choice of university teachers of various Marxist persuasions.

Only the XIXe, the XXe, and the XVIIIe have retained something of their original character, and Eugène Dabit's Belleville-Ménilmontant of the 1930s (*Banlieues de Paris*) can still be vaguely recognized, at least in accent, impudence, independence, and ingenuity at *bricolage* – every sort of repair and fixing – in the rue Ramponeau, or off the place des Fêtes, or on both sides of the boulevard de Belleville. *La Vie devant soi* was written in the mid-1970s, and still described a mixed population of poor Jewish tailors – mostly from North Africa – of Algerians, and long-limbed Sénégalais. But even here the high-rise flats are beginning to point up menacingly on the heights and halfway down the steep slopes. It does not seem very likely that Belleville-Ménilmontant, the Paris of the Commune, and la Goutte-d'Or, the Paris of the FLN, will remain for long undisturbed. The middle-class armies from the north will soon be spilling down the hill, engulfing the little artisans' two-storeyed houses of the rue des Amandiers, the rue de la Mare, the rue des Partants, and the rue Soleillet. When these north-eastern areas are engulfed, the traditional Paris, based on the *esprit de quartier* and on a series of villages, thriving on familiarity and gossip, and in which even shopping represents a social function, will be quite dead. Paris will have become more or less a single-class city, reserved for the very affluent and the very ambitious.

Where then have the Parisians gone? The older, the more recalcitrant, the most intractable have *died*. The rest have gone, reluctantly, to Alphaville. Professor Evenson does not attempt to disguise the full horror of Sarcelles – the biggest and most conspicuous of the *grand ensemble* projects which has become a symbol of both the physical and social shortcomings of these suburban developments. She describes the alienation, loneliness, monotony, and despair that French journalists have called *la sarcellite*, as if it were a disease, and she quotes to great effect Christiane Rochefort's eloquent novel, *Les Petits Enfants du siècle*, an account of growing up in one of the *grands ensembles* as described by an observant sixteen-year-old girl.

What she does not state *en toutes lettres* is amply conveyed in the horror of the photographs: the vast concrete coils of the development called la Grande Borne, with its enforced walking precinct, dominated by twenty-foot stucco statues of ducks and geese, huge wall-paintings of cuddly animals, immense wall-portraits of Kafka (of course) and Rimbaud (such a homely couple), a *panachage* of a French Disneyland and of a sociologist's *ville radieuse*, the rectangular blocks painted in bright colours. They are all there: not only Sarcelles, an initiative of the Prefecture of Police, but also Cergy-Pontoise (rewarded with a prefecture), Saint-Quentin-en-Yvelines (which also gets a prefect, a very eighteenth-century concept of giving an identity to a town) – particularly sad, as it rises on the edges of the jumble of small individual houses and villas that had once been the railway town of Trappes – Melun-Sénart, Marne-la-Vallée.

The social cost of Alphaville can be gauged from the high teenage crime rate in Sarcelles, with its rare café and its lack of an identifiable centre, in the *chronique judiciaire* of the Paris dailies and weeklies. No doubt any roof is better than none, any *grand ensemble* is preferable to a *bidonville*. Yet, time and again, Professor Evenson returns to the preference shown by the Parisian artisan, ever since the 1900s and the 1920s, for the single house, the tiny villa, even a converted railway wagon or an old bus or green tram, pathetic grabs at privacy and individuality that mushroomed along the main lines, often on quite unsuitable terrain, and denied most of the amenities, on the wide steppes north of Paris, and in sight of the Warsaw express and the *Étoile du Nord*: a jumble of irregularity, of artisanal fantasy, turrets, minarets, grottoes, plaster cloisters, Gothic towers in yellow bricks, that may be seen flashing by, in irregular lines, interrupted by the solid cube-like blocks of the *grands ensembles*, as one approaches Paris by train, from the north or the east. Life in the unfinished villa, in Drancy or Garches, as depicted in Queneau's *Le Chiendent*, was pretty uncomfortable; but at least one knew one's neighbours living up the muddy, waterlogged lanes; and there was even a wooden café that specialized in *bifteck-frites*. There is, after all, quite a rich literature of this chaotic type of *banlieue*, the scattered *bicoques*, or shanties, of the 1910s, the 1920s, and 1930s, in the valley of the Orge, in the Pays de France, in the valley of the Marne, from Landru to Queneau, from

Dabit to Ben Barka, from Simenon to Sarrazin, from Weidmann to Fallet, from *faux manoir normand* to crenallated Maison Larousse, the literature of individualism, eccentricity and of do-it-yourself, the jumbled styles of *le facteur* Cheval and his many suburban imitators, and the tiny follies below the railway viaduct at Viroflay. But, apart from Alphaville and Christiane Rochefort, what can one expect of the *grands ensembles* other than inarticulate despair, vandalism, and teenage violence?

Evenson's study is equally informative on the development of the Paris transport system. The suburban railway lines came surprisingly early: Sceaux, in 1846, Bourg-la-Reine and Orsay in 1857, Boissy-Saint-Léger, in 1859. The Invalides line to Versailles was electrified in 1900. The Petite Ceinture was started in 1851, the Grande Ceinture, in 1875. Predictably, ever since the 1930s, the Gare Saint-Lazare has remained far the largest point of entry and exit. There is an evocative section on river transport, the *bateaux mouches* and the *hirondelles*, the former starting as a Lyonnais venture. The author states that the *bateaux mouches* were suppressed in 1934, but I can remember taking one from the pont de Sèvres to the pont des Arts in the following year.

We move from the trams to the familiar snout-nosed buses, with their open rear platforms, an invitation to sociability, conversation, and verbal fantasy on the part of inventive *contrôleurs*, one of the few places where one could encounter Paris police on terms of affability, and the stage too of Queneau's wonderful *Exercices de style, ligne 24*. But Evenson is best of all on the *Métro*, and this is as it should be, for it is the most poetical form of Parisian transport. The *Métro* was carrying 400 million passengers by 1914, 761 million by 1938, over a billion by 1941, 1.5 billion in 1946, its peak year. Her account is one of steady advance and improvement, from grinding *rames* to the silent rubber-tyred trains of the present day. It would require considerable nostalgia to regret the passing of the old, clanging scalloped coaches of the Nord-Sud, as they emerged from under the Seine. But how I wished that she had evoked the little Dubonnet-man, and the flickering *Dubo, Dubon, Dubonnet*, the emblem of the late 1930s and the insistent accompaniment to the packed *métros* of the Occupation years! And how I wished that she had quoted the advertisements and *métro*-poems of Raymond Queneau! Generally, her account is so accurate and so well reseached, one hesitates even to question it; but the Gare d'Orsay did *not* connect up with the Gare de Lyon; it was the prolongation of the line from the Gare d'Austerlitz, so that, at one time, the Sud-Express, from Madrid, terminated in the centre of Paris.

I wish too that Evenson had made greater use of literary material in her descriptions of the city and its suburbs. Zola is all very well. But why Sartre? Why the boring, self-indulgent Gertrude Stein ('*we* lived', 'in our time, *we all* . . .'). What of *Poil de Carotte* and *Bubu de Montparnasse*, of Jean Galtier-Boissière and of Jules Romains? I wish too that she had taken greater care of the spelling of French words, especially in her bibliography, from which, unaccountably, she omits Louis Chevalier's powerful and angry *L'Assassinat de Paris*. For *that* is the subject of her own careful, beautifully illustrated, compassionate and very human book, the work, surprisingly, of a professor of architecture.

PART III

Impressions from Elsewhere

13

Ixelles[*]

IN MY earlier broadcasts† I have been concerned with the works of French novelists and of novelists writing in French about particular localities at certain periods of time; and I have taken the specific case of Raymond Queneau as a novelist of habit, of fixed and restricted itineraries, and, thus, of reassurance, the reassurance to be derived from the sheer unpretentiousness and prudent timidity of *la vie à petite échelle* (in Queneau's case, that imposed by the *promenade*, the *planisphère*, and the *ligne de Métro*). If, to take another example, René Fallet and his young friends occasionally venture out of Villeneuve-Saint-Georges, on their Vespas, acquired in the full flush of post-Liberation optimism, to display themselves in Paris, their point of entry is predictably the pont de Charenton, their maximum penetration will be Strasbourg-Saint-Denis. Queneau's *habitués* can take a Sunday walk to the Bois de Sainte-Cucufa, just as an inhabitant of Viroflay will find himself impelled, as on the lines of a tramcar, upwards, to conclude at the ponds of Ville-d'Avray. Or a *petit-employé*, living in a large block of flats facing on the *ligne de Sceaux* at les Baconnets, will be drawn, Sunday afternoon, towards the concrete-bottomed ponds, the minuscule concrete-edged artificial islands, connected to the mainland by tiny exotic bridges in cement, disguised as rustic and gnarled wood, and decorated by doll's-house *châteaux-forts* also in cement, and painted red, yellow, blue and chocolate, of the

* First published in *Promenades* (1980).
† See note on p. 56 above.

Bois de Verrière. Likewise, *Les Ibis*, a concrete-and-stucco-tamed jungle, the wild life provided by stone cranes and herons, bending forward in drinking position, three ponds, two islands, a footbridge in Japanese style, will draw out the family units from the neighbouring villas of le Vésinet and Chatou. What itinerary could be more predictable, more reassuring, and more banal, than that of the *promenade de dimanche* in the suburbs of Paris!

I am reminded, too, of the monumental diary kept by a French archivist, in several scores of schoolboy notebooks (all marked *Préfecture de l'Oise*), relating the clockwork mechanism of his inverted day: *me suis levé 18 h., me suis lavé 18h2, me suis habillé 18h5, ai mangé 2 tartines de pain d'épice 18h7, suis sorti sur le Cours 18h12, ai suivi le chemin des remparts, ai croisé au niveau du tabac M. un Tel, notaire, au gilet duquel il manquait le troisième bouton en partant du bas 18h19, ne l'ai pas salué 18h20*, and so on, day after day. In this instance, only the framework remained, left behind to his successor, with empty tins of Abeille, used for cooking, and rotting socks.

So I too want to propose the framework of a novel that has not been written and that I will not be likely to write.

The framework is the commune of Ixelles, one of the nineteen independent municipalities which, together, form what is called *le Grand Bruxelles*, or Greater Brussels. The period is from about September 1944, after the liberation of the Belgian capital, until sometime in the middle 1950s.

The axis of Ixelles, the chaussée d'Ixelles, runs steeply down towards the place Émile Flagey and then down towards two ponds. The ponds, known to the local inhabitants as *les étangs d'Ixelles*, are part of Brussels's lost river. They are edged with concrete and a narrow sward enclosed by chains – the permissible terrain of ducks, but not of couples or of children. The concrete paths round the ponds offer two itineraries: the northern route, skirting the RTB building, the Maison de la Radio, and the Église Sainte-Croix; and the southern route, via the avenue du Général de Gaulle. Before 1945, this was called the avenue de la Cascade: the waterfall runs through a concrete conduit from the upper pond into the lower one, at the level of the causeway which divides the two ponds.

At the opening of these two routes, at the western tip of the lower pond, is a very ornate statue, one I would describe as being in *le style Léopold II*, together with a fountain that no longer works, but which, at one time, must have been supplied with water from the lower pond. The statue is of Till Eulenspiegel and was erected in memory of Charles de Coster, the nineteenth-century Belgian writer who made Till Eulenspiegel an incarnation of the Flemish folk spirit. This statue is, I suppose, as reassuring to generations of young Ixellois and Ixelloises as that of Peter Pan in Kensington Gardens is to young inhabitants of London.

Whichever route one takes, the paths lead implacably towards the squat, chrome-coloured building of the Abbaye de la Cambre. This is set in small, formal, seventeenth-century gardens, with box hedges, an *orangerie* that is not doing very well in the damp climate, and three avenues of clipped trees. The central avenue was presumably for the local important people – *le gratin bruxellois* – and the two outer ones for the less important ones, *le menu peuple*.

It is possible to push on beyond the Abbaye de la Cambre: to climb the steep approach to the avenue Louise and thence to the Bois de la Cambre. Or it is possible to take an alternative route to the avenue Louise, a little lower down the street, reaching that particular *voie triomphale* of the Brussels upper bourgeoisie, at the level of La Taverne Louise, a very, very quiet place with plants in highly polished brass containers, and small alcoves in which there are tables bearing pink lampshades that give a pink tint to the pages of *Le Soir* and *La Dernière Heure*.

But the Abbaye de la Cambre is a frontier, an ultimate temple of reassurance at which inhabitants of Ixelles will turn back homewards. They can, though, extend their limits, in the other direction, by going back up the chaussée d'Ixelles, to the porte de Namur. This can be described as the checkpoint from the centre of Brussels into Ixelles, but I think the *maison communale*, the town hall, is a much better starting-point. This unpretentious, cream-coloured, three-storeyed building is clearly the centre of what is an identifiable small town, with its own *bourgmestre*, or burgomaster, and its own flag.

Les étangs d'Ixelles provide for the Ixellois a terrain designed for promenading, entertainment, deep conversation, vigorous exercise, meditation, and reading. Its iron or concrete seats provide opportunities for the closed conversation, *à deux*, of the approaches to love – the preliminary exploration of another person's life. The pram-borne population, too, has been given an ideal terrain. And, because of the presence of the very large and modern Église Sainte-Croix, it is a terrain for imposing funeral processions, headed by uniformed brass bands, playing Handel's Dead March from *Saul*, or the oddly unsuitable, fast-moving, and joyful 'La Brabançonne', the Belgian national anthem. Also to be seen are the early-morning and evening *pénitentes* and, on Sundays, families in groups, *en grappes*.

The complete itinerary, from the *maison communale* to the low-lying Abbaye de la Cambre, passes, as I have said, through the cascading chaussée d'Ixelles, which is a street lined with artisan establishments and small shops: *merceries, pâtisseries, ressemelage, blanchisserie, cordonnerie, papeterie, marchand de journaux*; shops selling the profusion of chocolate, tobaccos, cheroots, and small cigars that give to Brussels its specific rich odour and colour, and a great many cafés and *tavernes*: Stella Artois, Gueuse-Lambic, Bières de la Meuse. Interspersed between *le petit commerce* are the daily whitened front steps of dwelling-houses, more numerous in the village-like streets leading off the chaussée, rue du Couloir and others, small irregular houses in dark reds, whitewashed, cream-coloured to match the trams, lime-green, the windows picked out in black or in white surrounds, very solid, and low on the ground, with low roofs in curling red tiles; at the side of each door, two or three bells, with visiting cards beside each, bearing the double-names of families. It would be hard to find a more enclosed and predictable landscape: each artisan, each shopkeeper with a name, each householder with a double-name, each café and *taverne* containing its immutable clientele, seen through the large windows at all hours, the numbers expanding with evening. At the upper end, between the porte de Namur and the place Communale, hangs a pervading and rather appetizing smell of *frites*, the other component that, along with tobacco and chocolate, forms the specific and inimitable *parfum de Bruxelles*. The architecture of the chaussée itself, and even more of the streets at right angles to it, is semi-rural, such as might be encountered in the Tournésis, or in small towns like Leuze, on the road between France and the capital, or in villages in the province de Namur, houses the plastic qualities and the even colour-washes of which – beige, russet, lime-green, cream, white, dark green and black, red and black – seem to cry out for an appropriate painter.

At the level of the ponds, the *étangs*, though, the architecture changes. It is either *style Léopold II*, the Belgian equivalent to High Victorian, or the ironwork fantasies of Brussels domestic architecture of the 1920s, which is a period that marked the city more permanently than any other capital – at least that I know. There is a kaleidoscope of stained glass in diamonds and lozenges, *modern-style* fretwork, and hints of a discreet, fussy, and, perhaps, rather uninspired Anglomania of a purely bourgeois variety.

If the chaussée d'Ixelles is *artisanale*, the area adjacent to the *étangs d'Ixelles* is solidly professional middle-class, while the Abbaye de la Cambre keeps to itself, at the far end, surviving as a reminder of Flemish Gothic, with rather heavy but simple seventeenth- and eighteenth-century additions.

The chaussée d'Ixelles is the street that supplies all the basic family needs of the Ixellois; it is the equivalent to the main street of a provincial town. Though its walls are often covered with election posters, it would be very hard to discover an urban landscape more obviously unrevolutionary. Instead, there is the enclosed, protected, gradually discoverable domain of habit, prudent friendship, careful observation of the kind that addresses itself to the whiteness of the front step or to the brilliance of a brass door-knocker. Violence is controlled, with a recognized vocabulary of mounting insult, and is confined to the later hours of a Saturday night. The results are little more than broken glasses, broken chairs, and an exchange of blows.

To emphasize both the provinciality, the continuity, and the sturdy individualism of the family unit, Ixelles contains an unusually high proportion of domestic pets: dogs that, on Saturdays, get drunk with their masters; cats in attitudes of comfortable and possessive repose on front steps and window-sills; canaries and other tiny bright-coloured birds are displayed in elaborate cages in windows emphasized by a fringe of lace curtain. Unrevolutionary, self-confident, slightly old-fashioned and dowdy, Ixelles has been quite untouched by the ugly mushrooming of the nearby *quartier de l'Europe*, the area of the offices of the European Community.

The itinerary of Ixelles is one to be explored at dawn, when the mist is still lying over the ponds of the Abbaye de la Cambre, before even the dustcarts are out, and only those who have worked through the night are enjoying the peculiar luxury of a walk through the sleeping commune. A few yellow lights of cafés are already showing, a couple of ghostly trams huddle together and wait in the place Émile Flagey, and a scattering of lights can be seen at the top of the otherwise black and gloomy Maison de la Radio. A night-worker on the treadmill of the Saint-Nicolas trade or of that of Easter, has ready for delivery to L'Innovation, the chain store in the rue Neuve, a score of freshly painted toys. He is his own master and, like an eighteenth-century artisan, able to regulate his life to his own lonely, eccentric pattern of work, deadened even to the hourly changing sounds of the working day.

This is the hour at which, all at once, birds break into twittering and song, the ducks take their heads from under their wings and fly into the waters of the ponds, and the sea-birds appear from the north, a reminder of how close the area is to a sandy, indented coast, and to the wandering inlets of the anarchical river Schelde.

The hour approaching daybreak is the moment when cities show themselves in a different way from that seen in broad daylight. In Ixelles, privileged walkers see, deployed for their exclusive enjoyment, the squat contours cut out in the silhouette of the Abbaye de la Cambre; the modern Église Sainte-Croix with a disguise of the unpretentious outlines of a purely rural church; and the radio building lends the brooding menace of a place of torture, a place where terrible things happen in the night, the evidence of which is removed in the morning, along with the empty cigarette-packets and ash.

The pre-dawn light also reveals the stately magnificence of an empty and silent avenue Louise, stretching out to a full length, like an exercise in perspective, and its solid houses still dark cliffs, enclosing a black macadam stream.

These are the timid openings of a new day; one, for most, so full of hope, but also one displaying, like the offerings left, blandly and as if in laughter, on an early-morning beach by the receding tide, the unbearable evidence of crimes committed under cover of night. At the approach to the avenue Louise a tiny hand protrudes from the lid of a crammed dustbin, in front of an affluent, unsympathetic, tall, and over-ornate apartment block. When the lid is removed, a minute, doll-like, quite naked girl is revealed – a diminutive Bruxelloise-to-be that never saw the day.

And so there still lingers fear in an itinerary so reassuring in full day-light, when the gardens of the *abbaye*, in the hesitant half-light still dark jungles, are swept clear of mystery and of the suspected presence of objects hideous to see.

Apart, then, from the night-worker and his companions – those who sat up with him, as he worked at his lathe – who will see the urban dawn? First of all, the dying who, somehow, have managed to live through the night, not by choice, but from the doubtful mercy of relentless biological processes; secondly, the parents, husbands, wives, children, close friends of the recently dead who have been awakened at this hour by the incessant ringing of the telephone, followed by the implacable, unanswerable short sentence. The mourner dresses hur-riedly and rushes out into the silent streets in search of a taxi, to reach one of the vast hospitals on the periphery of the city – a building which is a mass of lights and enveloping warmth, a building which never sleeps.

Murder and death have taken place before the city has done its toilet and has tidied away such inadmissible and disturbing secrets.

The dawn itinerary offers the reassurance of an entirely predictable movement, hour by hour, as Ixelles, like a lightly sleeping Gulliver, slowly stirs from slumber. It stretches an arm or leg, sending out, like a prudent advance guard, a brightly lit single tram, its destination board shining a filmy yellow and black in the half-light, or sending out a fast-moving postal van, with a golden hunting-horn on its side.

Another advance guard is a boy on an elaborate bicycle. It has many gears, with a *dérailleur*, and has handlebars shaped like curling ram's horns. A kingfisher flash of yellow, blues, and greens, the boy threads his machine through the still lighted streets, delivering here *Le Drapeau rouge*, there *La Libre Belgique*. Each will have its readers in neigh-bouring houses in the same street.

In 1944 and 1945, the windows of those houses sprouted unaccus-tomed adornment, a rival to green plants in brass pots or to brightly coloured birds in cages: photographs of Léopold III in a general's uniform, or of his brother, Prince Charles, *en civil*, in mufti, announced, like flags, contrary allegiances. It says much for the placidity of the Ixellois that none of these windows was ever broken. In any case, there would not have been any point, as everybody knew, even without such display, where his neighbours stood on *la question du roi*: *Léopoldiste* or *anti-Léopoldiste*.

The huge tricolour flag flies reassuringly limp in the morning cold, or cracks merrily in the east wind, over the Palais du Roi. Delicious smells of rich coffee and of chocolate emerge from the early *crémeries* of the chaussée d'Ixelles. One or two *pâtissiers*, still in the white overalls and white caps of nightwork, can be seen coming out into the street to put the handles on the outside doors of their shops.

The ornamental gates of the Bois de la Cambre, surmounted by two lazy, yawning lions, are already open. The lions, each on top of his plinth, lie spread out, with claws outstretched, inviting isolated groups of men and women exercising their dogs, and athletes and enthusiasts running downhill through the mist, towards the big lake, which is still a great, whitish hole, like an inverted cloud, and soon lost to the sight of the runners as they disappear down the straight avenue of ghostly trees.

Perhaps if it is the specifically silent dawn of a Sunday, with an extra quality of stillness, accentuated by the absence of bustle, there might also be seen stepping gingerly along the chaussée d'Ixelles, holding on to walls, projections, and cornices, zigzagging uncertainly, as if deprived of rudder and internal gyroscope, a few rather battered figures, men in caps or dented bowlers, their feet catching in their woollen scarves. The debris of a Saturday night spent in the rue Haute or in other warm and noisy pleasure-spots of the quartier des Marolles, they are now washed towards home. Now they are in search of an ultimate drink, to enable them to put on a better countenance to a questioning or shruggingly resigned household. Or lonely British soldiers, cleared right out down below by implacably systematic Luxembourgeoises – contents of pockets, cigarettes, pay book, for Brussels is one of the world capitals of *faux papiers*, and any *pièce d'identité* will have an immediately negotiable value, there and then, *derrière le comptoir* or, at the most remote, at a café round the corner – and so full of anger and belgophobia, people best avoided, as they grope their way, shouting incoherent threats in thick Glaswegian, to the Leave Centres that, at one time, in post-Liberation years, existed place Sainte-Croix, a population unwelcome and fortunately transient, the presence of which, in my own account, is merely designed to fix a given locality in a specific point of time. Soldiers – save the rare Red Army ones – appeared incongruous among the solidly and tranquilly civilian population of the *commune*, a place that, one felt, would have liked, like so many of its unambitious inhabitants, to have lived right outside great events, or, at worst, on their more distant fringes.

But when I go back to Brussels and to Ixelles now, I find my narrative has been interrupted. There has been a death, perhaps several deaths, creating, here and there, holes behind façades, putting new, unfamiliar names on shop signs, new figures behind elaborately polished counters, serving new drinks, and making of myself a stranger all the more lost and wistful, once back in the geography so utterly familiar and apparently untouched.

A family, having lost the carpenter head of the household, has had a series of moves. At first, it was a series of moves within Ixelles, away from the comfortable familiarity of the rue du Couloir, in which the only previous move had been from one side of the street, No 19, to the house immediately opposite, No 24, a change entailing the rise from basement to ground-floor level. The next move, however, had been to an address one or two streets nearer to the place Sainte-Croix, and to the ponds.

This family of toymakers had always managed so well to live outside conventional time, outside work discipline, out of reach of the media, indeed, well beyond most collectivities, huddled within an underground of semi-basement or contiguous *rez-de-chaussée*, or on-the-level-with-the-street, topography. It was unthinkable, for instance, to imagine them living on even the first floor or having friends who reached up to such heights. It was as if a staircase leading upwards beyond the ground floor had always been something quite beyond their common experience.

They enjoyed a very exclusive circle of friendship, based on a rare combination of individualism and eccentricity, though eccentricity quite unstudied because it was quite unconscious, because they simply did not judge people as other people might have judged them, being totally, indeed quite joyfully, immune to the power of emulation and to the pull of envy. They were people joined together by relative lack of success, who could only move downhill, as if drawn to the ponds and to the church by the force of gravity.

Perhaps, too, the move farther downhill had been due to a veritable *dégringolade*, a tumble, as a result of the loss of the leading carpenter, the small master of the fragile yet utterly contented enterprise of toy-making for L'Innovation, the chain store in the rue Neuve. Or perhaps it had been dictated in some way by the *curé* of Sainte-Croix, about the only person vaguely in a position of authority from whom these people were willing to take advice and from whom, every now and then, out of the toy season, when there was little demand for toys, they would accept help beyond such meagre benefits as they may have drawn from the Belgian state.

Then, all at once, or so I gathered as I called here and there, ringing bells against which there were still familiar names, they had moved away completely, right out of Ixelles into an almost alien Uccle, and a long way beyond the frontier of the avenue Louise. The reasons I do not know, save that they must have been awful, and compelling.

Perhaps the move was dictated by need, perhaps also by some steady, implacable change in the social composition of Ixelles, no doubt subjected to pressures from below the hill, from the invasive, pitiless marshlands of *l'Europe*, sending predatory outriders of Eurocrats up the heights and then down the chaussée d'Ixelles, driving out the artisans and shopkeepers and independent folk and giving over the doll's-house-like buildings to readers of fashionable left-wing weeklies and fortnightlies.

I could, however, vaguely recall that Uccle had not been totally alien territory, at least to the carpenter's wife. She had been in the habit of going there once a month, to see the *commanditaire*, the sleeping partner, of the toymaking enterprise, a middle-class lady who was occasionally referred to, in deferential but quite impersonal terms, and who, for reasons that remained obscure, had something to do with the ebb and flow – more ebb than flow nine months of the year – of orders for the home-made wooden toys. Perhaps then, in the last resort, it had been this mysterious figure who had come to the rescue and had been the cause of the move to Uccle.

The façades of Ixelles are still much the same, but I no longer know what lies behind them. I can no longer look down through the iron grating of an area, to spy friends in a lighted room below ground. I can only walk alone in streets that were once inhabited by people I knew.

So I have, indeed, the *cadre*, the elementary framework, of a novel – one well set in time and place: the second half of the 1940s and the early 1950s, in the Commune of Ixelles. But how to conclude it? It simply peters out in emptiness, absence, indifference, and uncertainty: '*Oh . . . ils sont partis; il y a longtemps de cela. On ne sait pas où.*' Or: '*Cela ne doit pas être bien loin. C'était après que le fils a fait son service.*'

Left behind, and pathetically intact, is much of the décor; also, perhaps, a few scattered witnesses to the warmth, simplicity, and generosity of lives one once tentatively shared and explored. But life, change, ageing, readjustment to the sense of loss, do not respond to such artistic imperatives as might be dictated by personal memory and by the desire to take up the book again, perhaps after years of neglect, at the page at which one had left off.

The Commune d'Ixelles which I have tried to immobilize, at a precise point in time, I could then have peopled with a very enriching and completely illogical collectivity of *marginaux*, of marginal people, marginal because their ties did not, in any way, respond to the ortho-doxies of sociology, or politics, or common origins, or trade, or pro-fessional relations, or even sports activities, or shared leisure (only the father and the son took to the *pistes cyclables*, for trips to Malines and Antwerp, an enthusiasm not shared either by the wife or by their gener-ally sedentary friends, one of the most regular of whom no sooner mounted a bicycle than he fell off it); all they really had in common was a commendable ability to exist quite outside any known or accepted orthodoxy.

It is a story that has moved on without consulting me, but still leaving me with a heritage of enrichment, and with the warmth of once shared experience – a great deal of it bizarre, most of it quite outside the ordinary run of things.

Perhaps this is all one can ask of a place: to be the reassuring *cadre* of past exploration, and of the memory of common friendship and shared reactions over a regular, predictable, but inverted pattern of night and day – the febrile industry of November and December, and again of March and April; the terrible doldrums of a long, long summer and early autumn, with meals of bread, butter, *saucisson*, and coffee – beerless months.

We all live with history, and we live in history, and the frontiers between history and imagination are very little more than Chinese screens, removable at will. And a historian is a person who walks his chosen itineraries with his eyes open. It is up to the novelist to pick up the pieces, to tie up the loose ends, and to cap the edifice with a conclusion suited to what has gone before.

I have lingered in Ixelles, as much as anything else, in search of myself and my friends and of their compact circle. I have lingered in search of those who, during the German occupation, opted for the wrong side, without full awareness of what they were doing. It might have been merely for a pair of long leather boots, a very rare and prestigious luxury in the Belgium of 1942, or to satisfy some minor, passing, personal craving – for chocolate, tobacco, or coffee. It might have been motivated by the desire to get even with some Jewish middle-man for an imagined economic ill dating back to the late 1930s. All these actions were forgivable because the people who did them were basically innocent; indeed, eventually, these people were forgiven. I have lingered as much in search of them as of, as yet, an unwritten *roman ixellois* or, in the wider but surely more profitable context, of the very largely inexistent *roman belge*.

Neither, of course, is for me, a historian, a witness, and a fellow traveller with those whose greatest ambition was to be left alone to go their own, mainly unsuccessful way, to write. All I can do is to sketch in the framework, and to set up the stage sets and the scenery.

I can provide perhaps a dozen or so characters: Jean and Émilie; Poum, their son; Marcel; Charles; *la femme de Charles* (she did not appear to have had any other name); Reinette, Marcel's girl-friend; Marcel's mother (an extremely long-suffering woman); *le Cosaque*, a constant inhabitant of a fantasy world far removed from the rue du Couloir.

I can add a suggested chronology that is bizarre because it is mostly back-to-front, turning night into day, with the passage of the night-hours witnessed from below street level. I can even provide a basic dialogue of '*belgicismes*', illustrating a naïve and insistent nationalism, neither Walloon nor Flemish, nor even *bruxellois*, not even purely *ixellois*, but specifically Belgian; a nationalism one associates with small and rather self-conscious countries.

Then I can complete it with a topography that will include a childhood in Namur, a mother unidentified, but supposedly from the German-speaking enclave round Eupen (Jean's mother); another purely rural childhood in Marienbourg, of farming stock, and looking it (Émilie); common origin in Charleroi, with matching accent (Marcel and Reinette); Ixelles-born Charles and *la femme de Charles*; in the case of Jean, an apparently unrelated succession of jobs, including various unspecified ones in the port quarter of Antwerp, despite a total lack of Flemish.

There would be the seasonal descent to L'Innovation, and occasional sorties down to the quartier des Marolles, in search of collective enjoyment. Long walks would be taken, right through the Bois de la Cambre, to the *commune* of Boitsfort or even to the forest of Groenendael.

Finally, there would be the fabulous and never-to-be-forgotten adventure of *l'Exode*, in the summer of 1940, ending with six months or more in a sunny vineyard and small farm somewhere in the Département du Gers, in the south-west of France. This is an event which, through the years, has acquired the expanding proportions of a legend, endlessly repeated and embellished, and involving the earliest experience of the then infant Poum. A desire is often expressed to return to the Gers, to thank the farmer and his family, but this desire will never be realized because it is quite unrealizable.

Back, then, to reality, to the rue du Couloir and the firmly marked frontiers of that small enclave, the Commune d'Ixelles, a coloured island in a multicoloured agglomeration of nearly a score of other municipal republics, forming that strange, shapeless, and disputatious entity, gradually eating up the surrounding Flemish countryside, of *le Grand Bruxelles*.

And there is that even stranger, more varied federation of city states joined together by rich farmlands and by many watercourses, sandy pine forests, abandoned *corons*, or mining villages, like cities of the desert, pyramidal coal wastes, strung together by trams, buses, and trains of the CFB, the last two marked merely 'B', the most convincing of national affirmations.

The *royaume de Belgique* itself is a quilted patchwork of immense historical variety, tied together as much by intermarriage across the linguistic borders, by common cultural attitudes, by common reactions to others, and, above all, by common reactions to immediate neighbours: the Dutch are an object of constant criticism – a mean lot, given to endless litigation on the subject of the navigation of the Schelde; the French are seen as arrogant, patronizing, and even sneering; and there is a common indifference to most other nationalities.

This reaction to others is characterized, too, by a certain *esprit frondeur*; a desire never to be taken in; a very basic common sense; a refusal to be unduly impressed, whether by uniform, titles, or literary reputations; a large reserve of scepticism; a sense of humour, inclined to the scatological; drinking habits that tend to be uninhibited and, above all, very noisy; an appetite always considerable and normally not easily satisfied; a monarchy which is touchingly popular and middle-class.

Perhaps Ixelles is, at this very moment, secreting its own novelist. Or perhaps all such potential witnesses have become self-elected *émigrés*, who have moved west, right out of the comforting, and backbiting, circle of restricted national experience and national bickering, to evoke Ixelles with deprecatory laughter, and with apologies for a garment unfashionably provincial, despite its modern cut, and so to be discarded in the artificial, rather wearisome conformity of a zealously adopted Parisian ambience, speech, attitude, and condescension.

14

Marseille[*]

THE PLACE of Marseille in French literature is rather an ambivalent and a contrasting one, in that it figures in very different aspects. On the one hand, it is, first of all, a *lieu de passage*, a place to pass through, coming or going; and, on the other hand, it is a somewhat secretive resident community – a place to live in.

In the 1930s and, I think, until quite recently, Marseille has been good for a laugh, at least with Parisians; indeed, one might even say this was part of the city's export industry, along with soap and cooking oil, via Marcel Pagnol and his creations – Marius, Fanny, and César – and, of course, those two great actors and comedians, Fernandel and Raimu. And, again, there are the joke picture postcards of conversations on the Canebière, which is the main street of Marseille, leading down to the port, at the quai des Belges.

I am sometimes tempted to think that the joke was actually on the Parisians: the inhabitants of Marseille especially thriving under this convenient disguise of levity, loquacity, and mendacity, 'talking big', exaggerating, telling what the locals call *la galéjade* – the tall story. *La galéjade*, seen as a national southern characteristic, must have satisfied in some way the very relative verbal sobriety and reticence of the native-born Parisian, and of those recently converted to 'Parisianism'.

The mixture of much-publicized corruption and inefficiency, however, that seemed to characterize the municipality, the police, the

---

[*] First published in *Promenades* (1980).

Renseignements généraux, the fire brigade,[1] and the Prefecture of the Bouches-du-Rhône, as revealed in such national events as the burning down of the Hôtel de Noailles, boulevard d'Athènes, or the assassination, on the Canebière, of King Alexander of Yugoslavia and Louis Barthou, undoubtedly served to harden this Parisian vision of *manque de sérieux* when applied to the Second City (and there was even some suggestion of fraud arising out of that claim). It was also a comfortable way of discrediting, at least to one's own satisfaction, a place that, throughout its immensely rich history, had shown itself again and again quite capable of living and prospering in the *absence* of Paris and *without* Paris. Certainly, as a result of such firmly held attitudes, there was little hope of any eminent Marseillais (at least since Thiers) ever being taken seriously in the capital, as some of the leading Protestant politicians from the port were later to discover to their disadvantage. Indeed, twenty years or so after the king's murder, the appointment, as an *expert*, in one of Marie Besnard's three trials for murder, of a Marseillais toxicologist, with the unfortunate name of Médaille, was taken, by pretty well the whole of the Parisian press, as a guarantee that the *enquête* would go wrong, as, indeed, it did.[2] I can recall, too, at the time of the Liberation, the genuine indignation of my friends in Roubaix, people of widely different political beliefs, at the appointment, as Commissaire Régional du Nord, of a Marseillais; the Nord, they would complain bitterly, was a serious place, where people *worked*.

Indeed, I think what may further have contributed to this Parisian – and more generally northern – myth about the Second City and its inhabitants, extending it downwards to include Belleville, Ménilmontant, Clichy, and the industrial suburbs, was the creation of the *congés payés* in the summer of 1936. *La cité phocéenne* – already established as a particularly hoary joke, the North French equivalent of a shaggy-dog story – now further became associated, especially in retrospect, with leisure, with holidays, with walking about and taking

---

[1] Though doubts about its efficiency could be expressed also by inhabitants. '"Tant que nous aurons une mairie socialiste,"' states Pagnol's uncle Jules, '"il n'y aura pas de pompiers. Je l'ai dit cent fois à Joseph." Et c'était vrai, car il l'avait dit un jour sur la terrasse, en lisant son journal . . .' (Marcel Pagnol, *Le Temps des secrets*).
[2] See my book *A Second Identity* (1969), 'The Memoirs of Marie Besnard', pp. 287–95.

the air, with eating squids in the sun or swimming off one of the little, rather dusty beaches, below the Pharo. The Parisian holiday-maker, whether clerk or metalworker, in typical Parisian imperialism, could only assume that, as *he* was on holiday, everyone else must be similarly occupied, indeed, that the whole of Marseille, in its vast bowl facing seawards, had been especially laid out as a pleasure-ground for his benefit. And it would have been most unlikely that he would ever have torn himself away from the *corniches*, the Vieux Port, and the quai des Belges, to climb up to visit a soap factory in Saint-Louis.

In the late thirties, according to accepted Parisian lore, particularly as then expressed in *Le Canard Enchaîné*, a paper designed to accli-matize the provincial *instituteur* or *professeur de lycée* new to the city to the prejudices of *le bon ton parisien*, certain towns and the inhab-itants of certain provinces had as their principal function to contrib-ute to the formation of a sort of joke map of *l'Hexagone* (*Le Canard* would have more readily compared its shape to that of a schoolboy's *carte de France* on the sheet). The mere mention of the name Perpignan would release shock waves of hilarity: the very name, the accent, the alleged nature of the inhabitants, eternally *figés* as twenti-eth-century retarded Tartarins, wearing panamas or floppy berets, clothed from head to foot in colonial tussore, sipping *pastis*, playing *pétanque*, sitting arguing under the plane-trees, certainly never working or doing anything useful or serious, nor ever seen in the company of women, a purely masculine world, then, of boastful idle-ness and empty eloquence, barely living, and on what one could not tell. The sole function of the Perpignannais (not declinable in the fem-inine), it would seem, was to provide constant entertainment to the Paris-based schoolteacher, shopkeeper, *petit employé*, and intellectual. Much later in life, I was quite amazed to encounter in that town men with grave faces who never laughed and who dressed in black from head to foot, learned scholars and local historians, and teachers who devoted themselves to their work, about which they went with an air of austere gravity.

Perpignan was *the* joke town of the thirties (and perhaps it had already held that position in the previous decade). But there were plenty of others, most of them situated somewhere in the Midi, or in the Massif Central, and some in Brittany, particularly in the *breton-*

nant part of it (*Le Canard*, angling above all for a teaching readership, was one of the most effective instruments of French linguistic imperialism), and some again in Alsace, providing the paper and its readers with the everlasting joy of taking off the German accent in French, the open vowels and the *ang* endings of the different Midis, the alleged *chuintement* of the Auvergnats, and Norman peasant renderings of *-oir*. *All* peasants were more or less comical, all wore clogs, country priests always wore long, protruding shovel hats, all country churches had Norman-type wooden spires, surmounted by huge weathercocks that indicated north for south. And villages were awarded standard comic names. Some towns were funnier than others. Limoges was always good for a laugh, even declining and sprouting out into a small vocabulary: *limoger*, *limogeage*, a reference to Boulanger's posting in the previous century, and a relic, perhaps, of an even older horror of banishment dating back to the eighteenth century (and *what* punishment could be more dreadful than such removal from the centre of the universe?). So Romorantin would likewise qualify as an undesirable place of exile, a *voie de garage* to be avoided ('*je n'irai pas à Romorantin*'). Much the same could be said of the horrors of Gap, Mende, or Privas, Châteauroux, Langres, or Chaumont. *Aller à Niort* represented an ancient play on words, while Brussels was everlastingly associated with Mlle Beulemans, as well as with the midnight train from the Gare du Nord that would take the murderer, his hands still covered in blood, the swindler, and the burglar beyond the reach of French justice, adding the suggestion that one would never go to the Belgian capital for any reason other than to escape. Toulon also would provoke irresistible hilarity, at a period when its leading and extremely picturesque politician bore the extraordinary name of Escartefigue.

Equally indicative was the *absence* of certain towns and certain provinces from this apparently changeless map. There was nothing funny about Rouen, nor about Lille and the industrial towns of the north-east and the east. And if Dijon and Beaune would come in for a certain amount of good-natured ribaldry on the subject of wine-growing (*Le Canard*, a twentieth-century *Père Duchesne*, tended to equate libation with masculinity, promoting on its way the everlasting merits of *Juliénas*), Nevers and Moulins would not, perhaps because they would have appeared as too visibly melancholy. And there was

Midi and Midi. The comic *méridional* belonged, by right, to the south-east rather than to the south-west; certainly Bordeaux and Toulouse were well out of the comic zone, whereas Nice, Toulon, the whole of Corsica (*Le Canard* was inexhaustible on the subject of the islanders), Orange, and Carpentras were in it. As far as the Auvergne was concerned, Parisian humour would be directed at the *bougnat* from a rural area; the Auvergnat was the peasant *par excellence*, and so there would be nothing particularly funny about the Michelin factory worker of Clermont-Ferrand. In the geography of Parisian attitudes and humour, the Midi did not extend even up to Valence. As for Lyon, the deep-seated suspicion in which Parisians had long held the city would not have allowed it any such light-hearted favour. There was, apparently, absolutely nothing funny about Lyon, nor about the Lyonnais.

But a mixture of Parisian arrogance and Parisian lack of curiosity is far from being alone to blame for the propagation of a largely mythical Marseille, strictly *article d'exportation*, often consciously erected as a barrier to keep strangers out, and bearing about as much contact with reality as a Blackpool beach postcard has with the daily lives of the inhabitants of that other seaside town.

The result of this has been that the only truly evocative novelist of Marseille, apart from Pagnol, was a Swiss, Blaise Cendrars, who first approached the port from the sea. He took a line on the Fort Saint-Jean, on the left-hand side of the harbour, and was guided in from far out in the Mediterranean by the tower of Notre-Dame-de-la-Garde with its immense statue of the Virgin, the rocky, brownish-red hills, covered in scarlet undergrowth, beyond, a reminder, at least to the historian, that the old bandit country, the nightly killing country of the White Terror, at the end of the eighteenth century,[1] extended right down to the fringes of the town, the market-gardens and orchards of the upper slopes of the bowl, right down to the level of the main road east to Aubagne, as if, landwards, Marseille had been surrounded by a desert of another

---

[1] And, indeed, according to folk memory, much later. There must have been some background of reality to Pagnol's ghostly Grand Félix, who was said to have haunted the *pinèdes* above the city in the early years of the present century: 'il avait au moins mille moutons. Des bandits l'ont assassiné; ils lui ont planté un grand poignard entre les épaules et ils lui ont pris un gros sac de pièces d'or. Alors, il revient tout le temps, pour se plaindre, et il cherche son trésor . . .' (*Le Château de ma mère*).

sort of alarm and hazard. Cendrars came in the same way as that recommended by the Abbé Expilly;[1] and he had the same intimate,
almost loving knowledge of the prevailing winds blowing off the
dangerous sea, or, on the contrary, tearing down the Rhône Valley,[2]
making the approach nearly always dangerous, as the nautical-minded
southern priest. For Cendrars, then, the port quarter was a temporary
place of rest and relaxation and sunny enjoyment, an escape from loneliness, a plunge into verbal sociability, between long voyages, or from
service in the Legion, or from various adventures in the valley of the
Orinoco. If Marseille belongs to *anyone*, apart from its own secretive
inhabitants, it would be to the white-capped *légionnaires*, the hon-
oured freemen of the old Vieux Port, and certainly recognized as such
by the prostitutes of the rue Nationale, the rue des Couteliers, and the
rue du Petit-Saint-Jean. This was where the Legion, even more than the
fusiliers-marins, or the old colonial regiments, enjoyed *droit de cité*.
Cendrars, a former member of the Foreign Legion and a tireless traveller, a man never for long on land, and then only on the very edge of
land, was a particularly well-qualified observer of the small cafés and
the tiny restaurants, their dark entrances protected by fringes of green
matting, decorated with coloured beads, and of the varied inhabitants
of the anarchical Vieux Port. His novels, which are really autobio-
graphical novels, *L'Homme foudroyé*, *La Main coupée*, and his other
tirelessly picaresque works, ranging from the Mediterranean to the
Canal Zone, from northern Russia in the throes of revolution to
Venezuela and the northern tip of the Latin-American continent, offer
an always utterly convincing picture of place and people, of the influence of environment on a permanent or on a transient population; a
picture as well observed, warm, and fraternal as the scenes set in Braïla,
another great port near a vast delta, described, in novel after novel, with
tenderness, compassion, and humour by Panaït Istrati, another travel-

---

[1] L'abbé Jean-Joseph d'Expilly (1719–93), author of the celebrated *Dictionnaire géo-
graphique, historique et politique des Gaules et de la France* (Paris, 6 vols., 1762–70).
See under *Marseille*, *Martigues*, and *Provence*. The abbé is particularly informative on
the subject of the prevailing winds off the sea or the shore and on the currents at the
entrance to harbours.

[2] 'Toujours les petits pins au tronc noué penchés dans le sens du mistral, et les grandes
dalles de pierres bleues' (Marcel Pagnol, *La Gloire de mon père*).

ler and regional novelist, who likewise wrote only in French – rather than in his native Romanian (or Greek) – when attempting to describe a remarkably free childhood and adolescence spent in the harbour area, the markets, and the gypsy encampments of a port on the Black Sea.

The Swiss writer is completely at home in the steep little streets that lie in the shadow of the Hôtel-de-Ville and the cathedral. But his observation does not extend very far inland, not even as far as the fashionable shopping centre of the quartier de la Bourse, the Préfecture, and the great shopping street, rue Saint-Ferréol, and so his work has become very much a period piece, an eloquent but sad monument to yet something else that has been lost: the sunny, salty, peppery, aromatic fraternity of a maritime community, well adjusted to the comings and goings of sailors, fishermen, colonial troops – a community facing seawards and resolutely turning its back on the hinterland.

With the decline of the importance of Marseille as a great trading port, as the point of departure and arrival of colonial troops, administrators, and adventurers plying between France, Africa, and the Far East, with the shrivelling up of much of the Mediterranean inshore fisheries, most of the city of Cendrars and, indeed, of the city of the plays of Pagnol, has entirely disappeared. Even the Greek fishermen seem to have left the quai des Belges, to make way for tourists from the north and for extremely expensive fish restaurants and hotels and apartment blocks advertised '*avec vue sur le port*'.

One can hardly look forward to the further development of a maritime literature concerning giant petrol-carriers, as they ply between the oil fields of the Middle East and the Étang de Berre; and a present-day Conrad, a Loti, a Peisson, or a Cendrars would clearly be overtaken, and made completely irrelevant, by the constant speeding up of air transport (Marignane never occurs in any work either of Pagnol or of Cendrars), something that has killed the excitement of slow discovery, as made from offshore, or on foot inland, and that has reduced great waterfronts and once busy port areas to desolate industrial wastes of abandonment and rusty cranes. The Marseille of the old *pont transbordeur*, as depicted, for instance, in an unforgettable sequence in *Un Carnet de Bal*,[1] seems now about as remote as the Paris

---

[1] Film directed by Julien Duvivier, 1937.

of René Clair, the posters of Paul Colin (including that, representing the prow of a ship, for the Foire de Marseille), and that distant, almost fabulous period of French urban history when strange, rather frightening 'tomates' performed, with a wonderfully realistic jerky mechanism, with a hideously contrived fixed and automatic smile, as if painted on, accompanied by a drilled rolling of the eyes, in the windows of shops: immaculate, in double-breasted suit, hat, and polished shoes, as they pointed, at carefully measured periodical intervals, to the designated object of wonder and envy, to the mixed delight and terror of small Parisian children, in coloured smocks and berets, their *cartables* strapped on their backs, in the twenties and thirties. The *tomates* were so appealing, and yet so alarming, because they really *did* seem to respond to a hidden machinery, and because no amount of juvenile provocation, whether by word or by telling gesture, would make them lose their fixed clownlike grin, their hideous smile, make them alter the steep arch of their permanently amazed eyebrows, or cause them to abandon the jerkily mechanical slow progress of their movements from front to side, the arm with the pointed hand being projected as it were by the vibrating movement of the whole body. And yet one knew, in one's heart of hearts, that they really *were* human, just poor men who had chosen this peculiar way of earning a sort of living, and who, when the lights went out and the blinds and shutters came down, would step nimbly down from the shop-window, stretch themselves, scratch, resume the normal irregular flow of movement, before walking off to the nearest Bouillon Chartier, where, had it not been for their frayed and formal elegance, nothing would have distinguished them from the general mass of eaters who, in their speed to fill themselves with a poor fare, would themselves assume a mechanical movement of jaw and tongue itself reminiscent of the public performance just completed in the face of the street.

What, in French, one would call *la littérature de l'escale* – the literature of arrival and departure by sea – is thus as unlikely to experience a renewal in Marseille as it would in Bordeaux or in le Havre. Just as there is no longer any possibility of escape – and perhaps redemption – for Pépé-le-Moko,[1] or for some Parisian murderer, on the other side

---

[1] Hero of a film directed by Julien Duvivier, 1937. 'Moko' is argot for Marseillais.

of the Pyrenees, in the cosmopolitan dockland of Barcelona or Algiers, the criminal on the run is unlikely to find a semi-clandestine berth on a tramp steamer bound out of le Havre for the Canal Zone. MacOrlan, as much as Cendrars, has been overtaken by new forms of transport that have likewise destroyed the mysterious possibilities of the extinct Orient Express, the moving terrain of Paul Morand and Maurice Dékobra, of the *dame des sleepings* and the *contrôleur des wagons-lits* (a 1930-style Figaro), or the *salons dorés* of ocean-going liners. As an *invitation au départ*, Marseille now has very little to offer, apart from the official commemoration of a past when the port really was still the point of departure for North Africa, the Lebanon, and Indo-China: huge white monuments, facing seawards from the main *corniche*, to the colonial troops and the marines.

The change has been so rapid that it is really quite difficult to recall that, as recently as the 1950s and the early 1960s, the huge, barrack-like, noisy hotels of the cours Belsunce still witnessed a regular coming and going of tin trunks, proof against ants, rust, and the other multiple hazards of the African climate; trunks often of quite gigantic proportions, painted black, and with the names of the owners and the destinations – Oran, Tananarive, Sidi-bel-Abbès – painted on them in large white letters. Beside them were hatboxes containing green-lined, white pith helmets. Milling around were a baroque clientele of long-limbed Senegalese, their wives in lurid print frocks; venerable, bearded Arabs wearing golden slippers; and harassed and screaming families of French officials returning to the *douanes indochinoises* or to duties in Madagascar or in Nouméa. Even the novelist Céline's ghastly crossing, as described in his famous *Voyage au bout de la nuit* – the crossing from Marseille to Algiers – now seems a colonial period-piece, the polemics of which concern a shipload of ghosts.

Perhaps indeed all this is a type of 'homing' or of 'departing' literature which is likely, everywhere and in all languages, to see its days numbered, with the relentless shrinking of travel by sea and of the ready sociability and equally ready detestation – how important the seating at table assigned to one, the first night out, by the purser, an entry to bliss, to purgatory, or to boredom – of *la traversée maritime*. For it would be beyond the scope of the most imaginative novelist to reconstruct a conversation, much less a 'plot', set in an aircraft, however long and tedious the flight.[1] If the 'passage out', from Liverpool or Southampton, to Bombay, had so long served as a preliminary marriage-mart to younger daughters of English middle-class families, in France, too, Marseille must so often have been the predictable, indeed, looked-forward-to, point of departure of a tentative exploration, ending perhaps, if all went well, in marriage to a *fonctionnaire colonial*, to an army doctor, or to an officer in the *tirailleurs algériens*. Such standard plots – so standard as not even to qualify for a literary description as *l'intrigue*, because the plot was provided in advance, was there to be acted out – in the regularly repeated, yet significant, even touching, *histoire des familles*, have always remained largely unrecorded in works of imagination as in history itself (both equally hostile to the invocation of an imperial past), being confined to the semi-private archive of the devotedly kept family photograph album, itself an effort at groping reassurance, a bold and often pathetically inadequate claim on the uncertainties of a bottomless future (I can still recall being shown, while billeted with Polish officers in a small hotel next to the Pleasure Beach in Blackpool, in 1941, the albums of young lieutenants and sub-lieutenants, often their only visual links, apart from the odd *czapska* or the silver braid, rather frayed, sewn on to the collar, relics of uniforms that had survived many moves, with a past not at all distant in time – 1938, 1939 – but politically indescribably remote, even then – though none could then have known just *how* remote – processions and march-pasts, the white-red flags unfurled, the coloured chokers of youth organizations, the triangular caps, baroque churches, a flat countryside, squat cottages, whitewashed, with low thatched roofs, dramatic wells, armies of geese): '*voici Jacques en blanc*,' '*voici le commandant un tel, je ne retrouve pas son nom*,' '*voici le départ de Marseille; on voit Notre-Dame-de-la-Garde*,' '*voici la rade d'Alger*,' '*nous voici arrivés à Saïgon*,' '*voici la table du capitaine, c'est moi en smoking*,' as natural a frame for a novel of banality, habit, and reassurance, as the fixed itinerary imposed by the long, single street of Fontenay-le-Comte leading from the station, via the Sous-Préfecture, the Banque de

---

[1] But see the excellent story 'The Dull Man' by Noel Blakiston, in *The Collected Stories of Noel Blakiston* (London, 1977).

France, eight cafés, seven *notaires*, four *huissiers*, la Banque Agricole de l'Ouest, two hotels facing one another from opposite sides of the street, the Café-Bar des Sportifs, the *parc municipal*, with a pond, an artificial island bearing a miniature *château-fort* and connected to the mainland by a Japanese bridge, the *gendarmerie nationale*, and *commissaire de police*, the Pompiers, a group of Indochinese passing in the direction of the station, a group of nuns passing in the opposite direction, to the cathedral and the château at the far end: Simenon's *Au bout du rouleau*, the end of the line indeed, in its stark, French Primer predictability.

Each *escale* would offer a further stage in tentative exploration and emerging intimacy, the last night of the trip out, before landing, might represent an all-or-nothing risk, a desperate win-all or lose-all, which, in the former case, might result in inclusion in the photograph album, a measure of time that proceeds at a pace even more leisurely than that of the Messageries Maritimes or the Compagnie Paquet, but as predictable as the progress from port to port of a well-regulated steamship line. One is reminded of the no doubt common experience of the *soldat deuxième classe* Valentin Bru, in Queneau's *Le Dimanche de la vie*, whose personal geography of France has been confined parsimoniously to his birthplace in a Paris suburb, to Marseille, where he had embarked for Madagascar, to Bordeaux, where he had disembarked on his return, and to le Bouscat, a suburb of Bordeaux which housed the barracks of a colonial depot.

It could be argued that most such passengers would have been too pressed for time, too worried about their luggage, too afflicted by the first attack of the *mal du pays* and by the onset of fear of the unknown, or too eager to reach without delay a beloved home town or village, its virtues greatly inflated in the exile of Tananarive, Djibouti, Abidjan, Pointe-Noire, or Brazzaville, to have taken in the cascading, steeply terraced, ochre-coloured city, as glimpsed at a sudden bend of the railway line above l'Estaque, or diminishing slowly, falling into itself, first the two forts, then the dome of the cathedral, then the tiers of red-roofed houses, then the Virgin, and finally even the brown and russet hills, before all disappeared in the sea, sternwards: all the more so because departure and arrival would so often occur at unusual times, at first light, or in the middle of the night, as if further to emphasize the apartness of the maritime traveller and to separate him from the sleep of the resident inhabitants, that other great barrier that divides the night-worker from the sleeper. Yet how many times must such an impression have been indelibly marked on the retentive retina of personal or collective family memory! There can be no more dramatic, more significant introduction to New York or to Cape Town than that by sea; and a general view of Marseille, perched on the edge of its broken bowl, a huge amphitheatre open to seawards, must thus have marked, like the shutter of a camera, the departures and the arrivals of countless people, measuring out the regular course of a career in colonial service, with intervals of leave, new postings, gradual promotion, interrupted every now and then by alcoholization or the regular return of malaria, marked too, possibly, by marriage, during one of these periods of leave, following the placing of a carefully worded advertisement – personal appearance, age, health, tastes, leisure habits, moral qualities, present employment, and future prospects specified – written out while in Abidjan or in Douala, in a specialized paper, such as *Le Chasseur Français*, the dream literature of the lonely colonial, a paper passed around, closely scrutinized, and mulled over, *petite annonce* by *petite annonce*, so reassuring in the sheer mediocrity of mutual expectation offered and in the modesty of both those who inserted and those who, in small towns in metropolitan France: Parthenay, Issoudun, Châteauroux, Saintes, Laon, Semur, Marcq-en-Barœuil, Hénin-Liétard, Culmont-Chalindrey, Saint-Germain-des-Fossés, Lambesc, Pont-l'Évêque, read these pleas for companionship, for a sharing of experience, however uninspiring, these brief exercises in ideal double biographies, a strange dialogue, paid for at so much the line, and so allowing little room for poesy and fantasy, like small bits of paper, curled into a bottle, and thrown into the sea, as if the long arm of the BHV, the Belle-Jardinière, or the Enfants de la Chapelle had managed to reach right out into the green fastnesses of river outposts on the Congo or forest clearings in the Côte d'Ivoire, the faithful, banal *Chasseur* as much a familiar witness of provincial ordinariness as *l'Almanach des PTT*.

Each return would bring with it a sharp, rather bitter, and uneasy awareness of nationality – for Marseille would still represent a sort of France even for a Frenchman who still had ahead of him a thousand kilometres of travel before reaching la Bassée or Maubeuge, Mayenne or Concarneau – and an equally acute, and much more disturbing real-ization of change, after a long absence: the fact that the *agents* and the *douaniers* on the quayside wore ties and no longer had their tunics but-toned up to the collar, the fact that boaters and panamas had given way to berets, hats, and caps, that alpaca and tussore jackets in postman beige were beginning to be assigned to a museum of memory designed to house an already mythical Tartarin, that beards and pince-nez no longer designated the schoolmaster, the savant, the chemist, and the taxidermist; all visible and sharp reminders of having been overtaken by events that one had not experienced, that one had read about in newspapers months old, by subtle changes that one had not witnessed in their slow progress, of having missed out on a whole area of collect-ive national experience. That *classe*, for instance *classe de 38*, those young men who had remained with the colours, mobilized in the French Army, under the terms of the Armistice of June 1940, and who had, shortly after the formation of the Vichy Government, been shipped off, via Marseille, to North Africa, Syria, or Madagascar, serving in colonial troops until the Liberation, must have returned to a France bewilderingly unrecognizable, even in its deep and bitter divi-sions, into which they could not readily be re-accepted, for the simple crime of merely having been out of things for four or five years; neither *collabos*, nor *résistants*, nor even prudent *attentistes*, but absentees, involuntary deserters from a testing-time of choice in national history, cut off both from the humiliations of foreign occupation, the dis-comforts of the curfew and of privation, and from the small pride of refusal to accept defeat. Superficially, the language would appear the same, but many words would have acquired a new, hidden significance, a whole vocabulary that would serve to exclude the ghostly *revenant*. An experience of national rejection that must, over a century earlier, have been that of so many *demi-soldes*, so many *grognards*, back from the Grand Duchy of Warsaw, the Kingdom of Holland, from the Départements Réunis, and from the Illyrian Islands.

To such, Marseille, *la porte du Midi*, the southern sentinel of *l'Hexagone*, might present the same appearance from far out to sea: the two forts at each side of the mouth of the old harbour, the mosque-like contours of the cathedral, a place apparently of Eastern worship and rite, the huge Virgin at the summit of Endoum, the beige, russet, and mauve hills, the brilliant white of the Château d'If, on its stony grey and green island, even the cranes of la Joliette, giving a deceptive appearance of habitual activity. But, once disembarked, the immense space left where the Vieux Port had been, the absence of the *pont transbordeur*, giving to the old harbour an air of incompleteness, would underline the enormity of change and the chasm that would separate them for ever from the recent experiences of the Marseillais, and from that, as it were in advance, of the rest of their compatriots. A port lives as much in the memory and observation – always far more acute, always conditioned to a greater awareness and sensitivity to the concreteness of matter, to the texture of stone and wood, to the warmth of a wall, suddenly crossed by a darting lizard, to the aromatic plants growing in old stonework – of its passengers, of those who take ship and who land, as in the more dormant, more routinal, lazier, less intense memory of its permanent, land-based inhabitants. But each would be aware of a totally different town, of an urban geography quite unknown to the other. The distance from the height of a deck to the quayside is almost insuperable in mental terms; and to the ship's passenger, the lit-up destinations on the front of the blue trolley-buses and trams represent names that are meaningless, however poetic and inviting in their vagueness and unattainability – Belle-de-Mai, la Madrague, Saint-Jean-du-Désert – the end of the line of journeys that will never be taken, of small green oases of plane-trees and shutters, a fountain in a quiet square, a green fence overtopped by lilac, the *tête de ligne* of a numbered line of urban transport, where the trolley-bus can rest its long arm, unhooked from the overhead wire, and its driver and *contrôleur* can pause for a cigarette and a conversation, on a seat under a tree with its bark peeling.[1] A terminus then that cannot even

[1] Or one of the splendid blue trams, carrying the blue cross on a white background of the city's arms, of Marcel Pagnol's childhood, recalled in *Le Château de ma mère* (1958): '. . . et ce fut le départ pour la "gare de l'Est". Cette "gare" n'était rien d'autre que le terminus souterrain d'un tramway, et son nom même était une galéjade. L'est, en la circonstance, ce n'était pas la Chine, ni l'Asie-Mineure, ni même Toulon: c'était Aubagne, où s'arrêtaient modestement les rails de l'Est . . . nous sortîmes des entrailles de la terre, juste au début du boulevard Chave, à 300 mètres à peine de notre point de départ.' A municipal itinerary no more discoverable by the stranger passing through

be imagined, save in the promise of its evocative name, but that, to the traveller out, to the soldier or the sailor on his way back to discomfort, boredom, and loneliness, must yet offer a poignant and tantalizing mirage of domestic peace, daily routine, and the assurance that tomorrow will be like today: *la vie en pantoufles*, at the end of both. Even bitterer the contrast, and greater the gulf, to those who are sailing on the evening tide or at nightfall, and who cross the city by taxi, shut away from its population, at a time when the buses and trams are taking their packed shirt-sleeved and summer-frocked loads of people, at the end of the day's work, back to the suburbs, back to a *pastis*, a game of bowls, supper, and bed, and sleep, perhaps vaguely disturbed, or, on the contrary, even encouraged, by the muffled fog-horn of the ship about to leave. Most unbearable of all, the lights going on in the streets, then in a tall window, then in a mass of windows at different levels, conveying an intimacy, a sharing in the collective life of the city, as it settles down for the night, a sense of almost maternal protection, from which one is excluded, on the threshold of general sleep.

On the other hand, perhaps in an interval between hustling from the Gare Saint-Charles to the port of la Joliette, the transient, on his outward journey, might spend the night in a noisy, carpetless, stone-floored hotel in the cours Belsunce or in the quartier de la Bourse. But, in his flickering sleep, he would be drifting in a sort of geographical limbo or already ahead of himself physically, in a gently throbbing ship.

He might take a meal, or several meals, in a large restaurant facing on to the Vieux Port. On the other hand, he might take a meal in a deep narrow restaurant with an unassuming entrance facing on to the rue des Phocéens; and, like the chap opposite him, his *vis-à-vis*, he might order a *rosé de Provence* and fish soup, or, like the shop-girl or the country family opposite, he might have a plate of squids, *sèches à l'armoricaine*, or, like the old man at the next table, he might be reading the evening paper, in an effort, perhaps, to cling on to scraps of local

than *le train bleu* from Lyon to the Île Barbe. But the discovery of such local lines of transport gives the more permanent visitor both *droit de cité* and a sense of belonging in a municipal community. *Le train d'Aubagne* is as much a password to Marseillais particularism as *le train d'Arpajon* (or, more familiarly, *l'Arpajonnais*) would have been to that of Paris before 1937, when the train was replaced by a bus.

news: a brawl, a burglary, a wedding, a *pétanque* match, a *vin d'honneur* (a presentation on retirement) – the everydayness and guaranteed renewability of a land-locked existence. He, the transient, is rather like a drowning sailor who clings on to a piece of floating wood; as if some minor *revolverisation* in the quartier du Panier or an accident involving a trolley-bus and a scooter would actually put off the imminence of departure, granting him, as it were, a tiny bonus of 'territoriality'. He might then follow the conversations around him – indeed, he could hardly fail to do so – the pointed vowels as reassuringly local, fixed, and familiar as the violet-scrawled menu; and yet, despite such desperate exercises in immobility as his feet firmly set on the red-tiled floor, his elbow resting on the paper cloth, his nostrils taking in the aromatic smells coming from the kitchen, his eyes brushing over the busy, concentrated fraternity of the eaters, all engaged in the same rapid rites, his ears holding on to the fall of a sentence or to hurried greetings accompanied by a perfunctory handshake across the table – '*à demain,*' '*à dimanche,*' '*bon weekend*' – it is but a pathetic effort actually to lay hands on and to caress an immediate future totally inaccessible. Already, he is removed by thousands of mental kilometres from those sitting opposite him, those who might even have spoken to him as across an immense but invisible gulf, those who know the waitresses by name. And something of his apartness would be communicated to them, too. They would not be deceived by his close reading of the evening edition of *Le Provençal*.[1] The concentrated attention of the solitary eater to all that surrounded him – the arrival and departure of customers, the comings and goings in the busy, narrow street outside, the tour of the tables by a deaf-and-dumb man depositing at each place his printed biography: '*Je suis sourd-muet de naissance . . .*' (and coming back on his round to collect them again, most of them left unopened, sadly) or the tour of the tables by the lottery salesman – would reveal him for someone already on the brink, beyond the com-

---

[1] Pagnol's mother has a more practical use for the blue-titled paper; Marcel and his friend Lili are going out into the hills in bitter winter weather: 'Elle nous habilla. Entre mon gilet de flanelle et ma chemise elle glissa plusieurs numéros du *Petit Provençal*, pliés en quatre. Elle en mit aussi dans mon dos . . . Lili, bouleversé par ce désespoir, me prit dans ses bras, froissant entre ces cœurs désespérés seize épaisseurs du *Petit Provençal*' (*Le Château de ma mère*).

forting embrace of habit, of a fixed itinerary, even of a tiny participation in a collective routine.

Or perhaps, because of living in a port, they would scarcely notice him at all; they would simply write him off almost as a non-person, as one already outside the visible perimeter of the regular eating-place, regular eating-time, and regular leisure.

The result of all this has been that such literature as concerns Marseille has been written by strangers and by travellers on their way somewhere or other, whose only reason to be in the city would be to get out of it, and so only aware of the place as a point of rest or waiting, preferably brief, but always of uncertain and unwelcome duration. For Victor Serge, it is waiting for a visa to Mexico or somewhere else, a daily tour of consulates; for Arthur Koestler, the crowded febrile waiting-rooms of yet other consulates; for Airey Neave, a flat owned by a doctor, a member of a well-known local medical family, somewhere on one of the *corniches*, with a magnificent view seawards, that can never be extended or varied in any way – three dusty palms, a grey wall, a blue-and-white advertisement for Noilly-Prat, two islands out to sea, enclosed implacably in the frame of long-windows – because he cannot be allowed out, lest his accent or his appearance give him away, till means can be found to remove him by sea, from a nearby *calanque*, and transport him to Gibraltar; for Léon Blum and other Socialist deputies, a confusing wait, actually on board, on the *Massilia*, a ship that, in the end, never sails, as if reluctant to leave her home port, and part company with the city the name of which she carries; for Joseph Kessel, a *tournée de cafés*, not for pleasure or refreshment or for the enjoyment of company, but in search here of a liberating rubber-stamp, there of a ration card, here of a false identity card, there of a photographer, a tiring circular tour of specialized underground skills. All that Evelyn Waugh could retain of the place was the cheekiness of the prostitutes, as they leant out of windows to deprive his leading character of his hat – a ridiculous object – and the washing that hung from windows or, like bright-coloured bunting, on lines across the narrow streets. Few travellers, even French ones, seem to have been bothered to take in much more; and both French and foreigners appear, in their cursory glance, to have regarded the inhabitants of the port in much the same way as passengers through the

Canal might have thought of the Egyptian salesmen as they swarmed around the ship or the quayside at Suez. All seem to have been remarkably uncurious about the inhabitants of the second city of France; in return, the resident Marseillais seem to have been principally concerned to hold travellers and strangers at arm's length and to maintain the sharp distinction between the city as a *lieu de passage* and as a place to live and work in.

During the First World War the city would witness the brief passage of British servicemen, travelling overland, to take ship here for the Dardanelles, and that of those fortunate enough to make the return trip. During the Second it would perhaps just discern the coming and going of successive garrison commanders and high-ranking officials to and from Syria. Only the massive exodus of the *pieds noirs* from Algeria on the eve of Independence seems strongly to have impinged on local awareness of such movements, whether regular or exceptional, while the port could absorb, in its indifference, the constant comings and goings of patriarchal Algerians, carrying enormous bundles and accompanied, a few paces ahead, by small groups of veiled women, as they headed towards or away from the Gare Saint-Charles. And so, in general experience, it would be recalled as a place in which the *waiting* was above all demoralizing, as a sort of twilight zone in careers spent in the colonies or in the colonial armies: a threshold, neither one thing nor another, neither quite the *métropole*, nor quite the African or Far Eastern shore, but suspended in a point of time and space between the two, and so a time and place for uncomfortable self-awareness and self-examination, doubt, bewilderment, hope, and fear. Of such passers-through, there is no visible record, save perhaps in the well-worn steps of Saint-Charles,[1] though for those prepared to carry the search a stage further there might still exist at least the terse evidence of name and surname, several names and the same surname, the suggestion of a family on the move, nationality, passport number, whence coming and whither going – not that either would give away

---

[1] It was only those who stayed who might acquire a brief mention in local literature, as naturalized Marseillais: 'Joseph assimila son cas à celui d'un coiffeur berlinois, venu à Marseille pour trois jours, en mission syndicale, et qui n'en était jamais reparti', an instance flattering to local reassurance (Marcel Pagnol, *Le Temps des secrets*).

much – in the *fiches de police* filled in before a night's stay at a hotel: that so-and-so, claiming to have been travelling from Paris, had stayed one night, cours Belsunce, before embarking for Algiers. It would be as if they had never existed other than as staccato paper biographies filled in hurriedly at a hotel desk and ending up in some indifferent section of the Prefecture. And, for soldiers and sailors, of whatever nationality, who were travelling collectively, there would not subsist even that derisory monument.

Pépé-le-Moko gazes with tears and bitter nostalgia through the iron railings fencing off the port of Algiers, because he is on the *wrong* side of the Mediterranean, with his life-blood running out on to an unfamiliar *pavé* – because his dreadful, hopeless nostalgia has been exacerbated by listening to a few old records of Fréhel's songs, accompanied by Fréhel herself, a ruin of herself in a cracked alcoholic voice, and because the white ship, that he will not take, is heading for home, *his* home: Marseille, now a distant and desirable city, never attainable. But Pépé is an expatriate Marseillais (though he is in fact Jean Gabin, a native of the Seine-et-Oise, almost a Parisian), an exile, now stranded on an alien shore, like the sad, dejected, hopeless, alcoholized poor whites left behind for ever in the port quarter of Cape Town: Swedes, Norwegians, West Germans, Dutchmen, Scots, stuck there, with no hope of escape, cadging drinks from any unfamiliar customer. Very few Marseillais of Marseille would ever get near to understanding Pépé's agony; and perhaps the only inhabitants who might be able to cross that mental barrier would be the prostitutes who thicken in ever increasing clusters in the narrow streets approaching the quai des Belges and the rue des Couteliers, as a last reminder that this was the traditional, historical approach to the city from the sea right up to the nineteenth century, before the construction of la Joliette, and one still reserved for visitors of state right up to the present century, the unfortunate Alexander of Yugoslavia disembarking at the very foot of the Canebière, as if to save his assassins trouble and to be in ahead of time on his own murder, a few minutes after landing, a hundred yards or so further on.

By the nature of her profession, the prostitute will be in contact, above all, with transients. Even the gangling Bretonne or the massive Ardéchoise will represent the last physical link with *le pays*, so that *une passe*, in conditions however brief and breathless, takes on a much deeper significance, almost tender, maternal and lingering, long after physical contact has been broken. She will be in contact with a moving and primarily non-Marseillais population, men from every other area of France and from all of what had once constituted *la France d'outre-mer* – a momentarily complete racial integration – thus achieved in the queue spreading out into the street from the *hôtel de passe*.

Prostitutes are always the most reliable guides to the normal patterns of movement, outside those of work, within a city, and to the most commonly used points of entry to it and departure from it: a simple fact of urban social geography at one time illustrated in Paris, in telling simplicity, by the constantly crowded pavements and the many red pompoms of the French Navy, of the rue du Départ and the rue de l'Arrivée, on both sides of the old and modestly provincial Gare du Montparnasse, and the equally naval aspect of the rue du Havre, alongside the Gare Saint-Lazare, a reminder also that the Bastille and the porte de Vincennes, as well as Austerlitz or the Gare de l'Est, are railway or bus termini, that the porte de Clignancourt stands opposite the Reuilly barracks, that the now mostly demolished rue des Partants, in Ménilmontant, once stood close to a barracks, also gone, and that it contained a row of brothels, still recognizable as such by their blind outer walls of washable cream-coloured brick and by their lack of ground-floor windows, though they have long since been converted to serve other purposes; a reminder that soldiers and sailors, like provincials – and most of them *are* provincials – have always regarded Strasbourg-Saint-Denis and the adjoining streets, above all the rue d'Aboukir and the rue Berger, as the true centre of the capital: where *pleasure* is, *there* is the centre. But in Marseille, such concentration of pleasure will actually turn its back, as if in disdain, on the station, the Gare Saint-Charles, and will thicken from the level of the Chamber of Commerce and its neighbour, the naval headquarters, guarded by two sentries in white belts and white spats, as well as from the level of the Bourse and the Comédie, and acquire maximum intensity in the rue des Couteliers, behind the Hôtel-de-Ville, a street long familiarized to the white kepis of the Legion, to the long Sénégalais, to the tiny Indochinois, as well as, briefly, to the GIs of the American base.

How many *secrets d'oreiller*, secrets of the pillow, most of them of no value whatsoever to the DST, the French counter-espionage, or to the Sûreté Nationale, poor little secrets, banal tragedies, paltry inadequacies, mean, unimaginative little crimes sighed or whispered hurriedly on the sweaty, coverless bolster, or murmured while buttoning up, as the girl stands in front of the mirror to fix her lurid mouth or crouches rather perfunctorily over the bidet – a rapid gesture of orthodoxy rather than of hygiene, as if the customer were trying to get a little more for his money than had been bargained for, a sort of last-minute clutching at reassurance and intimacy, threatened by the menacing call of ships, in a lilac-papered and red-tile-floored bedroom on the third floor, flickering from the coloured lights of neon signs: Hôtel des Amis (as if in derision of the eight-minute lodger), Hôtel de la Côte d'Ivoire, Hôtel de Pézenas, Hôtel d'Alger, Café-Bar de Casablanca, Hôtel Miramar, Hôtel de Suez, Au Rendez-vous des Toulonnais, Hôtel de Nice, Hôtel de Sisteron, the blue, green, white, and red geography of several continents starting or ending from Marseille, of a score of *sous-préfectures* and *chefs-lieux d'arrondissement* emptying on to the city their surplus population (perhaps even in homage to the commonest home-towns of the girls themselves)! Brief Lives indeed, so many of them shortly to be terminated, with no final chapter beyond this strictly limited, commercialized pause of an intimacy well beyond the reach of family memory. And so what a store then of metropolitan and transoceanic experience, of the minutiae of a social history well below the level of significant ambition – merely that humble one of *du galon*, an extra stripe, or a single one, or that, simpler still, to survive and to return – below that of any chronicled importance, even in an obscure regimental history, yet a wealth of human material stored, briefly at least, in the confused and crowded memory of tired street-walkers, as they relaxed, in couples or in threes, in a bar on the ground floor of their place of work, for a *menthe verte* or a *grenadine*, for a short respite to chat loudly with colleagues, between a series of *passes* – five minutes, eight minutes (*strictement chronométrées*, for profit is in speed) – gaudily dressed, frayed *dépôts d'archives humaines*, walking on abnormally high heels, each life not even afforded the tiny luxury of a Christian or even a nickname, not even identifiable in the simplest police terms, and so recollected, perhaps, in some exotic tattoo on the chest – because the customer would not even have had time to remove his shoes, much less to undress. He is only vaguely and unhelpfully individualized as a sweaty face, made out as a grimace, a *rictus*, as if already rehearsing for death, looking downwards, and inquiring, in a local accent or in a French jargon, '*D'où tu es donc?*', in a sudden gabble of words designed even to cross the barrier imposed by such formal and ready *tutoiement*. Little then to carry the female witness, momentarily pinned down on the sheetless bed – covered by some grubby washable material – beyond the *tu* and the *toi*, a pair of eyes, a face little more revealing than an actor's mask, with tattoos on the upper arm or on the forearm, the unhelpful uniformity of a khaki shirt or a sailor's blue-and-white striped undervest. And yet, with so little to go on, an impressionism so sparse and as pared down to essentials as the furniture of the room itself, sometimes, almost unaccountably, leaving behind long afterwards the lingering memory of a man who had lost his way, who was frightened of the darkness ahead, and who was clutching briefly, like a child, at such commercially offered femininity.

But prostitutes, of course, do not write novels; though, if they reach very great eminence, such as Manouche did, they may have novels written for them, or about them.[1] Nor do prostitutes write history, save, every now and then, in the staccato records of *la chronique judiciaire*, the crime column, or, as it were, *par personne interposée* and at several removes, in the devitalized language of a *commissaire de police* or his secretary, following a *revolverisation* or a stabbing, an act of sudden vengeance so often adding a definitive conclusion to the life of the potential narrator. She was a woman who had made a sort of living by going up and by coming down, by listening inattentively to mumbled *bribes de conversation*, snatches of conversation, falling from the partner in a hurried ceremony and competing with a multitude of sounds coming through the walls on each side, together with the banging of doors and the distinguishable noise of masculine and feminine footsteps along stone staircases and passages, each word falling into a deep well of confused murmur, with perfunctory intervals to wash down below, the turning of the taps, the angry shudder of the gurgling water in the pipes, as if designed to acclimatize already

[1] See below, p. 235.

the customer, as he puts on his jacket and searches in his pockets for a cigarette, to the throb of a ship's engine. Her life of repetitive work ended, meriting, perhaps, a few lines in a local newspaper, with each sentence preceded by the word *encore* – *encore un crime du milieu; encore un drame de la jalousie; encore un règlement de comptes* – as if to deny the individuality and uniqueness of her death and her manner of death, a departure as discreet and as sparsely recorded as those, every few minutes, of her *pratiques*, as they hasten back to the loneliness of the functional and rather awful collectivity of ship, of regiment, and of barracks.

For such witnesses, the only recorded literature would be the weekly or monthly letter, written in mauve ink on lined sheets of notepaper bought by the sheet with a single envelope at the nearest *bureau de tabac*,[1] to a child regularly visited at great cost, inconvenience, and loss of precious working-time who had been put out to a wet nurse, *en nourrice*, somewhere in the countryside not too far away from Marseille, but as far away as possible from the girl's native town or village.

Already in the 1930s, Marseille seemed so irresistibly set up as a sort of national joke-shop that it would take the peculiar circumstances of the Occupation to provide the place with a literature of its own, although a literature written mainly by novelists and poets who were refugees from the north. Today, thanks to the development of the enormous new southern industrial complexes of Fos and l'Étang de Berre, the joke-shop image is dated and, rather mercifully, I think, *la galéjade*, for export northwards only, has gone the way of the once-thriving trade in dirty postcards. But this very complex, very hard-working, and rather austere city still has not quite managed to develop an indigenous literature representative of its apparently ready expansibility, its sociability – a sociability easily accessible, but in fact hardly

---

[1] Perhaps like the paper Marcel chose, in order to impress his little friend Lili, but that, in the end, he did not use: 'j'allai au bureau de tabac, et j'achetai une très belle feuille de papier à lettres. Elle était ajourée en dentelle sur les bords, et décorée, en haut à gauche, par une hirondelle imprimée en relief, et qui tenait dans son bec un télégramme. L'enveloppe, épaisse et satinée, était encadrée par des myosotis' (Marcel Pagnol, *Le Château de ma mère*).

extending beyond the café terrace or the bar and certainly never reaching back into the impenetrable secrecy of domesticity and of the family. Thus a very masculine form of sociability.

And I do not think an indigenous literature has ever grown up to express the innate pessimism and melancholy hidden behind so much verbiage. Perhaps the potential capacity for native literature has always been exhausted in advance – in speech, in the constant fount of conversation, in the rich and flowing delight of the spoken word.

The arts seem deliberately to have been expelled from the *cité phocéenne*, as the Marseillais like to describe their city, as a reminder of its Greek origins, to make more room for trade, industry, medicine, science, and technology, as a result of the division, in the course of the nineteenth century, of what is still called the University of Aix-Marseille, in order to concentrate on what the Marseillais would call *les choses sérieuses* – science, technology, engineering, and, above all, medicine.

This sense of cultural sterility is certainly confirmed further, visually, even to the most casual visitor, by the predominantly nineteenth-century, Second Empire, early Third Republic (both at their very worst) architecture of what, in fact, is the oldest town in France, making of the port the most profoundly nineteenth-century ensemble in the whole country. Indeed, it produces a sort of Third Republic rococo which achieves its most luxuriantly leafy ugliness in the cours Castellane, the triumphal exit from the city eastwards towards Toulon and the Italian frontier, and again, in the extraordinary luxuriant statuary of the museum and the park of the Pharo.

Furthermore, apart from its only too apparent architectural brashness and vulgarity, there is certainly nowhere in France where people dress more loudly, and where women's print dresses are more strident. The Canebière, in the evening or at the weekend, resembles a rural fairground, with a predominance of canary yellow, pinks, mauves, and acidulous greens.

But what most characterizes this Mediterranean port is its secrecy. The ready loquacity, the easy sociability, the old standard jokes are really screens, put up to deceive the Parisian and the visitor from the north and to exclude him from the reality of a sort of embattled family neighbourliness. The result is that Marseille can be, for the stranger, an extraordinarily lonely city. It would seem that, for generations, one of the principal concerns of the Marseillais has been to keep themselves to themselves, even at the price of putting out to the rest of France a commercialized standard image on the basis of the *galéjade* and the picture postcard. A genuinely Marseillais literature, *à l'usage des Marseillais*, might give too much away, so better not to write it down. Or merely leave it to an always revealing *chronique judiciaire* in one of the local newspapers.

Or possibly the old capital of the *royaume du Midi* has never entirely adjusted itself to the discipline and severity of a standard language, gradually imposed, through education and ambition, military service, and the railways, especially the PLM, from the north, leaving, as it were, the local *chose écrite* high and dry in a linguistic wilderness, and devitalizing the once thriving local, patrician culture of an eighteenth-century academic Marseille. Unlike Paris, the very cosmopolitanism of the city seems also to have helped to create something of a cultural vacuum, as each generation of immigrants has succeeded in preserving their own linguistic identities: the Catalan sailors from the orange boats, the phanariot Greek merchants who helped to finance Greek cultural revival and linguistic modernization, successive waves of Genoese and Corsican settlers, followed, between the wars and even since, by Tunisians, Moroccans, Algerians, Congolese, Senegalese, Côte d'Ivoiriens, and, more recently, *pieds noirs*, amounting to a linguistic diversity even more pronounced than that of Belcour and Bab'l Oued. Perhaps too it has been the misfortune of Marseille, from a literary point of view, to have come too late to have experienced a linguistic revival – or possibly, a recreation, *de toutes pièces*, such as occurred in the sister port of Barcelona, in the late nineteenth century, that is, at a time when social and economic links with Paris were already too strong to be broken, and when the ladder of ambition pointed so insistently, in the phrase *la montée à Paris*, northwards, for it still to be possible to justify a readiness to stay put. It may also have been that the city's prodigious commercial destiny had something to do with this literary indigence. In the past, the city has produced many writers; but most of these, from the Abbé Expilly onwards, it exported northwards; and the fact that Rimbaud died in the Hôpital de la Conception seems to have been a matter of indifference to most

Marseillais. After all, coming, on his last journey, from Djibouti, where else *would* he have landed? Marseille was a point of disembarkation as inevitable for the poet turned slave-trader as for any French traveller from North Africa, the Middle East, and the East African coast.

If, for the majority of the Marseillais, there was any sparse consolation to be had, in the terrible conditions of food shortage, cold, and scarcity resulting from the circumstances of the Occupation in the Mediterranean Departments, it would no doubt have been in the fact that Paris was no longer so readily accessible,[1] separated as it was from the southern port by an internal frontier, and, indeed, in that it was no longer the capital of France. Vichy could only be a different matter, owing to its proximity to the border of the old *royaume du Midi*; and it was bound to be more receptive to southern grievances. It might be argued, at least in terms of long historical memory, that the strange interlude of *l'État Français*, an accidental hiatus in French public history, represented, at least by promoting both Lyon and Marseille to the position of the two principal cities within the new bifurcated state, *la revanche du Midi*.[2]

A certain deliberate and rather touching parochialism is apparent even in a work of local history (part, however, of a general series of the history of the resistance movement in France during the Second World War, planned and published from Paris at a national level) such as that of a local historian, Pierre Guiral, *Occupation, Résistance et*

---

[1] That Paris was still very far away indeed, both in physical and mental terms, even after the construction of the PLM at the time of the Crimean War, is suggested by a passage in Pagnol referring to 1870: 'A cette époque, Paris était bien plus loin de Marseille que ne l'est aujourd'hui Moscou. Il y avait trois jours et trois nuits de voyage, une centaine d'arrêts dans les gares, et plus de cinquante tunnels' (*Le Temps des secrets*).

[2] It would not be altogether fanciful to suggest that, already under the Third Republic, and again, under the Fourth, the *revanche du Midi* could take the form of the colonization of the rest of France by southerners who climbed up the educational ladder and who, in doing so, often climbed northwards, giving to Norman schools southern headmasters and headmistresses, *inspecteurs d'académie* and *inspecteurs primaires*. The ascension of Pagnol's *tante Fifi* is characteristic of an ambition especially southern: 'Depuis sa vingt-cinquième année, elle était la directrice d'une école supérieure: elle y régnait en despote et se donnait toute entière à sa mission qui était d'instruire, d'éduquer et de former de jeunes citoyennes vertueusement laïques . . . Bref, c'était une femme de bien, ce qui ne l'empêchait pas d'être belle, et de sentir bon' (ibid.).

Libération, a work in which no one is really entirely villainous (Carbone and Spirito are, but they are expendable because they are Corsican immigrants), a work in which the relations between the local *Vichyssois* and the various brands of local *résistants* always remain at least correct, if not always cordial. Certainly, no breach ever seems to have been irreparable, no channel of communications ever completely cut off, so that a telephone call across the city, or a meeting by appointment in some discreet restaurant could generally keep all sides informed about what the others were up to, and prevent matters from ever getting out of hand – that is, out of the control of the various acknowledged leaders of the local community, including the members of the clandestine Communist party. Indeed, probably the man the least well informed of what was going on during the Occupation years was the Prefect of the Bouches-du-Rhône! It is a picture both convincing and reassuring in its generally prudent, unheroic dimensions, and a picture that carries the very clear message: *Que ceci reste entre nous, arrangeons les choses entre nous,* a habit of ingrained 'municipalism' that must have owed a great deal to past history and to long and bitter experience of interference from Paris.

Yet, one would think, in Marseille of all places, childhood must have represented a point of time particularly sunny and luminous, the perception of blinding light and of an almost visible heat, the darting green and yellow belly of a lizard among stonework, the ragged, diaphanous, and reddish *rascasses,* that peculiar Mediterranean fish, and the rainbow colours of squids in the fishermen's baskets, the blue-painted Catalan boats piled with oranges, in a city which, as an immense and stepped playground, spills downwards towards the old harbour and the little beaches, and peters out all at once on the edge of the desert, a wild, aromatic scrub, high above the deep inlets, the *calanques,* on the reddish cliffs between Marseille and Port Miou that dominate the sea, the approaches to the harbour, the three white lighthouses, and the islands lying out, their outlines obscured in a heat mist.

The sea is there to be looked at – a changing spectacle, with several shades of drifting colour – as well as there to be smelt. It is very doubtful, I think, if any of the residents would ever make the standard tourist trip to the Château d'If, and there are very few hints of the proximity of a port in the quiet rue Saint-Sébastien or among the market gardens, the soap factories, and the olive oil distilleries of Saint-Louis, Saint-Julien, and Sainte-Julie.

There is surely some negative significance in the fact that, in the four volumes of his childhood memoirs, Pagnol never once mentions either la Joliette or the Vieux Port; and there is nothing to suggest that the bright-eyed, very observant child had ever seen a ship, while the sea is only glimpsed at a great distance, reflecting the midday glare of a superb sunset, from the heights of the rocky *pinèdes* above Aubagne. What is more, it is always an empty sea. Even more surprising, the child never seems to have encountered a sailor, or, if he had, he does not consider the fact worthy of mention. His visual world is entirely land-locked, often confined to the heartless stone courtyards of school and *lycée*, but extending to the enchanted heights or valleys of the blue and tawny hills. An uncle had been to Rio, had indeed died there. But that is almost the only reminder that the boy was growing up in a great port. His father is entirely shuttered in by the conventional ambitions of the proud, but closed, hierarchy of the *instituteurs*. The mauve ribbon of the *palmes académiques* that beckons him on in his devotion to primary education and correct spelling, republican rectitude and conventional anti-clericalism, contains no hint of colonialism, nor of a *France d'Outre Mer*. Mauve is not the colour of departure, and, far from being an *invitation au voyage*, it is an insistent one to stay put within the familiar, safe territory of the *académie* and the reassuring geography of a *société savante*. It is as much a stay-at-home colour as the green of the *mérite agricole*. And its award will be duly mentioned in *Le Petit Provençal*, along with success in *boules*. Pagnol, it is true, does mention, *en passant*, the presence in his *lycée* of one or two Algerian boys, of two or three Annamites, even of a Japanese; but he does not feel that such exoticism is worth commenting on.

Equally indicative is his lack of curiosity about the parental back-ground of his schoolfriends at the *lycée*. Only many years later does he discover that the orphan Oliva, a scholarship boy like himself, had been brought up by his two elder brothers, the one a stonemason, the other a docker. 'De même je n'avais jamais soupçonné que le père de Zacharias possédait soixante navires.'[1]

---

[1] *Le Temps des secrets.*

When he wants to impress the little peasant boy Lili, who has apparently never come down from the heights of the plateau into the city, with his urban lore, the itinerary is entirely land-locked: 'je lui racontais la ville: les magasins où l'on trouve de tout, les expositions de jouets à la Noël, les retraites aux flambeaux du 141me [*not*, be it noted, a colonial regiment] et la féerie de Magic-City, où j'étais monté sur les montagnes russes . . .'

Very few land-locked Marseillais would ever actually have been on the quayside of the docks, unless they were dockers or employees of the Port Autonome, or unless, rarely, they had come to see off a relative; at best, their observation, from one of the *corniches*, or from the sea front at l'Estaque, might register the arrival of the mailboat from Corsica, Casablanca, or Algiers, merely as a reminder of the day of the week or the time of the day, an extra public clock set seaward, a reminder that it is time to go home or to keep an appointment, to buy a weekly, or to catch the bank, or that, much more impressive, of a liner or a troop-carrier from Saigon or Oran, outside the normal calendar, or the reminder of the month provided by a shipping company.

So *la littérature de l'escale* would offer little appeal to the resident Marseillais, any more than it would to the resident Havrais or to the inhabitants of any other French port, most of whom would be remarkably uncurious about what went on beyond the twin lighthouses at the mouth of their harbours and, indeed, within their sight. The novel of the sea, of *le grand passage*, of terrible storms, typhoons, and near-shipwreck, has always had a much greater attraction for those living well away from the coast and less familiar with the constantly changing surface of the sea and the ocean, and, above all, to the Parisian, who, though living in France's most important port, would scarcely be aware of the fact, beyond taking in, every time he crossed the pont des Arts, the flags of the Belgian and Dutch barges, clustering along the quays of the Left Bank, below the Monnaie, or, if walking by those beyond the Gare d'Austerlitz, the big English coasters, with their blue ensigns, of the regular service Paris–Londres. To look seawards would not suggest any awareness of the significance of maritime matters; and the skyline of the steep city, climbing around its semicircular bowl, in tiers of ochre-coloured red-roofed houses, their long green raffia blinds cracking in the wind from the hills, would not affect the inhabitants of the port in the poignant way it might the sea-borne traveller. There was no special wealth in a landscape that one could see the next day and the day after that. Notre-Dame-de-la-Garde and the Virgin of Endoum were unlikely to move overnight; and their special care was to watch over the departing or returning mariner rather than over those who lived in their shadow. The barrier between a land-locked literature and landed itineraries, and a literature that looks seawards, or that, from the other side of several seas, longs for land, will remain uncrossable.

As far as I know, apart from Pagnol's luminous memoirs, there has been no Marseillais equivalent of Henri Béraud, and no such childhood has ever been evoked in a novel or in recollections, and only once in a film, *Merlusse*,[1] mostly concerned with the eccentricities of a warm-hearted *maître d'internat*, an usher, and with the *internes*, the boarders, in one of the big *lycées* – the Lycée Thiers or the Lycée Saint-Charles – all living in an enclosed world of barrack-like discipline, Merlusse in his own peculiar tent in the middle of the dormitory, and all of them either strangers to the city or cut off from it.

Nor could one turn to the unhappy Germaine Roussier for as much as a hint of the physical awareness of her urban surroundings, of the port, its bright colours and its pungent smells. For impossible love for a teenage pupil and of a purely thematic, bookish education as a *professeur de lettres*, for whom literary characters possessed a reality denied to living people, and intellectual and theoretical discussion about generalities would obscure even a vague perception of what people might be saying around her; she was already as much a prisoner of her education and of her total intransigence while still living in freedom in a flat overlooking the port, as when, later, she was confined to the real physical prison of les Baumettes; and one wonders whether she would even have been conscious of the change of scene. How could she have sought consolation or derived joy in the appearance of a town that she never *saw*, that she was incapable of seeing, living as she did in a barred and shuttered barracks of committed left-wing totalitarianism? The *affaire Roussier*, as its title implies, was not just another French dispute over the nature and the course of justice; it was also a polemic, an argument, an intellectual debate between people more

---

[1] Written and directed by Marcel Pagnol, 1935.

concerned with ideology than with experience and observation. It offers no window on the town in which it took place, nor on its family life, all the leading participants being equally wrapped in the blindness of political fanaticism. So one cannot blame well-established Marseillais for expressing resentment at the publicity given to a human tragedy of starkly classical proportions merely because it occurred in a place of which most concerned seem to have been quite unaware. The *affaire* had nothing at all to do with Marseille, save that, owing to the bureaucratic decision that sent the impossible young woman as a *fonctionnaire* to one of the *lycées* of the town, it happened, or mostly happened, in or around the port. Marseille was merely a cardboard backdrop to Germaine's impossibilist fantasies; and, in any case, in most French provincial towns, the younger teaching personnel, coming mostly from outside, huddle together, like colonists cut off from their surroundings. Mlle Roussier is no more capable of witnessing, out of the depth of her myopic self-pity and total intransigence, for Marseille, than would Jean-Paul Sartre, in his Parisian arrogance, and from the depth of *his* loathing for common humanity, have been able to witness for the inhabitants of le Havre, the place to which he was sent for his first post and on which he attempted to avenge himself in *La Nausée*. It would be rather like asking Simone Weil to describe the wartime London in which she died. If the *affaire Roussier* has a lesson, from the literary point of view, it is that totalitarianism, whether of the Right or the Left, shutters the eye of the observer to anything outside that does not conform to an ordered, preconceived harmony, to the long dreary avenues, the squat, square mausoleums, the ice-cream blocks of Palaces of Culture, and the vast squares set aside for organized popular rejoicings; for the committed will only see with the regimented eye of a Le Corbusier, the perpetrator of *la maison du fada*, a blot on the Marseillais horizon, and the object of much popular derision. Germaine then can tell us nothing at all about the children of Marseille, nor about the inhabitants in general, living as she did in the isolation of utter fanaticism, and killing herself when a glimpse of reality at last impinged on her atrophied awareness.

Apart from Henri Queffélec's *Journal d'un salaud*, a wicked incursion into the local family network of *la bourgeoisie marseillaise*, family, like childhood in the Mediterranean city, has remained inviolable, an object of mystery, save once more in a film, this time one made in the 1960s, *La Vieille Dame Indigne*,[1] a charming, perceptive, and compassionate account of the sudden revolt and liberation of an elderly widow previously caged in by the greedy, self-interested, and constantly watchful solicitude of her two sons and her two daughters-in-law, with grandchildren brought in as scouts, outriders, and informers. Set somewhere in the eastern suburbs, among the scattered red-roofed villas and *bicoques*, in the general direction of Aubagne, it is a very happy and sunny story which allows the old lady, trotting with her young protégée from Prisunic to Marché Leclerc, from *corniche* restaurant to shady *terrasse de café*, a very good run for her money. Indeed, she is able to get rid of most of it by the time she has given her family the slip for good by dying.

The *galéjade* was for northern consumption, an *attrape-touriste* to keep the Parisian and the northerner happy, even to give him the nudging impression of being in the know, of being admitted into the closed world of elaborate private jokes, while the Marseillais went about their business. For evidence of the survival of an indigenous popular culture and of a popular speech, one would have to turn from literature to the *chronique locale*, especially in the bitterly cold, windy winter months approaching Christmas, when the eloquent street vendors from the foothills inland lay out the brightly painted figurines of the *crèches*: Provençal shepherds and *vignerons*, fishermen, Arlésiennes, lavender-women from Grasse, Niçoises with their flat black hats and dark blouses, chestnut-vendors, and sellers of clay pipes, on the wide avenue climbing towards the ugly mass of the Église des Réformés. It is perhaps typical of the quirks and deformations of the Parisian view of things, of Parisian assumptions on the subject of the inhabitants of two cities that are still capable, even *now*, of getting along without Paris, even – *ô crime atroce!* – of ignoring Paris, of turning their backs on the capital and of looking southwards or east-wards, along axes of communication that do not include the city of the north – it is typical of Parisian myopia that it should be the Lyonnais who are traditionally depicted as secretive, closed-in, inhospitable, and

[1] Directed by René Allio, 1965.

jealous, and the Marseillais who are represented with their mouths wide open and their secrets pouring out.

Of course, there was a great deal more to such Parisian attitudes towards Marseille than what one might call 'the professionalization of *la galéjade*' and a whole encyclopaedia of tried and very repetitive commercial-traveller jokes. There were the right-wing *nervis* – trigger men, gangsters, the Corsican protectors, including that irresistible duo of Carbone and Spirito, hiding under exceedingly hilarious surnames the exceedingly nasty reality of many gangland killings in the quartier du Panier, the underworld quarter of Marseille, and other places never too far away from the waterfront, and, later, torturers and murderers in the service of the French Gestapo in Paris.

Certainly, Carbone and Spirito were not a very presentable pair, wearing long, belted mackintoshes and pigeon-grey *chapeaux taupés* – velour hats. Certainly, they always had stubbly chins. Certainly, they were not devoid of a certain bandit chivalry: they gave lovely presents to Manouche, the protégée of Spirito and the subject of an extremely amusing biography-cum-novel by Roger Peyrefitte. But they were certainly not comedians – unless one thinks that Carbone's death, his legs blown off by a mine set by the Resistance at the side of the main line between Marseille and Dijon, is something which is good for a laugh.

An attitude of discretion in the presence of strangers, especially those from the north, can be readily discerned in Marseillais reactions to the very touchy subject of the city's changing, but generally thriving underworld. Most inhabitants would argue, rather fiercely, that the city was and is no more criminally inclined than any other great cosmopolitan port of its size and diversity, and it is, after all, a clearing-house for the whole of the Mediterranean, the Near East, and Algeria. In fact, they would argue, it was and is quite as safe as other French cities, and crimes of violence remain restricted to the professionals, the *gens du milieu*, but that Marseille has always suffered from undue publicity in the national press as France's capital of crime.

Yet, at the same time, in a spirit of proud localism, the very same people would expatiate, rather knowingly, on the subject of what went on in the quartier du Panier and would refer, with a touch of affection, to the multiple activities of the old *clan Guérini*, before it was finally broken up as a result of a series of murders, most of them committed in the rocky, hilly outskirts, and as a result of the defection of some leading members of the gang.[1]

The Guérini at least, though of Corsican or Genoese origin, clearly enjoyed *droit de cité*, the reward of long residence, complete integration, local intermarriage, and extensive charity, including the interests of the local football club, and a very touching respect for local interests and local hierarchies. They very much formed a well-established part of an oral literature on the theme of *Les Mystères de Marseille*, a sort of twentieth-century chap-book, a *livre bleu*, reserved exclusively to local story-tellers.[2]

But any interference from Paris was liable to provoke a stonewall of silence or even positive impediment, both reactions dramatically illustrated by the attitude of Sébeille, a local police inspector and a native of the port who, as a consequence, became something of a local hero, at the time of the prolonged inquiries into the Drummond murders in 1952. Lurs was well within the province of the Marseille-based *police judiciaire*, and the presence of Parisian inspectors, and a highly critical corps of Paris correspondents was deeply resented, as a further example of Parisian meddlesomeness and interference. It is thus not difficult to understand why Simenon, a very discerning man, although a northerner, should never have risked the flair and experience of Maigret in these unpromising waters. It is rather as if he had decided that l'inspecteur Maigret, though he had been launched on London, New York, Geneva, and Lausanne, would never have been given any chance to make even the slightest progress in Marseille. Maigret, who certainly is no stranger to the Côte d'Azur – after all, he has been to Antibes, Nice, Juan-les-Pins, Porquerolles, where he even sought very improbable excuses to prolong a quite blissful stay – has always given Marseille a miss.

---

[1] There is an excellent section on the Guérini clan and on the traditional *milieu* of Marseille in Lucien Bodard, *Les Plaisirs de l'Hexagone* (Paris, 1971), 'Néant à Marseille', pp. 280–334.

[2] Something of this inbred provincialism is indicated by the social ascension, from lover to lover, of Bouzigue's sister, in Pagnol's account: 'un chef de dépôt des tramways, puis . . . un papetier de la rue de Rome, puis . . . un fleuriste de la Canebière, qui était conseiller municipal, puis enfin . . . le conseiller général . . .' She was moving *upwards* all right, but within a purely Marseillais framework. (*Le Temps des secrets.*)

Nor has any other detective-writer in French pitted his talents against such an apparently recalcitrant and taciturn milieu. The French detective-story writer Exbrayat, in a whole series of *romans policiers*, has made, on the contrary, most effective use of the topography, the speech, the accent, and the cuisine of Lyon, and the familiarity displayed with all four is entirely convincing; but there is no equivalent for Marseille, even at this harmless level of light entertainment. Yet, in the last few years, according to the detailed investigations carried out by *Le Progrès*, the local newspaper, Lyon would appear to have overtaken Marseille as a European centre of crime, profiting from its proximity to Geneva and from its accessibility from Paris and Dijon. This has not prevented Lyon from retaining its own school of detective-story writers and of semi-professional criminologists, the successors of the famous Locard and Lacassagne, criminologists of the 1920s, and what, I think, is probably the finest *musée du crime* in the whole of Western Europe.

If a Marseillais were to object that Pagnol may have got things wrong, may indeed have fabricated caricatures for sale on a national market, the Parisian would probably shrug off his objections as ill-informed or, possibly, as inspired by some ticklish local conceit, just as the Parisian would take a great deal of persuading to accept the fact that Marseille liberated itself in 1944 with only a minimum of American help, because it would be an article of faith with him that it was Paris and Paris alone which had succeeded in such an achievement. And so, if a group of Ustaša gunmen chose Marseille as a base in which to assassinate, in 1934, Alexander of Yugoslavia, if Carbone and Spirito first emerged on the national scene in the port, and if Germaine Roussier opted for Marseille as the place for her suicide, the Marseillais, in each instance, were in some way to blame.

I myself early acquired a view of France tempered by what might be described as *une mentalité 75* (though, before the war, Paris had a letter, or a series of letters, rather than a number, the initial letter always being an R – for *rassurant?* – as can be ascertained from any film by René Clair on the 1930s). Soon I could only see France through borrowed Parisian blinkers, for, save for a memorable visit to Rouen, regular weekends at Samois (here one woke to the gentle chug of the French and Belgian barges, as the house was right on the river, within sight of the pont des Valvins), and several summer visits to the village of Saint-Germain-de-la-Coudre, on the edge of the Orne and the Sarthe, and reached either on foot from the main line of the État, or by Citroën bus from la Ferté-Bernard, a village in which the children were extraordinarily polite and still wore clogs, Paris represented the totality of my geographical experience.

I have dwelt, at considerable length, on the Parisian view of Marseille and its inhabitants, at least in the present century, because I believe it is quite fundamental to any understanding of Parisian assumptions about provincial France in general, and the Midi and the south-east in particular. I think it would be very interesting to take such an inquiry back into the previous century, as a further exploration of a very long background of misunderstanding, conditioning the mental blockage that has so much to do with the emergence at the level of Parisian awareness of what Parisians would call *le problème du Midi*, the problem of the south: a problem which is often of northern creation and, certainly, one of which most southerners are not aware, for I have never heard, in the Midi, any reference to the *problème du Midi*.

At the time of the Second Restoration, in 1815, the Prefect of the Bouches-du-Rhône and the garrison commander of Marseille, both of them from the north, commented with rather condescending amusement, as if they were describing a tribal dance, on the childlike joy of the inhabitants of Marseille as expressed at a great public festival held on one of the *cours* for the fête of Saint Louis. Of course, they went on in their enthusiastic report, they were well aware of the traditional attachment of the ever loyal Midi to the legitimate dynasty of the Bourbons, and did not need reminding of the terrible sufferings that the inhabitants of the port and of its wild hinterland had undergone during the dreadful years of the revolutionary wars. They further declared themselves deeply moved by such spontaneous manifestations of popular devotion to the Bourbon house: the women wearing their gayest colours and carrying green, white, or red silk parasols and pretty baskets of flowers; the fishermen dressed in their narrow jackets, wide blue velvet trousers, and dark hats covered in oilcloth; the children holding hoops and hobby-horses or pulling wheeled toys, clothed in striped waistcoats and brightly coloured frocks; the dancing of endlessly energetic farandoles; the whole vast concourse revolving hand-in-hand and facing inwards in ever widening or suddenly narrowing circles, to the sound of the fiddle, the flute, the *vielle*, and the shepherd's pipe, '*tout un peuple joyeux et en liesse*'; the huge white flags waving merrily in the sea-wind, while shouting boatloads of seamen and fishermen in long galleys, and armed with poles, jousted offshore, at the far end of the Canebière, in the old harbour. A splendid occasion indeed, and rendered all the more memorable by the presence of the duc d'Angoulême himself, the husband of the only surviving child of Louis XVI, the lieutenant-general of the faithful Midi, and the hero of ultra-royalism.

Yet, underlying the comments of the prefect and of the garrison commander, comments voiced *en style dithyrambique*, in inflated official prose, is the unstated assumption that the Marseillais are not to be taken entirely seriously, even in their perfectly genuine expression of joy at a great political change, long awaited, that had brought them immediate advantage and honour and the promise of many more advantages and many more honours. They were regarded as being like little children: enthusiastic *tout en surface*, naïve, changeable, and unreliable. And also like children, their moods could easily darken from *allégresse* and song to cries for vengeance and acts of bloody violence, so that a farandole, begun in light-hearted good spirits, could easily degenerate into a series of lynchings. They were quite unpredictable, not to be trusted, blown this way and that by the contrary winds off the sea or off the chilly mountains of the Lubéron; at one moment, full of courage and *plein d'élan*, at the next, running away like cowards. They were shallow, mendacious, boastful, unindustrious, content to bask in a prevailing sunshine and giving little thought to the morrow. In fact, they were some sort of colonial people, childlike yet cunning, largely immune to sober reason and judgement, incapable of prolonged effort, readily bought off by some highly coloured trinket or gay bauble that would match their brilliantly coloured clothes.

What they did not add, but what they no doubt thought, and what many of their predecessors from the north, and from the west, from Thibaudeau onwards, had both thought and, in fact, stated, was that they were little better than Hottentots and Zulus, which, of course, to the Parisian or to the northerner was hardly surprising, since they faced on to the African shore and turned their backs on what they would describe as *la civilité septentrionale*.

The attitude of these two officials echoes that of the novelist and Paris imperialist, Restif de la Bretonne, a great and enthusiastic convert to *le bon ton Parisien*, who, when all at once confronted with the horrible sights and sounds of the September Massacres of 1792, had no difficulty at all in consoling himself with the comfortable reflection – on the subject of those who would go down in French history as *les septembriseurs*, members of the massacring mob, many of whom he had heard roaring through the streets of the Left Bank between 3 and 4 in the morning – with the comment, '*Aucun n'avait l'accent du parisis.*'

15

Normandy*

Rouen – A First Sketch

Rouen, April 1935. It was a very important experience for me, for this was the first time I had ever gone off on holiday on my own. You can imagine what this would have meant to a boy who had spent a matter of years at prep school and public school and had never had a moment's privacy. It was all the more exciting because this was also the first time that I had to cope, unassisted, with a stay in a French provincial town where I knew no one. There *was* some assistance: the Hôtel Louis XIII, in the rue Beauvoisine, was recommended to me by a friend of Mme Thullier[1] who had a bookshop in the rue Thiers, and it was suggested that I should take a *demi-pension*, that is breakfast and dinner, leaving me free to have lunch anywhere. I remember the hotel both for its whiteness and its quietness. Everything was very white: the walls of my room on the first floor looking out on to that narrow, ancient street that cuts the city in two on a north–south axis, from the suburbs to the Seine. The bedspread and the curtains were white, the table-cloth in the little dining-room on the ground floor was startlingly white, the table in the window of my bedroom had a flower-patterned white cloth over it and gave forth a sort of white glow when the afternoon sun fell on it. The whiteness, the luminosity, that I can still recall. And the quiet. It was a

---

* First published as chapters 2, 8 and 10 of *The End of the Line* (1997).
[1] With whom I had been staying, and her two sons, in the boulevard Bonne-Nouvelle, Paris; see above, chapter 1, p. 7.

very silent, still hotel, the only sound the bell when the outer door was opened. At the other tables there were elderly couples, their white napkins tucked up under their chins. They looked as if they were full *pensionnaires* and lived there perhaps all the year round. They had their napkin-rings in little boxes. They talked in low tones, there was no talk between the tables. The atmosphere was decorous and restrained. I felt a bit prominent at my little table alone, but there were three or four other people who also sat alone. The waitress who took the orders, a very blonde girl with pale blue eyes, dressed in black with a white-laced smock, black stockings and mauve bedroom slippers, whispered the menu as if afraid of being overheard or as if 'raie au beurre noir' had been a secret code (my love of skate dates from that Easter holiday). I generally got in early, sixish, worked on my sketching-pad till the dinner gong went; then, after dinner, walked down to the quays and had an evening calvados on the terrace of the big Café Victor, from which I could watch the Finnish, Norwegian, Soviet and British boats being unloaded. I put lumps of sugar in my calvados, then sucked them. Sometimes I had a second calvados. I remember the banknotes, they had on them a female Republic with rather gauzy draperies hanging off her; she was, however, quite decent, nothing much was showing. She seemed to be stretching, as if she had a stiff neck. I enormously enjoyed my observatory, the lights of the ships, the ferries, the *pont transbordeur* taking people across the broad river to the industrial Left Bank. I walked up the rue Beauvoisine past sleepy *crémeries* and quiet little antique shops, pushed the door with its bell, picked up my key, and went to bed tennish, perhaps reading a bit of Maupassant.

Each morning I would head for the bus station near the river and take a little brown Renault bus, Les Cars Normands, to Caudebec, or Dieppedalle, the Forêt de Roumare, or the Forêt de la Bouille, carrying my sketching-pad. I liked taking this form of public transport, there would be voluminous adults with baskets, and talkative children. I would listen, finding that I could understand almost everything. For lunch I would go to a *pâtisserie* and buy some cakes and a bar of Chocolat Meunier. Once, in a village in the forest, I gave my Meunier to a small boy wearing a blue peaked cap; I had to buy another bar. Then I would get down to sketching. I sketched in the main square of Caudebec: a Decorated church, half-timbered houses, an old car, farm carts; I was closely watched by a small group of children in black smocks. I have lost the sketch – a pity, for Caudebec was bombed in 1944, it nearly all went. On the other bank of the Seine, near la Bouille, I remember going to a café with a terrace overlooking the huge bend of the river; the café black-brown-and-white timbered, *faux manoir normand*. The waitress, in black and white, had wonderful, caressing black eyes. The café was next to a very modern brick École Communale that looked as if it had just been built. I had some conversation with black-eyes and felt myself blushing purple, and she laughed at me, not mockingly, but I suppose encouragingly, to put me at my ease, but she didn't. I hated myself for my shyness, but could not do anything about it. Later, perhaps another day, I lost my temper with a taxi-driver who had overcharged me, and I realized that I could speak French.

In a fortnight, I did about twenty sketches, some of which I did not complete in pen-and-ink, leaving them in pencil outline. I remember one of a Finnish ship unloading wood, the *Suomen Poika*, which a member of the crew who spoke English told me meant '*Son of Finland*'. He was, too, and looked it, a very tall man with a sandy moustache and very pale blue eyes. I enjoyed each outing to the full, going to a different place each day, sometimes just staying in Rouen and sketching ships. Once, I climbed up the steep hill of Bonsecours and did a panoramic sketch of the whole of Rouen, l'Île-Lacroix in the middle of the river, the big bridge, the *pont transbordeur* and the iron spire of the cathedral. Panoramic sketches were not my thing, I was much better on small detail, a half-timbered house, pear and apple trees, a line of washing; especially a line of washing, there was something invitingly domestic about it, it seemed to be taking me in, telling me not very exciting secrets. Mostly I went through the day without speaking to anyone, save to ask for my bus ticket. But then I did have the long conversation with the red-faced docker, who was a Communist. I went back once to la Bouille, the café there, hoping to have another glimpse of black-eyes, but she was not there, just a rather surly waiter with acne.

With my meals in Louis XIII, I always took a *quart* of white wine (I think it was included), I generally opted for a sweet Graves or a sweet Entre-Deux-Mers. If I had had a very good day sketching or walking or both, I would boldly order a second *quart*. Tastes change completely over the years. Then, and later, as an undergraduate, I went for sweet white wines, Tokays, and that sort of thing. I can't remember when I switched to red.

What might have been the high spot of my Rouen stay was attendance at Pontifical High Mass on Easter Sunday in that fantastic cathedral. I remember a very old Archbishop, Mgr de Villerabel, all bent up, lines of white-robed monks from Saint-Wandrille, choirs, etc etc, the organ growling, in fact *the works*. I was fascinated and repelled; it was a bit like being in the enemy camp: there were young women with faces of extreme devoutness, one of them, quite close to me – I had got myself a chair on the aisle – suddenly went down on her knees, in the middle of the aisle, and kissed the Archbishop's large reddish ring, she kissed it *gluttonously*, almost as if she were going to eat the whole hand off as well. But the Mass was not like going to the cinema or sitting on the terrace of the Café Victor, for it did not give me the impression of *belonging*; quite the contrary, I felt alien, an interloper, I was even afraid that I might be caught out, exposed, as a fraud and a spy, by doing the wrong thing, crossing myself the wrong way round – or with my left hand (which would have seemed correct, it was, is, my *important* hand). Throughout the service I had been a bit apprehensive, it seemed so likely that I'd put a foot wrong, be kneeling down when everyone was standing up, or the contrary. Here was an aspect of France that made me feel very much of a foreigner, even very English. The cathedral, however, is very beautiful. A Governor of Normandy, a Plantagenet, the Regent for Henry VI, is buried under the high altar (but I didn't know that in 1935; he was discovered after the cathedral had caught fire in the summer of 1944).

I had come to Rouen from Paris, by bus via Pontoise and Magny-en-Vexin (the frontier), and I went back the same way. It was very hot and dusty on both journeys. I enjoyed both: *la route haute*, the old coach road, between Normandy and the Île-de-France, and the two Vexins. I had been quietly happy pretty well all the time. I thought that I should have more holidays on my own, the formula seemed to work, left me free to do what I wanted, to observe and listen; it would not have been nearly as much fun with a companion, then there would have been disagreements and arguments. It was wonderful to think that really no one knew where I was, though I did send my mother daily postcards;

I still have them, the postmark 'Rouen RD' is accompanied by a circle with dates, and a box containing 'VISITEZ ROUEN VILLE MUSÉE' – it was that, too, but a great deal more as well. Once or twice in the evenings I had gone to the public library; I liked the large frescos depicting nineteenth-century textile factories and the raw cotton at the quayside. I also liked the company, which was varied and unassuming. The public library did give me the feeling that I belonged.

I am still very fond of Rouen, though the Hôtel Louis XIII and the quays have gone. I suppose it is the abiding memory of having been so young, so inquiring, so excited, so much enjoying my own company, exploring the place on my own, seeking out things to sketch, and having no fixed plans, apart from returning to the white bedroom, the white dining-room, the pale walls of the hotel, 'HÔTEL LOUIS XIII' in gold letters on a black marble background shaped like a palette, and something like 'EAU CHAUDE DANS TOUTES LES CHAMBRES', though in smaller letters than the pious monarch's.

Rouen from the Sotteville Tracks

Most of the time that I spent working, in the rue de Crosne, on the criminal archives of the courts of the then still Seine-Inférieure (and yet unaware of its degraded designation) and of the État-Civil of Rouen and its satellite communes, I was put up in an SNCF hut, wooden with concrete floors, erected by the French Army in 1938, amidst the marshalling yards of Sotteville-lès-Rouen, and offering quite acceptable accommodation to twenty lodgers, ten a side, with ten wash-basins facing each row of ten beds. The beds were not bunks, but real beds, with pillowcases and sheets, and covered with thick dark-grey blankets marked in red with the letters 'SNCF'. Each bed had an accompanying small wardrobe and drawer. At the far end of the long wooden hut, there were two showers and five lavatories with seats. For the time I was put up there, the weather was warm, and the big coke stove remained unlit. The other nineteen lodgers were young trainee *cheminots*, mostly future signalmen. They were friendly, but not very communicative. On Friday and Saturday nights, I was left in sole possession of the hut, my fellow lodgers gradually trickling back in the course of Sunday evening. They all had families in the Rouen area, mostly in the Left Bank suburbs of Grand and Petit Quevilly.

Over the far side of about twenty tracks and trip-wires, and the long slow-moving lines of six to eight coupled trucks – long silver containers: Vins Gévéor, Vins du Postillon (a huntsman with a twisted horn), Bières du Lion, Dumesnil (both with lions, the former, red and with curly braided tails; the latter, a yellow, shaggy head), petrol, a liquid gas, toxic fuel – there were about thirty red Michelines, each opened at the end, like a raised snout, showing a mass of pipes and all their innards, in front of the rather precarious-looking driver's stool: cross-country via Serqueux to Amiens, or, via Bernay, Lisieux, to Caen; some also, via Maromme and Clères, to Dieppe. But nearly all the strings consisted of the huge containers, pushed indolently by shunting engines with zebra stripes, and some all at once taking off, clanking, apparently moving on their own, then stopping for a rest. The gasping Michelines, like open-mouthed pikes, were over by the main lines from Paris to Rouen-RD (Rive Droite), before the first tunnel. There were no passenger carriages in sight, and the big Also-Thom Fives, diesels, also no doubt opened up to display their complicated insides, must have found a resting place further down in the direction of Paris, between Sotteville and Oissel.

There were no waiting trolley-buses on Sundays, so one had to walk over the wires and sleepers to near the dark entrance of the first tunnel, taking care to avoid the sudden burst of air-pressure from the fast-moving Paris train, then cutting down the steep slopes of Bonsecours, through a maze of little brick houses, to reach the level near Eau-de-Robec and Saint-Ouen.

The red trolley-buses waiting at their weekdays terminus the far side of the tracks carried on their sides the city's crest, a white Holy Lamb, trussed up by its legs, beneath a fleur-de-lis on a blue shield, far into the Communist-dominated industrial suburbs of the Left Bank, the two Quevillys, and so on, and the big Centrale: the main prison for the whole of Lower Normandy. The city's escutcheon carried a timid message that was perhaps not even noticed, or just taken for granted, by the early-morning passengers. What would the Holy Lamb be doing in one of the Quevillys or in Saint-Sever? My own route to the rue de Crosne would take me to the rather impersonal rue Jeanne-d'Arc, at the stop by the big Café de la Poste.

From the black wooden SNCF hut one could see, at some distance, and beyond all those obstacles, wires and suddenly moving strings of trucks, the waiting trolley-bus, its cable unhitched, as if resting. Then a *wattman* (or driver) in peaked cap and smart blue uniform pulled the drooping cable into place on to the overhead electric wire, indicating an early, but leisurely, unhurried, but silent, departure, the red bus soon filling up two or three stops beyond Sotteville: a muted progress suited to a muted city (only in the markets would one hear a raised voice), the passengers mostly silent, whether seated or holding on to the rail at roof level. There would be a lot of wet umbrellas, making the red floor of the bus very slippery, and the smell of wet rubber and damp clothes. The dank smell would be partly overlaid by cigarette smoke from rolled-up Rizla paper. The windows would be misted over by the third or fourth stop. But the passengers knew their stops, pushing their way through the puddled wetness, to reach the opened swing-door, and trying to avoid the torrential flow of the paved gutter.

On Sundays, there was no waiting bus, Sotteville seemed sleepy in the still silence; but there was still the intermittent clanking and coupling of the small strings of ten or so containers; coal trucks spewing over, or long low-slung chassis bearing tree-trunks, all at once deciding to make a move down a slight incline, then stopping and going into reverse. You had to keep your eyes about you, in every direction. The little strings seemed to be tracking one by stealth. Apart from the discreet clanking and the low rumble of wheels, a Sunday silence (almost palpable) was all at once broken, in unison, by church bells coming from the deep bowl of the city: the grave, clanging ones of the cathedral; less insistent, but recognizable, those of Saint-Ouen, Saint-Nicolas, and Saint-Maclou; the tinkle from many small shrines on the slopes to the east and to the north. And a Sunday rain, even more implacable than a weekday one. It was time to break my own rules, as I slithered down the steep muddy banks, and put on a blue beret, with a coloured silk lining (Basque, probably), that had been tucked in the pocket of my mac, along with the two heavy keys that would open the green *porte cochère* of the rue de Crosne, giving me Sunday access to the huge minute-books of the État-Civil of Rouen and of some of its communes: Sotteville itself, Darnétal, Bonsecours, Déville, Oissel, maybe others.

Early on Sunday, I had swept thoroughly right through the long hut, cleaned the wash-basins and the lavatories with Javel, and shaken out the yellow SNCF mats. My weekday companions were very neat and tidy; perhaps they had PCF mothers back in the two Quevillys, and I wanted to impress them. I enjoyed the lonely activity of the quiet, wet Sunday morning, as if I possessed the hut. I even had a go with bucket and mop, opening the main door to look out on the gentle warm rain. First thing Sunday was to wash out my socks in my basin and put them to dry on the bar at the end of my bed. The rest of my clothes would go to a *blanchisserie*, open on Sunday morning, over the bridge beyond the far platform of Rouen-RD. The young trainees would turn up in the early evening with big Monoprix bags containing their washing, to last them out till the Saturday morning. They would also bring large black containers divided into compartments, which contained their food for the same period. There were no heating-rings in the hut, and they took the containers to the *cheminots'* canteen beyond the tracks, in a brick building near the Mairie, in the main street of Sotteville itself, which also contained a Decorated church with delicate fan vaulting. Sotteville had a pre-railway past.

The rest of Sunday I would be alone with my dead *fileuses*, later just numbers to figure in my only graph, drawn up with the expert help of Jean Meuvret and appearing, both dramatically and rather unfeelingly, in an article republished in my book *Terreur et subsistances*. La Moulière was shut; I had to make do with a restaurant of only four tables run by two almost identical red-haired ladies – in fact, mother and daughter – who took it in turns to cook. There was only one *plat du jour*, *petit-salé aux lentilles*, which marked out Sunday like the steady warm rain; almost invariable *radis beurre* (salted) and Camembert. The occupants of the three other tables ate there all through the week; they had credit, written on a slate. None was from Rouen, they were elderly couples from the centre of France, two men had lived in Senegal and spoke nostalgically about restaurants and cafés in Dakar. The tiny restaurant was in the rue des Mauvais Garçons. Whichever of the redheads was doing the cooking would talk through the hatch, with her sleeves rolled up, addressing herself to the couple from Moulins. The other lady sat on a lonely chair, smoking Gitanes. The single table had been left for my use: 'le jeune homme au petit-salé'.

But they had paid me no further attention. Each place had before it a full litre bottle of Gévéor, which seemed appropriate. Whether you drank it all or left a bit would not make any difference, you still paid for the whole litre (not at all expensive), and there would be another bottle laid before one's place in the evening, with the second round of *petit-salé*. Sometimes the two ladies changed places in the evening.

One Thursday, La Moulière was closed for some reason. The little table was occupied and I was told to come back in an hour. All the litre bottles were empty and the six 'regulars' had moved on to *café-calvados*. I was assigned the tail-end of Thursday's *plat unique*: *bœuf au gros sel* (and waiting litre of Gévéor). Dakar was on the menu again. One of the redheads had rolled herself some Dutch tobacco in Rizla paper. It would have been interesting to identify the other five days and their accompanying *plat*, the faithful Gévéor as a sentinel (and a reminder of the long silver bullet that rumbled through the night); but I was frozen as 'le jeune homme au petit-salé'. Was Friday *raie au beurre noir*? Did *tripes à la mode* have a day? Was *la potée champenoise* a Monday or a Tuesday? I never found out. I had to stick to La Moulière in the week: I had my place there, at a single table, right at the back; a *pichet de cidre* laid out, but one which the waitress, in a flowered plastic smock, would at once replace by a *demi-Côte, vin du patron*.

In Sotteville, as in Rouen, rue Fontenelle, or rue de Crosne, I was a prisoner of habit; I *liked* my prison, especially getting back at night by the trolley-bus to the terminus, then crossing the trip-wires and the rails, under the arc lights and the winking yellows, greens, and reds, the strings creeping up in shadow, and the *berceuses* of the night's rumbles and clinkings and the gentle breathing and occasional exclamations of my nineteen companions. I had six weeks in the hut and my regular Sunday routine. I even worked in the Archives Communales of Sotteville in the Mairie. The *secrétaire* told me I was the first person ever to have consulted the minutes of the *conseil général* for 1793 to 1795. There had been a royalist riot there in the spring of 1795, the Sottevillois (and Sottevilloises) had reopened the handsome church, sawn down the Tree of Liberty, burnt the wooden Déclaration des Droits de l'Homme, and then marched on Rouen down the steep slope of Bonsecours, and besieged the Hôtel-de-Ville, demanding both bread and a King. I wrote a short article about the riot for *Annales de Normandie* and sent an offprint to *la secrétaire*.

I had been happy in the hut as well as in the Sunday freedom of the rue de Crosne. I had found the trainee *cheminots* much less demanding (and much cleaner, they all slept in pyjamas) than the occupants of bunks in a Nissen hut provided by the British Army in 1942. They did not ask me questions or confront me with *L'Huma-Dimanche* or 'la vie soviétique'; but I was very grateful to the PCF deputy of one of the two Quevillys – or maybe of both – who had fixed me up with this long stay, free of charge. Much later, I acted as interpreter for him at the time of *les événements*, when he confronted a group of Balliol Maoists, whom he infuriated when he described the Billancourt activities of their Parisian counterparts, mostly from the XVIe, as 'ces enfantillages'. He was a Rouennais born and bred and knew his way about the industrial Left Bank, and the *other* termini of the trolley-buses bearing the Holy Lamb. I think he got on very well with the eminently sensible and pragmatic Waldeck-Rochet.

I liked living on the fringes of places and organizations, and 'lès' always seemed a good sign, something to go for, in its tricky relationship to the larger unit: Sotteville-lès-Rouen, the scene of a major anti-mobilization riot in August 1914, led by the *cheminots* and their wives. Sotteville reminds me of past happiness, the excitement of local archival research, the rumble of wheels and buffers, and being alone throughout warm, wet Sundays, rue de Crosne, with the huge green-bound *registres* marked, in pale, browning ink, 'Rouen' or 'Darnétal', or my subsidiary identity as 'le jeune homme' (I was thirty-five or so) 'du petit-salé aux lentilles' or 'le jeune homme du dimanche' – especially those last, despite the absence of the trolley-bus.

The SNCF had done me proud.

Rouen and Dieppe

Twice Rouen (mostly Rive Droite) had given me the taste of freedom and being on my own, in the spring of 1935 and again in that of 1952 or thereabouts. Both were pretty wet, though in 1935 there had been enough dry days for me to use my W & N sketching-pad.

By 1977, the *voie piétonne* had killed off both those streets – the long one north to south, the very short one leading off it east to west – as means of getting from one place to another, in a vehicle. La Moulière had survived, but not as a cheap *restaurant d'habitués*, most of them alone, with *Paris-Normandie* propped up against the regulation brown *pichets de cidre*, in a *quart* or a *demi*. Cidre, even *bouché*, had gone, to be replaced by a long, white, wine list enclosed in a mica protective folder. The menu in blue and red handwriting, reproduced by some simple process, had been abandoned in favour of a long printed, menacing affair, with a picture of La Moulière on top. But the picture did not make up for the easy familiarity of the service of the red, blue, and mauve menus of cyclostyled days. Now you sat where you were told, and to be alone and wanting a table for a single (rather apprehensive – once placed, there would be no escape; too late to flee) customer were not what was wanted; family parties of six or eight might cause the bullying waiters even to smile and to deal out the long menus like a powerful pack of cards, while a wine waiter hovered above a responsible-looking, self-assured occupant of the middle chair.

The chairs had also been changed; no longer the rather rickety wooden round-backs, with their slippery perforated yellow wooden seats, but padded chairs with rather threatening arm-rests. The paper table-cloths, so easily whipped away and replaced in a single swish, had given way to real cloths in red-and-white checks, to match the fanlike napkins. All the warning signals were on display. The fish was still very good: best to forgo the opening item, but the waiter would frown and the entrée would be a very long time in coming, necessitating a second *demi-bouteille* of Côtes. At the end of it all, a coffee without a large very dark calvados (3 Palmiers) would cause the waiters to smirk knowingly. *Not* the sort of customer one wants in a neo-La Moulière: it would have to be just one evening in the week. One would have to fall back on *chinois* or *vietnamien*; they too had prospered, rue Beauvoisine. And they were generally quiet, without intruding mummers and guitarists. 1977: *l'ère pompidoulienne*, a very bad time for the solitary evening eater, with *Ouest-France* to read (in Chinese or Indo-Chinese semi-darkness).

Still, La Moulière had survived, and the rue de Fontenelle and the rue de Crosne still had uneven paving stones, were open to traffic and the gutters running merrily. And there *were* cheap *lunch-time* restaurants near the market, rue Paul-Louis Courier: the market people, the police from a *commissariat*, and even some middle-aged female owners of clothes shops (not '*boutiques*') ate there off paper tablecloths. Lunch *had* survived for the *habitués*; it was a matter of looking: Martainville, La Rougemare, or even beyond the boulevard des Belges, near the abattoirs – large men with large appetites, not Gévéor, but a litre of *vin du patron* (always good) and very abundant helpings.

So a prospect not wholly bleak, indeed, a sort of adventure in patient research: markets, slaughter-houses, *commissariats* (to be recommended), *mairies*, *dispensaires*, laboratories, and *not* anywhere near the cathedral or the Grosse Horloge. And there was always Rouen-RD itself, with its two classes of buffet, both well-lit and even offering *petit salé*, *choucroute*, or *saucisse*. One could linger and watch the passengers through the Exit and try to guess where they had come from, particularly those from the red Michelines: Amiens perhaps? Or Barentin? Undistinguished luggage, a lot of baskets, children in tow.

In 1977, I had taken the non-stop St Lazare–Rouen-RD train (*avec supplément*). The Quai d'Orsay Relations Culturelles was paying for my trip, and I had the first part in cash; notes for huge sums in hundreds, bearing the portraits of literary figures (Hugo, rightly, scored very low, Flaubert topped at a prestigious 1,000; I had never seen the note before and it frightened me). The marshalling yards were still as extensive as ever; trains like bullets were open at their sides, halfway along their right flank, displaying their twisted guts, as if they had just undergone some elaborate surgery and had not yet been sewn up again – and the surgeons had gone off for lunch. Gévéor, Les Vins du Postillon, and Bières du Lion were still moving gently, survivors in a Coca-Cola age. I did not have time to make out the black hut: the non-stop train was still going too fast before it entered the first tunnel – but then provided a startling second appearance of Bonsecours, the iron spire of the huge cathedral and the Île Lacroix, the cluster of barges and the long bridge across the wide river. Then it was engulfed by the second tunnel, stopping gently, with a very slight jerk, at the steep left-side platform, the one nearest the exit, very briefly lit from above. The passengers for le Havre were waiting, well-dressed and with cases in real leather. Maybe the hut *had* survived from my time over twenty years before.

Now the Quai had booked me in at the Hôtel de la Cathédrale; an enormous wooden double bed with two armchairs in chintz covers and a little fridge containing mini-bottles, *quarts de vin*, gin, Armagnac, a dark, rich calvados – I decided to start my three-star stay with that and my latest Boileau-Narcejac, this one set, suitably, I thought, in la Roche-Guyon.

Then I walked down to the far end of Martainville, where the white lobes and the round stone obstacles ran out and the street became normal and open to traffic. The market people were beginning to pack up, stands folded and their contents – dresses, pinafores and shirts, boots, shoes, caps, berets, crates of apples, plums, pears, bottles of wine and *cidre bouché* – were being stacked into trailers, and the shouts and encouragements had died away. From the *terrasse* – it was sunny for once – I looked inside the big *café-tabac*; the waitresses were laying out the paper table-cloths on most of the tables. Now was the time to move and stake a claim to a round-backed chair with a per-forated seat at a table set for two. I wanted to face outwards; the street was being cleared of cauliflower stalks and skins of plums by a man in green with a long-handled brush. Men wearing caps in tartan with pompons sprouting from their tops, women still in their flowered smocks, stood at the long *zinc* for an *apéritif*, the men a Ricard, the women a Banyuls, all shaking hands with the blue-smocked *patron* and smoking. An oldish man in a corduroy jacket took the seat at the little table, with his back to the street, its gutters running.

'Vous permettez?' It was a formal question. I asked the waitress what was on: *pommes à l'huile*, a choice of *assiette froide* or *lapin chasseur aux carottes*, Camembert or Pont-l'Évêque. There was no menu, but it was an inviting choice. I went for the rabbit (despite the bones), the sauce was delicious. My *vis-à-vis* got through his meal – *assiette froide* as the main dish – in a quarter of an hour and got up to pay at the bar. He was not a talkative man. I ordered a bottle of *vin du patron*, lingered over cheese, offered myself a pale calvados with my very strong coffee, paid and went back to the *terrasse*, where I fell asleep. I was told there was a market Wednesday and Friday, so that looked after lunch for those two days. They didn't serve food the other days. Friday was always fish: sometimes *sole dieppoise*, poached. In the evening the *tabac* was almost deserted. It would have to be *chinois*, I had spotted two beyond La Rougemare. Over my first lunch I had paid with the Flaubert note, I was keen to break it up. The *patron* took it without comment, he must have been used to large denominations, especially on market days. I went off with a wad of notes depicting other literary figures.

I avoided the Hôtel de la Cathédrale as much as possible; it was just a place to sleep and to read my Boileau-Narcejac. I had my croissant etc in the *tabac*, then walked across the bridge to La Tour, heavily guarded by CRS, on the Left Bank. The Archives Départementales had been moved there, and the friendly rue de Crosne had been taken over by a tax office. La Tour was very efficient, but quite impersonal.

Rue de Crosne, I had made two close friends, both Rouennais (I loved that sonorous open 'e', brought out to its full value by the two 'n's that followed it, giving the name an expression of asserted pride, though those who responded to it were no boasters, but rather taciturn). There was the *sous-archiviste*, slightly dotty, the Giver of the Keys. His brother had been keen on Pétain. My friend's wife had a children's clothes shop, Le Petit Bateau, opposite the redheads' restaurant – which had, by 1977, been turned into a bar: Le Trou, or something like that. My other Rouennais friend, André Dubuc, was a retired schoolmaster, an *érudit local*, wearing the mauve ribbon of *les palmes*, who contributed numerous *glanes*, with commentary, to *Annales de Normandie*. He never missed the annual October meeting of the Normandy *sociétés savantes*, which, throughout the 1960s, I also liked to attend, always managing to stay somewhere in Rouen, either in a hotel the far side of the station, near my little *blanchisserie* (and starcher) or in what appeared to be a private house, in a quiet street beyond the boulevard des Belges, where, sleeping beneath a palm cross, I would be woken up at 8 a.m. by the noise coming from a children's playground that my room faced on to and that added to the illusion that I was sleeping in the big bed of what had been a married couple. I think that, along with the palm cross, there was a dried *couronne de mariée*. There was a framed picture of St Christopher carrying a child across a tiny stream – not at all like the broad frontier between RD and RG. In the morning, I left my heavy bedroom key at: 'Sonnez pour l'office svp.' There was a bell, but there was never anyone at the hatch. I hung up the key on its numbered hook; there were four other keys in place. I let myself out of the heavy door and went into the quiet street. There were three nuns on mopeds, their skirts rolled up to reveal long white woollen stockings, the avant-garde perhaps of a more extensive ecclesiastical presence further up in one of the big grey buildings to the west. The nuns were going fast, as if trying to race each other. Each had ten or so baguettes protruding from their two black saddle-bags; but the nuns were in brown with white-edged head-dresses. Although it was early – 8.30 or so, on a weekday there was a Sunday feeling about the long cobbled avenue, with a *boulangerie-pâtisserie-confiserie* at an intersection halfway down. Women in black dresses and thick black stockings, and coloured slippers with pink pompons, hurried along westwards, baguettes and *ficelles* sprouting from the voracious mouths of their shiny, waterproof black *cabas*. There was a green dustcart in the distance, its hygienic brightness accentuating the universal grey-ness. A tall, nonchalant Sénégalais, loose-limbed and ebony black, zipped up in green – to match his cart – was sweeping out the gutter with a long-handled broom. Unlike the nuns, he was not in a hurry, taking his time and pushing the water ahead, almost caressingly. He was puffing at a cigarette in crackly yellow paper and seemed quite alone. A yellow postal van – a brighter yellow than the browning cigar-ette – went by very fast, without stopping at a line of six post-boxes on concrete stumps; it seemed anxious to get away eastwards. Les Belges marked out some sort of unstated frontier; to their west, an anonymous diminishing grey perspective, tall houses with closed rolling-steel shutters at ground-floor level, and that gave nothing away save a hint of desolation and a more positive mistrust, a discreet and unwelcoming stillness, closed, steel-covered front doors surmounted by Second Empire Gothic fantasies: corbels designed to catch the rain, and to proclaim a seedy, suspicious piety somewhere in the dark *entrées* on the far side of the embattled entrances. Anaemic green plants, yel-lowing at the ends, and waxed polished floors up a few dark steps. No trolley-bus came this way, one was safe at last from *voies piétonnes*, an area *beyond*, best employed as place of sleep. I think now that the noisy children may have been those of a *patronage*. On Sunday, the long avenue would no doubt come alive: the insistent tinkle of small bells, lines of well-dressed families emerging, this time, not with baguettes, but with pastries or *tartes* done up in little cardboard boxes held with gold string, after a service in a Gothic church. For that matter, the street – nameless, as far as I was concerned – was sad enough to have accommodated an undecorated, bleak-looking *Temple*, with a glass-framed notice-board outside, and more family groups carrying little boxes tied up in gold string.

Rouen in 1977 seemed an *early* city, with most places, including couscous restaurants and wine bars closed by 11 p.m. and the chiming of the Grosse Horloge the only sound. So, beyond Saint-Ouen and at the far end of La Rougemare, I was surprised to see ahead of me, lighting up the shiny black blocks of *pavé* with a yellow light, the blazing windows of a huge corner café, neon-lit, apparently crowded with dimly seen moving figures, in black silhouette, like animated cut-outs. I went into the brilliant yellow light, a challenge to the long night still outside, another three or four hours of inky darkness. The triangular place, like a wedge shoved into the surrounding black, was thick with cigarette and cheroot smoke, and there was a powerful sharp smell of brandy, calvados, strong coffee and stale Kronenbourg.

Behind the constantly wiped semicircular bar there were four large men, dressed alike in long blue tunics and wearing light-brown corduroy caps. It looked as if they formed a team, they moved together with unhurried ease. All four had drooping sandy moustaches and very pale blue eyes. They pulled the pumps of Bières du Lion with the casual skill of seasoned drivers. Two had anchor tattoos on their long, hairless arms.

Men stood four deep at the counter, some breaking hard-boiled eggs on its edge and salting them generously. Most likewise wore caps. Trays, and fresh croissants in their wicker baskets, from a neighbouring bakery that lit up a moon-shaped bit of wet *pavé*, were being handed along. Many of the standing men and seated women were waiting for the *chasse-marée*, the refrigerator lorries from Dieppe, due in the early hours between 2.30 and 4. Most of the women wore long plastic overalls in blue-and-white stripes. But there was also a sprinkling of merchant seamen and *mariniers* from the long petrol-container barges, the latter due to head upstream at first light. The ships, docked below Maromme, would have to wait for the tugs to take them out midstream – there was a dangerous current at the level of the two Quevillys. Outside, one could hear the wooden shelves being put up ready for the array of silver fish, pale-pink *crustacés*, pale oysters, and black *moules* that would come a few hours later.

I sat at a table occupied by three Finnish seamen, in peaked caps bearing in front identical flags and capital letters (SKR); they had brought up a full cargo of wood pulp and were waiting to take on a load of vintage wines (*not* Gévéor, nor Postillon) and spirits. They had already been drinking a generous selection from their future cargo, putting down *fines à l'eau* with a rather sullen persistence, indicated by gesture, as the waitress, her hair running into her eyes with sweat, as fast as she could, brought them fresh glasses. They had laid out thick wads of notes – some of them green US dollars – on the watery plastic table, causing them to stick to the damp surface. The waitress disengaged them one by one, slowly working downwards. None of the three could speak a word of French, and they did not have much to say in English, nor, for that matter, to each other. They were not there for conversation. The wad looked as if it would last them out to first light.

There was also a small group of women in identical long aprons in blue-and-white stripes that looked, in their exact repetition in triplic-ate, a bit like a uniform, which indeed it was. The shared purpose of their waiting presence was further emphasized by their drinks: three large pale-brown *bols* of *café au lait*, with small brimming glasses of calvados to the right of the insipid-looking liquid, in the role of col-lective supporters, not assertive, but present all the same, ready on the touch-line. All three must have been right-handed, judging from the thrice shared position of the glasses, reflecting, in the crude neon light-ing, an almost golden yellow. The supporters could wait too. One of the three was studying a big black notebook, like a large schoolgirl doing her sums, occasionally putting her Biro into her mouth, then sucking it reflectively, taking it out, adding a figure, and closing the notebook with a snap that could be heard at the curved bar. Their common appearance and the triply shared identity of their drinks – even drunk down, so far as I could see, to exactly the same level – left no doubt that the three of them were waiting for the Dieppe lorries. If the *chasse-marée* arrived early, the market would open early. The stands were already set up, the fish market was just beyond the blazing lights of the triangular café. All three women had powerful arms, with their sleeves already rolled up, and their thick legs harnessed in shining black rubber. The three sat in a row on the red banquette at the far end of the smoky café. The banquette had large rents from which unhealthy-looking wisps of whiteish stuffing protruded. The three women, now engaged in animated conversation, and shaking with vigorous laughter, their notebooks stuffed away in the immense pouches of their striped tunics, seemed unaware of the dubious stuffing. Perhaps, being all three well-covered behind, they did not even notice it. They had an authoritative way of sitting down, and it was clear that the red (or *reddish* – it had dark stains) banquette was their well-established waiting location. There was still an unclaimed area of banquette to the right of No 3: perhaps one of the small squad had taken the night off. I did notice, from my own distant, standing position at the bar, that the sweating waitress did not take any orders from the red-faced trio, simply putting down the three steaming bowls and the first lot of the brimming right-handed golden sentinels.

It was a place for *waiting*. But some of the older men standing at the bar, three or four deep, were merely lonely and eager to talk, so as to see out the night. One, in a shiny, stained blue suit, had a red rosette in his lapel. He had a well-brushed head of white hair and had begun offering people rounds. I chose a *ballon* of alleged Côtes, but I think it was a Postillon or Nicolas product. At dawn, he would go to bed somewhere. The bed would be uninviting, certainly unmade, and the sheets greying. He told me he came every night, generally after 11, 'when things warmed up'. He knew the four blue-smocked men behind the bar, shaking the hand of each in turn. They referred to him familiarly, but with a nuance of affection, as 'le père François'; so he *did* run to the luxury of a Christian name. I don't know what he did on Sunday nights, when the big café was closed. But he could see out the night the rest of the week. Sunday, like Christmas Eve or the *réveillon*, was always a difficult, bleak time for the lonely. In Paris, I would make for a vast, deep establishment, with marble-topped tables and, in an inner recess, a desolate, unheated billiard-room, the green baize lining torn its full length and hanging in sad strands, at Strasbourg-Saint-Denis. Two years in succession, I had met there, standing at the crowded bar (among the hurried prostitutes taking a brief break, some of them in tears), and drinking Ricard, an oldish man wearing a green tie and the ribbon, in green-and-red diagonals, of the Croix de Guerre. He always stayed till 7 or 8, I was told by one of the waitresses as she hurriedly washed out glasses and wiped the long counter. I would take the first *métro*, which, on Christmas or New Year's Day, would be almost empty when it opened a bit after 5 a.m., the sliding iron bars pushed aside and the sudden breath of hot air welcoming in the bitter cold, the wind from the north-east funnelled through the two black arches and across the wide boulevard. Only after midday would it fill up with people dangling little boxes on gold string, accompanied by tired, whining children.

In the Rouen café I met two men in smart blue uniforms and wearing peaked caps marked SNCF in red on the front. They were to take out a very long goods train of gas canisters and oil through the two tunnels and the main platform of Rouen-RD at 3 a.m. Perhaps they had been in the black hut in my time. It seemed unlikely. They were cheerful and gobbled three hot croissants each, chased down with the almost inevitable *pousse-café*, one of them wiping his sandy moustache on the sleeve of his blue jacket. They were in a hurry, they had to walk back along the tracks to the Sotteville yards, then form up the convoy; the first passenger train was due in at 5, so the goods train would have to end up at a siding above Maromme. I had become quite familiar with the daytime and first-light logistics of a busy station that had only five platforms and that served six or seven different destinations in addition to the Paris–le Havre main line. Thanks to the daily section in *Paris-Normandie* devoted to 'Mouvement du Port', I could learn the times of the arrival and departure of the ships, mostly Scandinavian or Soviet, to be taken downstream or to be docked in the post-war port, visible from the train, far below Maromme. The knowledge seemed to include *me* in the unrestrained fraternity offered by the long night; much handshaking across the constantly wiped bar, Christian names: Robert, Dédé, Jo, Charles, Bob, Alphonse, Lise, Louise, Mado, Danielle, Rose, Gaby, followed by questions that required no answers, and a general cross-café *tutoiement* and phrases exchanged the full length of the wedge-shaped room, like fast-delivered tennis-balls. Everyone seemed to know everyone else's business, and to rejoice in that shared bond.

But it would not include *me* even in my temporary night status. That might have come later, after a week or a fortnight. But I could not have formed myself (as I had once in HQ L of C) into a *permanent* night-worker. My identity, either as a *rosbif* or as a Scandinavian, had been easily spotted by the waitress when dealing with the three Finns. Could I help out as they did not seem able to speak any French? Twenty pairs of (not unfriendly) pale-blue eyes were momentarily directed at me and my blue overcoat as I shouted, across the hubbub, in what I took to be my *français de Lille* accent, that I *would*, leaving my drink at the counter and going over to their table to sort out their (ongoing) order for the rest of the night till sailing time.

But this was in 1977. I did not get the *ruban rouge* till the last day of 1984. *That* would have done the trick, admitted me, *à part entière*, in my attempted identity. All there would have recognized the brilliant red on a blue lapel, it was like a sort of passport, albeit a false one, of course. But it generally did the trick, especially in *restaurants d'habitués*, when my *ruban rouge* confronted another *ruban rouge* across the narrow frontier of the freshly laid paper table-cloth. No questions would be asked, that would have been rude; but the red ribbon would put me on my mettle. My *vis-à-vis* would score though: he had a yellow ring, a napkin, and a numbered box. He was also in a hurry.

The Rouen yellow lighthouse was a startling discovery in a city that seemed muted at any time of the day. The noise was deafening: shouted orders through the hatch; boisterous laughter; a sandwich or a huge plate of *moules* (once the Dieppe lorries had arrived), hot soup served after 4 a.m. In fact, unlike Paris, Rouen had managed to preserve a night heart, or maybe more than one. This time, in the spring of 1977, I decided to see it out till 6, cracking large prawns. I did not have a train to catch till an afternoon express to Dieppe-Maritime on the next day and it didn't seem worth going to bed for the morning.

From inside the brightly lit café, I had been able to see (and hear) the actual arrival of the eagerly awaited *chasse-marée* from Dieppe. It took the form of a whiteish and silver-grey long lorry that displayed on both its sides a blue-and-black fish, bent in a wide arc, as if struggling to break clear from an invisible line or net. It could have been a salmon, or a common plebeian cod. It was certainly not a skate – with its unprepossessing, spiky profile, and in no way emblematic. This one was just a *fish*, as proclaimed the capital letters, in a chilly marine blue, 'POISSONNERIES DIEPPOISES'; the firm was housed in a vast building in silver-grey metal at the edge of the inner harbour of that port. The lorry was driven by a man in white overalls and a white cap with a long peak, with his fellow similarly clothed in hygienic purity and chilliness. Down came the big doors at the back marked with the same lettering, but without a fish, followed by a cascade of baskets containing a variety of fish of different contours, some ugly and rather threatening, others elegant, and all that seemed to shine back, reflecting, in various colours, the powerful arc lights and the brilliant, sizzling kerosene lamps. The baskets did not conform to any uniform size or shape or colour: fish quite flat, alongside fleshy-looking monsters of the deep, finned with sharp and scaly protuberances; maybe sea bass, and even swordfish. Not a moment was lost, the Dieppois driver and the man sitting next to him, and the figures, male and female, in blue-and-white aprons and long black rubber tunics and boots, moved with the precision of a well-trained *corps de ballet*. There was a crash of released chains hitting the yellow-shining wet *pavé*, as the contents of the baskets were stacked, at last, like to like, flat to flat, assertive to assertive, sword to sword, and, thus regimented, found their allotted places on the waiting trestles, to claim their price.

The long lorry was only five minutes late: not quite a record, but good timing that must have suited everyone's book. It was all over in about ninety minutes, leaving the inside of the deep lorry sopping with ice-cold water that ran out to form yellow-shining pools running in channels between the uneven *pavé* and the empty baskets neatly stacked inside. Then the tall man with long brushes moved in to clear away the scaly debris: heads with mournful eyes (in a Simenon novel they would have been described as 'glauques', a compulsive adjective that, perhaps in an hour's time, or a little more, could equally be applied to a reluctant, murky Rouen dawn). But Simenon did not have much time for Rouen, other than as a terribly dull place to get away *from*; you would not go there voluntarily, but you might have to go *back* there.

The *chasse-marée* had been and gone, the clearing-up had been concluded. But some of the regular participants lingered on. The three striped figures returned to the reddish banquette to look through their black notebooks, have their *bols* replenished and their right-hand yellowish sentinels refilled by the attentive waitress. Then, without a word being spoken, they shook hands with the men at the counter and moved off, in a squadron of three, into the still inky black night. Perhaps they lived together. Maybe they had a vehicle parked somewhere a little further out. They would be back for the next market, perhaps in fuller strength; four or five occupants of the reddish-brown outer fringe, for there had been loud inquiries hurtling across the smoky room, for Lulu and for Zoë.

I decided to see it out till a bit after first light. There was no particular hurry, I had avoided the three-star Hôtel de la Cathédrale, so as not to break into the larger notes still surviving from *la caisse noire*. I had booked in for the coming night at the Hôtel Saint-Nicolas in the street of that name. It had only one star. Then I walked down towards Martainville and, already pretty tired, sat down on a wicker chair at the *terrasse* of the big *café-tabac*, rue Paul-Louis Courier, ordering a strong coffee and a small calvados. After perhaps an hour, I woke up with a start; my coffee was quite cold, but the glass of calvados was shining a brownish gold in the pale sunlight. Its sharp taste revived me and I prolonged the taste by sucking on the sugar lump that I scooped up from the bottom of the curved-lipped glass. But there was not much to watch, I was the only occupant of the *terrasse*, and the street was almost empty, save for a few women in flowered aprons carrying black shopping-bags. There was a *boulangerie* open a little further down the street. The women must have lived near by, for they were all wearing slippers, one with pink pompons, the others in check patterns. The *pavé* had been given an early morning hosing, but it was now quite dry. The big *tabac* was open, two men in corduroy caps were buying cigarettes and *loto* tickets. A postman in a smart blue uniform brought in a pile of letters in bright yellow envelopes and trade magazines tied together in elastic, pushing the packet through the little window reserved for cigarettes and cheroots, hastily shaking hands with the female *tabagiste*, and then hastening on his rounds all the way down the street; some of the shops were still shut: he pushed the packets under the closed doors or wedged them in the space between the glass front and the wooden lintel. One packet, containing a thick wad of blue envelopes, he handed over to an oldish man in a crumpled blue suit who was walking a black-and-white dog on a lead, the dog stopping every now and then to raise its leg. The dog was wearing a tight-fitting tartan jacket; it seemed much smarter than its owner, who stuffed the blue packet in the pocket of his suit and shook hands with the *facteur*. I could see the little blue postal van parked at the first intersection. The postman must have made a habit of doing this section of his round on foot, at least on mornings when there was no market. I banged on the window behind me and eventually drew the attention of the *patron*, still in shirt-sleeves and wearing a tartan waistcoat – tartan seemed to be taking over men's caps, women's slippers, and dogs' jackets: it would be shopping-bags next, then the covers of school exercise-books, then, in triumph, the intimacy of men's trousers and girls' skirts; and it all seemed to be Royal Stuart, though I could not be too sure. But the tartan take-over did not have it all its own way. I ordered a Kanterbrau, which came in a long glass and had a frothy top. While I was paying for it, a lady with her hair still in curlers came by, hobbling unsteadily; she was wearing high-heeled black shoes, and the heels kept catching in the declivities between the *pavé*. But she managed to pursue a tottering course in the same direction taken by the blue-suited pensioner. She was accompanied by a white poodle held on a thin lead. The poodle, which had a pink bow in its curly and no doubt freshly rinsed hair, was wearing a tight little black jacket with white buttons.

Further down the road, the owner of a small haberdasher's shop had put on the handle of the glass door, and picked up her pile of letters and brightly coloured circulars tied in elastic. She was shaking a mat, which gave out small clouds of dust, and was banging away with a broom. The bangs offered a peaceful accompaniment to the stillness of the scene. They were not impatient or threatening. I could not see the *mercière*; I imagine that she was wearing a pinafore over her severe black dress.

It was that uncertain time suggestive both of leisure and waiting: *les heures creuses*, somewhere between 9 or 9.30 and 11.30, after the early-morning torrent of 7 to 8.30 had receded, and before the sudden, almost universal, tidal wave of midday, announced in booming tones by the cathedral clock, released the hordes of all conditions heading for lunch. The quiet street, almost empty, save for the odd handcart as it bumped noisily over the *pavé*, a reminder that life had not completely stopped, was like a film run slowly and in muted colours: a film that would have a gently soporific and rather agreeable effect on its rare audience, enjoying the respite offered by unexpected inactivity and absence from what should have been hours devoted to work – a holiday feeling that would make you lazily aware of small details, a cat darting across the *pavé*, a shaft of sunlight accentuating the contrasting black and white of Norman wooden eaves, a large rat disappearing down an arched culvert.

This would be Maigret time, as, fresh from the station, and having selected a wicker chair, on the empty *terrasse* of a smallish café offering a view of both the main street and an intersection, he sniffs out (*flairer*) the air, and drinks a local white wine: a pleasant combination of work and self-indulgence. The Commissaire, between sips of his *ballon* of local *Anjou blanc*, will idly question the blue-aproned *patron* (who also wears a cap) about this or that. Slowly drinking my Kanterbrau, my eyelids drooping, I have no such excuse. Just a holiday feeling while most work, a quietness soon to be shattered by the midday rush. No market, so no lunch in the café to my rear; but it soon fills up with hurried people who make do with long sandwiches: ham, *rillettes*, salami, cheese, followed by a rapid *pousse-café*.

I follow one of the tides, uphill, along the pedestrianized rue Beauvoisine, to Rouen-RD, to book for the fast train, *avec supplément*, for Dieppe-Maritime, which gets in at 3 p.m., giving me an hour before the arrival of the *Villandry*, the SNCF boat from Newhaven, on which Margaret is travelling. I have already checked with M. Vée, the big, red-faced *patron* of the café-hôtel Au Roi de la Bière, Arcades de la Poissonnerie, in Dieppe; there is a big round sign hanging from the vaulted roof of the Arcade depicting Le Père Kantor, in black Tudor cap, putting down a frothing glass of Kanterbrau. M. Vée has told me that we can have our usual room on the second floor.

It is a huge, old-fashioned room that could qualify as a *Dictionnaire Larousse* 'Chambre', or better still a Gaston Leroux old favourite: *Le Mystère de la chambre jaune*. But there is no mystery, no hint of violence; the room is not yellow but has a flowered wallpaper of pink roses and green leaves, picked out with pink borders, a motif running from ceiling to floor. It might have come straight from Oberkanth's factory in Jouy-en-Josas. There is even a key protruding that opens on to a shallow wooden shelf for socks and handkerchiefs. The door of the secret shelf does not interrupt the pink-rose pattern. The top of the window is in the form of two small arches that are above the Arcade and that filter a little light from the quayside street. There is a huge bed, covered in a quilt decorated in red roses. To the right of the bed is an enormous mirrored wardrobe that must be of Cauchois origin and that contains a score of coat-hangers and a number of large keys that seem to have lost their vocation – there is only the one little secret drawer. I don't think the pink roses, their green leaves, and the horizontal pink stripes of the *toile de Jouy* cover any more secrets, apart from the little shallow drawer the existence of which is indicated by the tiny, discreet key. I could poke about a bit more, banging the wall in search of a responding hollow echo indicating the existence of another, deeper recess. But I don't poke about. The roses have been in place, to my own knowledge, for at least eighteen years, and seem to have guarded their singular innocence, though they are perhaps badly in need of cleaning, a careful sponging down, to restore their freshness. They give the big room a borrowed, early nineteenth-century veracity, 1805 or so, to match the house, a bit older, that rises above the vaulted stone arcades while incorporating them. When the night boat from Newhaven (Harbour) gets in, between 4 and 4.30 a.m., the whole room trembles and vibrates to the deafening sound of the ship's engines. The ship seems to be entering the room itself. It is not entirely an illusion, for its grey sides, rising high above the quayside cafés and restaurants, are only about fifty yards away from the big bed, the wardrobe, and the pink roses. When the boat has docked and has been tied up, the pulsating engines go silent. There is a brief (and deceptive) interlude of total quiet. Then comes the rumble of heavy iron wheels, producing the clanking of couplings. The noise ends with the fierce roar of the snout-nosed train: a snake with two identical heads. The driver has moved from the head facing seawards to the head facing inland. Whoosh! The serpent very slowly gathers speed, the shattering sound diminishing as it skirts the handsome white terminus of Dieppe-Ville. Dieppe-Maritime is an illusion. There is no station: just a couple of railway lines that come to an end on a stretch of *pavé*; no buffers even;

the end of the line, without fuss, with nothing to show for it, other than that it *is* the end of the line. A few feet beyond, the train would become derailed. The gradual silence is comforting, you turn over and resume a deep sleep, still vaguely registering the fact that the night boat has been tied up and that the train is heading for Rouen-RD and Paris-Saint-Lazare.

A flowered screen, liable to fall over, the flowers blue and red, hides the wash-stand, the lavatory, and the bidet. There are thin strips of unmatching carpet both sides of the bed and opposite the wardrobe mirror, covering the uneven red tiles of the floor that sinks slightly in the direction of the quayside street and the two arched windows. It is a welcoming room – the big key on its hook, at the bottom of the steep stairs – because you know exactly what to expect and that every familiar object will be in place.

It is about 4. The *Villandry* is in, securely tied up. A big green crane has brought up the gangway, and the sailors from the boat have secured it to an exit that opens on the second deck. The trickle of passengers turns to a struggling flood. Soon I can see Margaret, and she can see me, standing just by the first carriage of the train, on the very edge of the quay. She is wearing a stunning new outfit and is smiling. She is the only passenger to go through passport control, in a steel eyrie high above a line of metal steps. We check in at Au Roi de la Bière, she shakes hands with M. and Mme Vée. We have ahead of us the inside of a whole week: time enough to establish a routine and to discover at least a little about how the town breathes, the days of the market held in the long square leading from the lovely late-Gothic Saint-Jacques and dominated by the hatted, prancing figure of Duquesne.

The first morning, when we come down to the big café, the fish market is still in progress: the fish are laid out on wooden trays, with metal words in black on a white background pinned on to each section of the tray. It is Les Arcades de la Poissonnerie, and there is a market there every day save Sunday and Monday. There are many customers, mostly women with big black bags. Their purchases are wrapped up in newspaper, and we can see them carrying them off, as they cross the swing bridge to le Pollet. The fish market just outside lasts from a bit before 8 to 9.30. Once it has been cleared away and the *pavé* hosed down, it is replaced by an untidy man in a long mac and wearing an old brown felt hat. He lays out three or four wooden troughs containing second-hand books, most of them in yellow covers with a black mark in the top right-hand corner. No one buys his books, but he seems to be a popular joke figure. There are many interchanges between the regulars at the tables within the café and the bookseller. He brings his troughs and books in a wheeled wooden *voiture à bras*, which he trundles off about 11 o'clock, apparently quite happy about the lack of customers.

Coffee or a beer on a big *terrasse* facing away from the quayside, then perhaps the shingle beach between the casino and the château. Margaret chats to a lady from Paris, who has brought her large tabby cat in a basket which she opens up so that the cat can look around at the gulls. On the stroke of midday, a man with a pointed nose comes from the rue Saint-Nicolas with a bathing-dress wrapped in a towel. He talks to himself quite loudly and distinctly, in a surprised tone, as if he were two people. I can hear him. 'The water will be cold for the season. There is a lot of floating scum on the surface: seaweed mostly.' He swims powerfully for ten minutes, dries, and dresses, still talking.

We have lunch in a restaurant up a flight of stairs, on the first floor, off the narrow rue Saint-Nicolas. The restaurant has its *habitués*, all with rings in numbered boxes, fifteen to twenty of them. They are from the *commissariat* and the Hôtel-de-Ville. The *patron* is a former petty officer (*quartier*) in the Free French Navy. He excuses himself for not being able to talk to us in English, but he has never learnt any. This comes as a relief. His wife does the cooking. I choose a half-bottle of *le vin du patron*, which is very good. He asks us if we have seen the glass-fronted Hôtel Windsor; that is where the English go, he states. Most of them are permanent residents. They have to start their lunch at 11.30 sharp, owing to staffing difficulties. The single waiter has to go off at a quarter past twelve. The Windsor behind its glass offers a scene belonging to the mid-1920s that has somehow become frozen in time. There are fifteen single tables and there is only one for a couple; at the singles, old ladies in pink, blue, or emerald dresses, one has a green bandeau like Suzanne Lenglen. The men wear blazers without crests and cavalry-twill trousers. One has on blancoed white tennis shoes. On each table are quarter or full bottles of Évian, Vittel, Vals, Badoit and, scoring highest, Contrexéville (*pour les reins*). The table for two has a timid, almost apologetic *quart de rouge*, dwarfed by a bottle of Vichy-Célestins three-quarters full. We tell the *patron* we have looked through the glass front on our way back from the steeply shelving beach, but had not been tempted to try and eat there. Probably there would have been no table for us, in any case. The petty officer laughs. The next day, we are a little late for lunch: there is a notice on our table near the door from the stairs: 'RÉSERVÉE'. The PO shakes our hands and smiles. He recommends what is on for that day.

In the afternoon, we cross over to le Pollet and walk along the far quayside to the deep black caverns dug into the greyish cliffs that had housed the enormous German naval guns set on railway chassis. They are empty now, even of squatters. Then we climb up to the little chapel, post-1871, ugly but touching. There is a minutely accurate model of the *Maine*, a troop-carrier of the French Navy that went up on a mine, all hands (mostly Dieppois) lost, in 1916 or 1917. On the walls there are more than thirty memorial plaques bearing the names (in gold) and the photographs of drowned seamen and fishermen, several lost off the Cornish coast. There is also an old sepia photograph of the *Maine*, which looks like a converted destroyer. Some of the plaques have fresh flowers in the little metal baskets placed beneath them. An old woman in a flowered dress and a headscarf is watering one lot; the man in the photograph above it has a big, shaggy moustache.

Two afternoons, we walk as far as Pourville-sur-Mer, another pebbly, shelving beach, with more monuments to officers and soldiers, of Canadian regiments – here, in Pourville, French Canadians; Mont-Royal. Or we walk along the top of the cliffs, beyond the fierce-looking turreted château. The Buvette du Château beneath the black landmark is still closed, its green-stained shutters down: too early in the season, like a lot of things. But the casino and the Société des Bains de Mer are open. I don't think they ever close. Along the top of the cliffs we can walk to the next inlet; not as far as Veules-les-Roses, but I can't remember.

In the evening, a tiny restaurant, served by a girl of fourteen, the cook (her mother?) invisible beyond the hatch; there are only four tables. The restaurant is hidden away from the harbour and the Gare Maritime (*sic*) in l'Enfert, a semi-secret enclave. But at the other tables there are generally English lorry-drivers, some wearing blazers *with* crests and asking loudly for bacon and eggs, sausages and beans, and drinking bottles of Kronenbourg. Most are driving to northern Spain. They are anxious to talk to us.

Later, a drink, or several, in a tiny bar – two tables, four chairs, a *zinc*, run by a talkative woman whose husband is also a long-distance lorry-driver and does not have any time for Yugoslavs, Bulgars, and Turks. Nor does she. She does not warm to Nord-Afs either. Are *we* invaded too?, she asks. Then she gets into a conversation with a man standing at the bar who works at the abattoirs. Before we leave she gets a phone call, the line is bad, but her husband tells her that he is on time.

I buy a beige corduroy cap at the market by Saint-Jacques. It fits beautifully and has a warm pleated lining in yellow silk. But it doesn't much help young Vée, whom I have known ever since he went to *la maternelle*, and who is now a philosophy student at Rouen University and asks us out to his flat in a modern block, Neuville-lès-Dieppe. He wants me to write a piece about horse markets for *Autrement*. I say I will, but I won't.

The next morning, we take the midday boat, after a drink at the big café that faces away from the quayside and on to the Grande Rue. We have bought some glasses and a bowl in Strasbourg china bearing a chirpy red cock on a leafy green background. The boat is heading the wrong way, the ugly chapel on the hill and the black château are getting smaller and smaller. We can still have a French meal in the Self-Service, the boat is the *Versailles*. I even know the barman, M. Lecarpentier, by name. He has very pale blue eyes and lives in the rue d'Écosse. In two or three hours, the white Seven Sisters will be rising up, bigger and bigger. Perhaps there is no escape from J.B. Priestley *et al*. But I have tried, and Margaret has helped. I am enormously grateful to her. We have fully shared the memory of that week. I am grateful, too, to Douglas and Madeleine Johnson: he, a *normalien*, she a *Sèvrienne*, the marriage in fact of a semi-coded educational network. Douglas is the last holder of the University College London Chair of French History. He gave the Chair the lustre of expertise. Madeleine is Norman. I want them both to know the affection and admiration which 'Le Cobb' feels for the two of them. Now, as at Dieppe-Maritime, it is the End of the Line. But this one does at least have buffers.

Index